CHARACTER AND STYLE IN
ENGLISH POLITICS

CHARACTER AND STYLE IN ENGLISH POLITICS

J. H. GRAINGER

Senior Lecturer in Political Science
Australian National University

CAMBRIDGE
AT THE UNIVERSITY PRESS
1969

Published by the Syndics of the Cambridge University Press
Bentley House, 200 Euston Road, London N.W.1
American Branch: 32 East 57th Street, New York, N.Y.10022

Library of Congress Catalogue Card Number: 69-10428
Standard Book Number: 521 07350 2

Printed in Great Britain
at the University Printing House, Cambridge
(Brooke Crutchley, University Printer)

CONTENTS

PREFACE

A few years ago I gave a broadcast talk on politicians on the BBC Third Programme. From this beginning has grown this study: an essay on the conduct of English leading politicians, a bold enterprise, not undertaken, I think, since F. S. Oliver wrote *The Endless Adventure* more than thirty years ago, and, appropriately, even in three volumes, did not complete.

The tone and content of three books have particularly influenced me: Herbert Butterfield's *The Englishman and his History* (Cambridge, 1944); Irene Coltman's *Private Men and Public Causes* (Faber, 1962); John Carswell's *The Old Cause* (The Cresset Press, 1954). But in a book of this kind debts to other writers must be very great. I hope that they are adequately acknowledged in the footnotes.

I owe thanks to my wife who typed the manuscript, advised on structure, and helped to clarify the successive drafts.

J.H.G.

August 1968

NOTE ON FOOTNOTES

At the outset I anticipated that a book such as this, which is at once illustrative of political conduct and a commentary upon judgments passed on it, might become overloaded with footnotes. I have therefore followed a broad convention of dispensing with them whenever the politician discussed was himself speaking or writing and his words are in the standard histories and biographies. I have appended a footnote, however, when I owe the politician's words to a particular secondary authority, when the politician's writings are diverse or remote, or when debate on his actions and motives is part of today's politics.

I

INTRODUCTION

There is an ancestral gallery rather than a typology of English politicians. The leading men, it is true, operate within particular conventions and tread well-beaten paths to office. There are affinities of temperament and one politician easily catches the voice and adopts the stance of another. Yet within the political arena where a mark may be made, 'every man', as Sir Walter Blackett declared two centuries ago, 'carries his honour in his own hand'.[1] There his deportment, conduct and action are judged in the light of standards developed by those politicians who preceded him. The judgment is that of an informed political world.

Within that ambience there is an inside view. Men did not meet one fine day to acclaim a hero of the provinces or of the press. The leader has always been 'evolved' within a knowledgeable circle. In a genuine parliamentary system this must continue to be so—even if the evolution is overlaid by formal democratic election within the political parties. In dispensing, until very recently, with a ballot for choosing their leaders the Tories were doing no more than recognizing the need for precise selection. For the Tories, the leader required no projection in an election campaign: he was known and acclaimed. This is the mode of the club with its experienced appraisal of character and style. It is a method barely explicable in functional terms, has results not easily predicted, and, because it is esoteric, confounds lobby correspondents and political scientists. For there is no necessary acknowledgement of long and honourable service. Business capacity may be useful, as may charismatic authority, but the club is not primarily concerned with recognizing either.

What there is, however, is a funded knowledge of style, character and current form—no more exact than but as immediately irrefutable as the knowledge of the stables. It is reliance upon such knowledge that distinguishes Britain from, say, the United States, where a new President looks unfledged even if he has graduated

[1] L. B. Namier, *The structure of politics at the accession of George III* (1929), London, 1957, p. 11.

from Congress. For, in spite of greater journalistic freedom to penetrate the recesses of its 'inside', the American political system often presents the electorate with candidates to the highest office who are unknown and untested politically over any decent period of time. Or so one must assume if Theodore White's book, *The making of the President 1960*, has a ring of truth. For here we have recorded with the omniscient detail of the novelist, the confrontation of two relatively untried young men before a public hardly capable of judging between them. (The French choice of De Gaulle, a known man with an unambiguous record in war and politics, was rational and knowledgeable compared with this.)

The English parliamentary system is one which produces politicians who can be trusted to do what they have to do because they have long been within the circle of eligibility, have been schooled for so long. Between the wars, J. A. Spender could declare with confidence that 'a public man in this country is above all things a Parliament man'[1] and Sir Lewis Namier, while ruling out any high motivation, asserted that 'for several centuries the dream of English youth and manhood of the nation-forming class has remained unchanged; it has been fixed and focused on the House of Commons, a modified, socialized arena for battle, drive and dominion'.[2]

Namier's last words may mislead. 'Battle, drive and dominion' are appropriately associated with Chatham, Gladstone, Lloyd George and Churchill in their more strenuous moments, but even in these men the will to power was muted by parliamentary modes of persuasion. The moving of a free assembly needs more than force of personality; the members have to be exposed to large and generous ideas. And memorable articulation of political issues requires either sincerity or art. These, even the 'great' politician cannot have all the time: Churchill floundered in second-class prose for years; Gladstone found his grand style only after many years in Parliament. Melbourne once confessed to having made 'a bothering, bungling speech at a bad moment'. And of Lloyd George's Budget speech in 1909, of all things, Hilaire Belloc could say that 'he spoke like a man in the last stages of physical and mental decay'.[3]

---

[1] J. A. Spender, *The public life*, London, 1925, I, XIII.
[2] *The structure of politics at the accession of George III*, p. 1.
[3] Robert Speaight, *The life of Hilaire Belloc*, London, 1957, p. 233.

Style is style in the vulgar yet absolute sense of self-conscious application of force, elegance and brilliance to making a mark in the world. It is the chosen words of a man who is, or seeks to be, consciously illustrious. At the root is passion, but it is passion schooled by responsibility and shaped by art. Only two or three ideas need possess the mind. No remarkable perception was needed by Chatham or Burke to understand the grievances of the American colonists, by Gladstone to see the moral issue of Ireland, by Churchill to apprehend the German threat in the 1930s. Such simplicities can nurse a whole rhetoric. Bolingbroke, that great *forgotten* stylist, became formidable not through learning but by shouldering his way through the material. He was always capable of giving a quick answer.

Political style, then, is manners and words. But it is only assured when manners and words are durable. And durability depends upon limited circulation. Style is difficult when words are reproduced, plagiarized and indiscriminately assembled. Style then becomes what the journalists call 'brilliance', meaning quick recourse to what is unremarkable metaphor, invective or repartee or possibly the flourishing of the remnants of a literary education. For Labour politicians it commonly meant the regurgitation of hours in a public library or (as in Aneurin Bevan) the assumption of the part of Junius: all ministries are the worst since Lord North's.

It would be mistaken to think that the great stylist forms himself solely to meet the demands of the political market. There is little that is modish about true style: it is self-shaped and stems from the desire of the politician to express himself as he sees himself rather than as editors and managers or audience would have him. It is not true that arguments in public speech and political writing are put forward solely to maximize support. They may be the expression of a distinguished political sensibility. The orator may not merely seek to persuade; his vanity may drive him to attract lasting admiration and thus to sacrifice the undiscriminating following that might raise him to power. There is no better example than Churchill. What audience could he conceivably have been addressing between the wars with all that senatorial ardour, in that archaic republican style?

Style is fabricated, *made*, but nevertheless implies honourable commitment to action. That is why it has become so difficult to achieve. For nothing has become more hazardous than political action. To have style and fear action is to be humiliated.

Because style is so consequential it becomes less and less possible for politicians. Formerly style was slowly acquired and meant living perilously by the heart and by the head. The managerial politician of today lives by the head alone. Style becomes an encumbrance, an impediment to survival. What goes by the name of 'style' means either pretending to consistency or predictability—constructing an 'image'—or merely a characteristic way of performing duties. In this last, very limited sense, 'style' has no qualitative meaning at all; every politician has a 'style', a particular way of doing things.

Style is not just *l'homme même* but rather something *added* (not as ornament), in Stendhal's sense:

'*Le style c'est ajouter à une pensée donnée toutes les circonstances propres à produire tout l'effet que doit produire cette pensée.*'[1] Style is also self-conscious; it may begin in sincerity but the practising politician may soon see his own sincerity objectively and exploit it. For constant use he fabricates a style. Stylish politicians from Chatham to Bevan deliberately make politics out of their own sensibility. For them politics is a means of expression, and does not need provocation.

Political style diversifies politics, creates political worlds. It compels imitation of tone, manners and stance but it flourishes only in a milieu sufficiently sophisticated to produce a common reader of politics. Yet in the past it has given life to politics even for the inattentive.

Style 'stands in a direct relation to a core or nucleus of emotional and intellectual experience'.[2] The ground upon which style is raised is character. By character I do not mean either what is peculiar to a man or the peculiarities in him. Nor do I mean that which reflects the inner historical development of *any* individual, the customary ways of reacting of *any* ego, or that which is merely functional, i.e. defends 'the individual against inner and outer demands which threaten him',[3] but 'moral qualities strongly developed or strikingly displayed; distinct or distinguished character; character worth speaking of' (the twelfth meaning listed in the

---

[1] Quoted in J. Middleton Murry, *The problem of style*, Oxford, 1922, p. 3.
[2] *Ibid.* p. 19.
[3] Philip Selznick, *Leadership in administration*, New York, 1957, p. 39.

OED).[1] In this sense, a 'person', writes Mill in *Liberty*, 'whose desires and impulses are his own—are the expression of his own nature as it has been developed and modified by his own culture— is said to have a character'.

It is likely that character in politics will come out of set ways, rest on convictions not often analysed. It may even be a kind of obtuseness, a resistance in and to politics. Essentially it is a willingness to take the consequences of moral vigour. But it is a moral vigour that has to be provoked. The politician of character does not make politics; it comes out of him. He communicates, feels on his feet. He does not aspire to office; he is called to it. Office is an obligation, not an aspiration, and for this reason he may very well emerge from a political class to which politics is an avocation only, or possibly from those who have been drawn into politics but whose fortune or reputation has been made elsewhere.

In the word 'character' there are overtones of virtue. Character often means 'good' character. The adjectives used by William McDougall[2] are 'strong , 'stable', well-knit', 'trustworthy', 'dependable'. But it is easier to say what character does than what it is. It is self-value revealed in action. We rightly associate character with the power of self-direction, with *will*, but you are more likely to find a crisis of identity in a politician of character than a will to power. His politics comes out of his private judgment. There may be a distaste for politics: perhaps even an incapacity for sustained attention to parliamentary duties. There may be a lack of facility with words. Lord George Bentinck would say that 'before he could speak, he had to make a voice, and as it were pump it up from the very core of his frame'.[3] There may also be hostility to mystification and obstruction through words, as when Campbell-Bannerman ended Balfour's parliamentary

---

[1] In *The edge of the sword*, London, 1960, De Gaulle's concept of character is close to, if perhaps more positive than, the one used here. The essential element in a leader of men, he says, is *character*, 'the virtue of hard times', the creative force in all successful enterprises. The man of character is the responsible man who 'draws to himself the hopes and wills of everyone as the magnet draws iron'. In crises he has 'recourse to himself' and his self-reliance is necessarily 'accompanied by some roughness in method'. He is too sure of himself merely to wish to please his superiors; within him, there is always a certain recalcitrance. Yet to those under him he is benevolent, 'for he is a born protector'.

[2] *The energies of men*, London, 1935, pp. 185–6.

[3] B. Disraeli, *Lord George Bentinck* (1852), London, 1905, p. 59.

fencing with, 'Enough of this foolery!' Yet rugged eloquence is available under pressure. Indeed the politician of character claimed the first real audience in English politics among the up-country members of Elizabeth's Parliaments. He was still retaining it in the eighteenth century among the English country gentlemen— among the 'consuls of the county republics'.

Character in politics is typically not so committed as style to specific action in the future (Peter Wentworth, Cromwell, Baldwin are instances). Yet the politician of character does stand firm and can meditate his speeches. In great crises he is troubled and will not sleep as soundly as Churchill. Churchill is primarily *style* in politics. Character and style may co-exist but in order of time character is prior in English politics. Character is not identifiably Tory or Whig but has its roots in the up-country party. Character at Court must be as powerful as Strafford's if it is to make a mark. In the closed politics of a Court, neither character nor style flourishes. There the king or prince monopolizes both; the politician is instrumental. 'At court, if a man hath too much pride to be a creature he had better stay at home.'[1] Honesty at Court turns to rancour as in Thersites or to academic detachment as in Enobarbus. Yet there is a sense in which English constitutional history is largely the story of how character was taken into Court while retaining its base in the Country. Country 'character', which had been so recalcitrant in Stuart times, becomes, in the eighteenth and nineteenth centuries, a kind of domesticated independence and honesty in politics, well represented by that 'hesitant and in-elegant debater'[2], Lord Rockingham, the Whig leader whose virtues, said Burke, were his arts.

The distinction I have made is far from being absolute but it is a simple differentiation made in life and play. In cricket it is possible to talk of an innings of character, pertinacious and coura-geous, in which grace is subordinated to the necessity of the occa-sion; or, on the other hand, of an innings of style, by which we mean smooth proficiency in which graceful execution runs to rhetoric. These are valid distinctions in the developed politics of England. And what about intellect? Intellect is credited to the spin bowler on a hard wicket.

[1] 'Political thoughts and reflections', in H. C. Foxcroft, *The life and letters of Sir George Savile, first Marquis of Halifax*, London, 1898, II, 507.

[2] Earl of Albemarle, *Memoirs of the Marquis of Rockingham and his contemporaries*, London, 1852, I, 141. 'He lacked the outward graces. He possessed the inward power.'

In the embarrassing political richness of the contemporary world, merely to study the varieties of the political apparatus, to ascribe success or failure to favourable or unfavourable political climates or soil, thus to moralize on Brazilian federalism or Ghanaian democracy, is not very profitable. Such a study of the mere prosody of politics confines us to externals. To evaluate a political system means that we must have canons which will enable us to judge whether or not within political traditions, identified historically or anthropologically, politics is well or ill done.

What are the criteria for such assessment? One, obviously, is the confidence to rule to be found within the élites. Another index is the capacity to engender and sustain opposition. Another is the extent to which politics attracts talent; beyond that, the depth of support for the leading contenders within the political nation. Then there is the kind of sustained debate which the system admits, the relation between words and action, between ideology and achievement. Important, too, are opportunities for the unpolitical to make themselves felt during great crises. All these reflect the nation's capacity for free politics. But an even more immediate touchstone than these is the quality of the political leaders.

A literature is a closed world within which a writer can achieve a consistency of vision and statement to which even the 'world-historical' statesman cannot aspire. The politician's materials are obdurate people, not the figments of art. 'He is a potter who cannot choose his clay, a painter who cannot mix his own paints, a composer who must score for a brass band what he perhaps intended for a string quartet.'[1] The politician who treats his task as a kind of *œuvre* will probably end in megalomania and—it is to be hoped—outside politics. The politician has not much freedom to choose his theme; and he is judged immediately, if not ultimately, by the efficacy of his actions, and not on the honesty and sensibility which took him to the heart of the matter. He cannot expect the same fullness of response as the writer or artist. The audience are much less attentive; their judgment less concrete. The politician can seldom afford an unalloyed sincerity. But he is not so delimited that he cannot, even 'within the contagion of current language', make a new summation of history

[1] Henry Fairlie, 'The idea of leadership', *The Spectator*, 1 March 1963.

to reframe the issues and to decide their priority; he can create new issues out of barely articulated desires and discontents.

A novelist explores beneath the official, the political levels of consciousness and there sets up an interplay between one awareness, one understanding, and another. He brings together not the outer but the inner lives of men. Unlike the politician, he has not to find 'proximate solutions to insoluble problems'. Nor does he grub, like the politician, among the rubble of worn-out language. Yet he must admit restrictions on himself. Unless he conceives of his sensibility as purely exploratory or his function as simply technical, he must choose themes which are central, engage the moral sensibility and judgment of his readers in an active and discriminating way. Moreover, his common reader is more active than either the man in the crowd or at the back of the omnibus. Like the politician, he too can become a hack, turning out work that will evoke stock responses and making an undeserved reputation from it. Yet both artist and politician, at their most strenuous, are concerned with reducing the inchoate, the irrational, to some kind of rule and order. Both simplify through the imagination. In the words of Erich Heller: 'Ideally speaking, art shares with politics precisely that which distinguishes both from the deliberate rationality of science and the blueprints of ideological programmes: that it springs from the elemental human need to discipline into articulate form and communicable convention the inarticulate and rationally incommunicable forces of life...'[1]

Moralizing on English politics was a major intellectual activity in the nineteenth century. But most critics sought a standard outside politics rather than within it. The vision of Carlyle is too apocalyptic to matter very much; the change of heart which he demands is beyond politics. That of Ruskin is too authoritarian. 'It did not greatly help the Glasgow undergraduates to be told by Ruskin, when they suggested to him an election address, "You have no more business with politics than you have with rat-catching...but I hate all Liberalism as I do Beelzebub, and with Carlyle I stand, we two now alone in England, for God and the Queen."'[2] Arnold's standards in *Culture and Anarchy* are civilized, his strictures, for example, on Bright's appetite for an inferior kind of politics apposite, but he is not sympathetic to the English

---

[1] *Thomas Mann, the ironic German*, New York, 1961, p. 129.
[2] Ernest Barker, *Political thought from 1848 to 1914*, Oxford, 1947, p. 174.

political tradition. Bagehot gives us a qualitative assessment in *The English Constitution* but at the heart of it there is, I think, a doubt of the durability of liberal politics, which leads him to praise both stupidity and social deference.

In this century there have been hardly any evaluations of English politics to compete with these; although Oakeshott has on occasions indicated what we may look for and Butterfield, elegiacally, sometimes lugubriously, has sketched the distinctively English approach to politics in a tiny volume of 1944.[1] Although there has been plenty of scholarship explaining the rules of the game and, now that the sociologists are moving in, 'the system of action', there is singularly little attempting a criticism of the English political experience. Even the extensive works of Sir Ivor Jennings are marred by a failure to take the English political tradition seriously, a curious unawareness of the predicament of the leading politician, and a scepticism about all political passion.

It is sometimes said that there is a great tradition in English politics: that there are conditions in which creative politics and politicians flourish, and that these are no longer with us. When the best politicians we have seem remote and ineffectual, their words fustian or threadbare, their filtered expositions banal, we may take it that political vigour is waning—and with it the nation's capacity for freedom. The sights are set for this current historical phase, all we need to do is to keep on as we are going. Only one or two fundamental choices remain; after them the administration can take over.

It is a good time to survey the ground upon which we stand. *Ich habe meine Gründe vergessen...* But which foundations? The Whig view of history has been built into our culture; we are only too well aware of our constitutional inheritance and the rules of the game. Lord Radcliffe finds it difficult to forgive those who have 'left us the mystique of Parliamentary supremacy with no comparable assertion as to its purpose'.[2] The purpose belongs, he insists, to men rather than institutions. What we are losing is the sight of men whose energy and conviction kept politics alive in the nineteenth century. These were the men, says J. A. Spender, who not only 'performed miracles of cleansing and purification' but also 'firmly embedded in the mind of Parliament and the

---

[1] H. Butterfield, *The Englishman and his history*, Cambridge.
[2] Lord Radcliffe, 'The purpose of politics', *The Times*, 24 February 1958.

nation that indefinable idea of the public interest which is the sheet-anchor of honest statesmanship'.[1] These were the large 'slow-moving public men' who gave public life a repute which it had never had before and has never had since.

This is an essay on political sensibility, on the political manners or character developed by our leading politicians in the modern period, particularly during the latest age of popular politics. I shall be concerned not with institutions or theories of government but with the stance which the politician found it possible to assume, in particular the way in which, by words and action, he sought to impress the reasonableness of his vision on a widening audience after the old political order broke down in the nineteenth century.

This is not an attempt at a sociology of politicians. It may be that a sociology of politics is possible, that, by intellectual effort, we shall in the long run be able to see all political creeds and attitudes emerging logically from specific social situations and thus be in a position to achieve a true political science. Thus we shall concede in time, a time which has taken all the stuff and stuffing out of politics, that the Blues and the Greens, the Roundheads and the Cavaliers, the Hats and the Caps were all right and all wrong, even at last have the consolation of knowing that

> 'All those large dreams by which men long live well
> Are magic-lanterned on the smoke of Hell;
> This then is real, I have implied,
> A painted, small, transparent slide.'[2]

Historians have long been incidentally sociologists without knowing it. History is rewritten to deepen political analysis, and unearth more facts about the structure within which Elizabeth and Cromwell and Gladstone found themselves. But, unlike the sociologist who will purge away the dross to discover persistent uniformities, the historian, though possibly less confidently than formerly, remains concerned with individual achievements, individual decisions, within the annals of the parish.

The sociologist can hardly be concerned with the quality of politicians at all. His business is with the structure and accommodations within that structure, with what holds society together

[1] Spender, *The public life*, London, 1925, I, 27.
[2] W. Empson, 'This Last Pain', *Collected Poems*.

in terms of forces rooted in interests. For him the particular exists only to be aggregated. The emergent, the free, those actions which constitute history, are random in his timeless pattern.

Sociology, which was born of political science and the philosophy of history[1], has long since returned to tyrannize over its parents. History and politics now absorb general theories which, harsh or bland, put the individual in his proper place. It is true that Marxism has a function for the hero, for him who gives power to the elbow of inevitability, but he is a strange, less than human, wooden oracle, dismantled at need by the currently dominant priesthood; even while he endures, both his presence and command over events are unreally superhuman. He is, nevertheless, more heroic than the politician revealed by Western political analysis. For in this, the preoccupation is with the field of force within which the political leader operates rather than with the leader, at most, with measuring his reactions to group pressures, his lines of least resistance.

Such analysis studiously penetrates 'the sea of words' in which political movements swim, to what men in groups actually want and do. 'When "ideas" in full cry drive past, the thing to do with them is to accept them as an indication that something is happening; and then search carefully to find out what it really is they stand for, what the factors are in social life that are expressing themselves through the ideas.'[2]

This seems salutary advice, laying many ghosts and confining us to the basis of those ideas and feelings actually expressed in the public realm. The raw material of politics is activity, the activity of group interests, pushing, pulling and adjusting. Government is one activity, one group interest among others. Feelings, ideals, climates of opinion, intellectual movements are not causes; they are not subject to scientific analysis. Nor is there any 'pure public spirit'; it too belongs to the pre-scientific realm of 'animism'. It is hard to measure the inner compulsives of politicians. What matters and is measurable is the force relationship among competing interests. Political science thus becomes the study of mediating, transactional processes among men who are, in effect, the agents of competing and coalescing groups. The tracing of the processes of their interaction, the measurement of pushes and pulls, alone constitute a feasible science of politics.

[1] M. Ginsberg, *Sociology*, London, 1959, p. 24.
[2] A. F. Bentley, *The process of government*, Evanston, Illinois, 1949, p. 152.

The same kind of rigour has long reigned in the sphere of *technical* history, and for much the same reasons:

> It is recorded somewhere that the group of men who founded the Royal Society in seventeenth-century England resented the waste of time that was liable to occur in their discussions when...every topic would be carried back to the region of first principles and fundamental beliefs, so that the debate was for ever returning to the same issues and they could not discuss the ordinary operations of nature without perpetually coming back to their basic theological and philosophical differences. Only when these men learned to keep their conversation fixed upon the mere mechanical operations of nature...could they short-circuit that tantalisingly unprogressive form of general debate.

In historical science and particularly in the upper regions of the study, a similar policy of abstraction has become customary. Historians, limited by the kind of apparatus they use and the concrete evidence on which they must rely, restrict their realm to what we might almost call the mechanism of historical processes: the tangible factors involved in an episode, the displacements produced in human affairs by an observed event or a specific influence, even the kind of movements that can be recorded in statistics.[1]

The rigorist of the new political science admits that politics is played according to the rules of the particular 'habit background' but insists that 'there is not a law that is passed that is not the expression of force and force in tension'.[2] It is a process in which it is difficult to find a place for the creative politician, for judgment or justice. What is crucial is the strength or obduracy of immediate pressures. 'Whatever happens at a given time and place within the field depends only upon the values of the field quantities existing in the immediate past, and the proximity of events under observation.'[3]

Within this science, the leading politician is functional. He is a man making rational decisions and this often means following the paths of least resistance. The environmental factors which have gone to his making, the social forces to which he reacts, are seen not so much as he perceives them but as if they existed objectively.[4]

---

[1] H. Butterfield, *Christianity and history*, London, 1949, p. 19.

[2] Bentley, *op. cit.* p. 202.

[3] Norman Jacobson, 'Causality and time in political process: a speculation', *The American Political Science Review*, LVIII (1964), 15.

[4] See J. M. Burns, *Roosevelt, the lion and the fox*, London, 1956, p. 485. Burns insists that 'the environmental political factors that affect the leader's personality should not be treated as inchoate and indistinguishable forces impinging on the emerging

Because these 'forces' can be accurately analysed they are given more prominence than the actual qualities of the leader. He is seen primarily not as a man with an attitude, endowed with volition, but as a register or calculator of quantities—although as Bentley admits he will never 'make a plain statement of his estimates; indeed it is rare that he knows how to tell...'¹

We have some idea of what the politician will measure—votes, financial support, military force, press backing, élite approbation, great and powerful friends and so on. Yet these have never the same intensity or explicitness. They are not weighable in the same balance. In the House of Commons in December 1965, Mr Harold Wilson had to use a mixed metaphor to describe the situation in Rhodesia. 'What we are trying to do', he said, 'is to go straight down the middle of the road in a four-dimensional situation. There is the dimension of Rhodesian opinion—and that is not uncomplicated; the dimension of public opinion in Britain, and that is not entirely uncomplicated; the dimension of the Commonwealth, and the strong views that our Commonwealth colleagues have; and the dimension of world opinion as expressed particularly in the United Nations where it can take the form of a mandatory and possibly dangerous resolution. Somewhere among all the pressures, we hope that the right answer will be found; and I think I can say with confidence that it will be found somewhere between the demand of the O.A.U. [Organization of African Unity] and those perhaps of the Monday Club [a right-wing Conservative club].'²

Canny assessments of the forces at work do not, however, give a firm indication of what politicians are likely to do. There is always something to take politicians forward when calculations have locked, a moral judgment possibly made some time ago, an obligation to maintain their own coherence. 'Their inspiration comes from their homely interests or dominant prejudices, from the contagion of current language, or from private predispositions.'³

'Scientism', which concentrates upon the measurable, comes to very much the same conclusion as hostile ignorance—that politics is a carve-up with 'the last appetite' or the longest purse winning.

---

leader but in terms of that leader's *perception* of their existence and of their relative importance'. ¹ Bentley, *op. cit.* p. 202.
² [722] H.C. Debates, p. 1932, 21 December 1965.
³ George Santayana, *Dominations and powers*, London, 1951, p. 17.

Neither the unedified nor the detached are conscious of political predicaments. Like Aristotle's beast and god they are outside politics. Yet in our personal experience we all face predicaments which cannot be resolved by mustering the forces. The predicaments arise because what is to come is incalculable. The politician has to bear the burden of a decision which will carry him into the future. It is at this point that his conception of what he is doing within the political tradition matters. The role may even dominate the situation. The inexorable pressures become merely context. There are rare occasions—in 1940 in England and in 1958 in France—when it seems as though obstructions melt away before imagination and heroic energy, as though the authority of the pioltician radically changes the situation.

This plastic power can only function in rare situations and for short periods. 'England has not known the *prima donna assoluta* of statesmanship,' wrote Ernest Barker.[1] The tradition has on the whole been resistant to the notion of the politician as 'history's commanding officer', the 'effective focus of a multitude, [making] the inward form of [his] own personality into that of whole peoples and periods. . .'[2] English statesmen do not, like Bismarck, habitually 'navigate upon the stream of time'. Except in the rarest of crises they do not 'transform the life of the nation'.

Such a conception of free creative power runs counter to the long movement from the seventeenth century, when men, bristling with refurbished ancient rights, sought through the High Court of Parliament, the established organ of co-operation, and through the law courts, to rationalize the royal prerogative. The will and reason of courtier statesmen who knew the common good and had merely to find an echo and obtain supply from among the estates of the realm now had to come to terms with the awakened will and reason of a broadening political community. Between rulers and ruled there was now slowly but firmly formulated a classic relationship of responsibility, with penalties attached. Not only could the free assemblies interrogate and impose sanctions on Strafford, Laud, Clarendon and Danby; they could also indicate the broad directions of public policy which the royal ministers could only ignore surreptitiously. The growth of group and then of party eased the strain on the individual. Sus-

---

[1] *Essays on government*, Oxford, 1945, p. 29.
[2] O. Spengler, *The decline of the west* (tr. C. F. Atkinson), London, 1928, II, 441.

tained by friendship and by group, aided by the steady depersonalization of the monarch in politics, the leading politicians were able to make politics out of their own experience and personality. This politics they had to make explicit in Parliament. It had to contend publicly with the politics of others.

Without party, the voice and policy of the leading politician would have been lost. Moreover, it was party which 'inspired our statesmen with the great spirit of public debate...furnished the nation, in virtue of the vicissitudes of party triumphs and party defeats at the polls, with a succession of contrasted yet complementary statesmen who diversify and enrich the general national record'.[1]

By the middle of the nineteenth century, the leading politician had acquired great versatility. Parliamentarianism was based on the assumption that political questions could be resolved in the same way as proposals in a debating society. Discussions in political assemblies produced truths in the same way as the inner dialectic of conscience. However romantic the postures of the liberal politicians of the period, their real strength lay in the thrust of their debating powers, their authority in Parliament.

They were not demagogues exciting the great beast, but statesmen addressing the political nation. At the same time they had to perform more administrative tasks—England had to be governed —with the support of an inadequate bureaucracy. Debating, oratorical and administrative athleticism were all demanded from the great governing politician of the nineteenth century. There was, it is true, another kind of politician, with up-country roots only, who never came to court, lived only as a critic, and found his real source of power outside Parliament, on the public platform or in journalism. His career, often illustrious, was uncomplicated by the responsibilities and chores of office. Indeed we know that Cobden found agitation so exhilarating that he did not desire office at all.

Democratic politics demanded even more from the leading politician. He now had to maintain his hold not only in the party and in Parliament but also on the nation. The diffuse general politics which for a while excited the newly enfranchised at the end of the nineteenth century yielded in time to a pattern in which aspirations were concretely resolved into tangible claims made

[1] Ernest Barker, *Essays on government*, p. 29.

by collectivities within an increasingly bureaucratized society. Faced with diversity the politician became more flexible. He had to move from role to role to identify with all those who sought recognition. Thus it became more difficult to discern his central purpose. In this thickening political medium, unity of character or style was endangered.

As the gap widened between the stated objectives, the manifestos of the politicians and their real strategic aims (a gap not so wide in Britain as in other political cultures but necessarily wider for Liberal and Labour politicians than Conservative), so scepticism grew about the capacity of politicians to make policy. 'Classical' democracy, which presupposed rational man making rational choices within alternatives posed by responsible leadership, seemed more and more of an illusion. Discussion inside and outside Parliament seemed to do little more than secure acquiescence to policies already decided. The real decisions were taken by ministers, civil servants and interests. Government came into its own again, drawing its primary force partly from the electorate and partly from ancient prerogative, but negotiating directly with the estates, pressure groups and syndicates.

In our own time, government is regarded more and more as a mechanism for making collective choice, as a means of adaptation, a product of joint, not divisive, intellectual effort. Debate is considered a waste of time unless the social facts are well known. 'Discussion', it has been said, 'frequently complicates social difficulties...arouses a psychology of conflict which produces obstructive, fictitious, and irrelevant values.'[1] Liberal institutions have become embedded in a governmental structure whose precise outlines are never traced. And upon this congeries of departments, quasi-governmental bodies, pressure groups, advisory committees, party research organs and press influences, only a general politician of remarkable architectonic power can make a deep impression.

It says much for the persistence of the classical liberal stereotype that the politician is still thought of as being formative, active and comprehensive:

If politics means anything, it means an all-embracing interest in the total affairs of the community. It means the interconnection of everything and an attempt to get a perspective of the whole. It is that com-

[1] Harold D. Lasswell, *Psychopathology and politics*, Chicago, 1930, pp. 196–7.

prehensive function which gives to politicians their greatest satisfaction and which—even more than the prospects of power—keeps them enthralled by their work. To identify the problems of contemporary society, to locate the men and women who are working for a solution, to evolve policies from ideas, to organize mass movements, to campaign for these policies, to convince the people to accept them, to carry through the programme by consent, lubricating the process with wise compromises without losing sight of the objective as he goes along—these are the tasks of the politician.[1]

The assertiveness of this declaration betrays, perhaps, some of the difficulties under which political leadership currently labours. Does the politician really hope for solutions? Is it not more exact to say that he takes decisions and hopes for a satisfactory outcome, all the time aware like Lord Salisbury that with the results he has nothing to do?[2] The 'interconnection of everything' seems more an enterprise for the academic political sociologist than for the politician. The politician, after all, has to act. And is it so easy for a politician to develop an 'all-embracing interest in the total affairs of the community'? Is it not true that political energy today works from a narrower base, that significant politics is to be found not in time-honoured areas but in spheres that were formerly designated 'private', within 'corporations, trade unions and even universities'?[3] The politics of these sectors has more technicians than artists. It is precise and grinding but there is little that is 'all-embracing' about it.

Yet it cannot be a politics of pure empiricism; such, as Oakeshott has said, would be an approach to lunacy. Its values may be few, simple, and seldom invoked, but there must be issues demanding a wider justice which must go on appeal to the judgment of the

---

[1] Anthony Wedgwood Benn, *The Guardian*, 20 March 1964.

[2] From the well-known passage in Lady Gwendolen Cecil's biography of her father: 'He was about to start upon a walk and was standing at the moment at the open door, looking out upon the threatening clouds of an autumn afternoon. "I don't understand", he repeated, "what people mean when they talk of the burden of responsibility. I should understand if they spoke of the burden of decision,—I feel it now, trying to make up my mind whether or no to take a greatcoat with me. I feel it in exactly the same way, but no more, when I am writing a despatch upon which peace or war may depend. Its degree depends upon the materials for decision that are available and not in the least upon the magnitude of the results which may follow." Then, after a moment's pause and in a lower tone, he added, "With the results I have nothing to do."' *Life of Robert, Marquis of Salisbury*, London, 1921, I (1830–1868), 119.

[3] Sheldon S. Wolin, *Politics and vision*, London, 1961, p. 353.

realm. Treaties among the groups will have to be signed; 'all-embracing politics' will be involved in their external relations.

The groups cannot in fact create a polycentric society in equi-librium—the implicit quietus, perhaps, of American political science—and are not likely to. There will still be a need for general politicians, although perhaps not so many of them or such a diversity. Moreover, they will have to work much harder. Ideology will not do. Yet the technocrats have not taken over: the politician's occupation has not gone. In some countries, in Ghana, Egypt and Indonesia, there must be indeed an uninhibited cult of the master politician. The master politician has been rare in Britain but no one could say, in the century of Lloyd George, Baldwin, Chamberlain and Churchill, that this country has been without political virtuosity. It is likely that the politically innocent will continue to ask for the right man with the right words.

What there is in Britain is a long line of short-term alternating politicians (short-term but not too short because of the party system) of complementary skill and high integrity. There is also a great wealth of political biography; much can be learned from those concluding chapters in which the biographer evaluates his subject —not merely as behaviour or image-inducing behaviour in the way of the new political science, not as role within system or sub-system, but in his own autonomy within a tradition, not as prototype but as exemplar. Leading politicians provide instructive behaviour for those who come after. It has long been the practice to trace with care the relations between their personal bent, private thought, public persuasion, and deed. It is the critical response to these, their relation to a scale of values, which estab-lishes the reputation of the politician. There must be frequent re-valuations; one can no more exactly define the influence of a poli-tician on his audience than one can that of a book on its readers.[1]

In this book the intention is to evaluate those politicians who have contributed something to the political tradition, its tone and expectations. The series which emerges is a concrete one formed by other politicians similarly assessed.

The critic's aim is, first, to realize as sensitively and completely as possible this or that which claims his attention; and a certain valuing is implicit in the realizing. As he matures in experience of the new thing he asks, explicitly and implicitly: 'Where does this come? How

[1] See René Wellek and Austin Warren, *Theory of literature*, London, 1963, p. 102.

does it stand in relation to...? How relatively important does it seem?' And the organization into which it settles as a constituent in becoming 'placed' is an organization of similarly 'placed' things, things which have found their bearings with regard to one another, and not a theoretical system or a system determined by abstract considerations.[1]

How the politician was selected, his relationship to the élite, the accessibility of power are all interesting subjects for investigation. But no causal study can do the politician full justice. He lives by a certain coherence, by attitudes and words precipitated in the memory. The statesman is not there before us like the poem on the printed page. Yet although present only through record, monument, gossip and the judgment of historians, he is as concrete as anything we have in history. It is possible for him to become much more than he was, but he claims our attention because he briefly embodied what men accepted or expected in political conduct. And, because, in England, he acted within an unbroken tradition, he can be 'placed'.

Leo Strauss[2] has written that 'ordinarily a political man must at least pretend "to look up to" something that at least the preponderant part of his society looks up to'. What men look up to gives society its character. There are different views of what is 'highest' and therefore there are qualitatively different régimes. What we are concerned with here is not what is common to all political communities but with what is markedly English.

It used to be said [wrote Lord Bryce[3] in the closing pages of *Modern Democracies*] of the British House of Commons that its tone and taste rose or fell with the Prime Minister who was guiding its deliberations. This applies to the body of the people also. A great man may not only form a school who assimilate and propagate his ideas, but may do much to create a pattern for the people of what statesmanship ought to be. If his honour is unblemished, his ideals high, his temper large, tolerant and sympathetic, his example is sure to tell.... He may, without being a Washington or a Lincoln, a Pitt or a Fox, not only deserve to be gratefully remembered as a light of his time, but may, like Lord Althorp and Peel, in one way, Cobden and Bright in another, so influence his younger contemporaries as to strengthen the best traditions in public life and maintain its standard.

[1] F. R. Leavis, *The common pursuit*, London, 1962, p. 213.
[2] 'An Epilogue' in *Essays on the scientific study of politics*, ed. H. J. Storing, New York, 1962, pp. 317–18.
[3] Lord Bryce, *Modern democracies*, London, 1921, II, 614–15.

And if we wish to compare political cultures we shall perhaps get at least as much from studying Gambetta, Clemenceau and De Gaulle or Gladstone, Lloyd George and Baldwin as from the close examination of French or British institutions. There is little that is quantifiable here, but the quantifiable would tell us little about the fund of human character, resources of style, which have made those institutions work in the way they have.

2

COURT AND COUNTRY POLITICIANS

In the emergent politics of Tudor and Stuart England we find character flourishing in the localities but expressing itself with difficulty in the king's presence in Whitehall or Westminster. Those like More, Fisher, Latimer and Ridley who stubbornly retained character at Court drew their strength from far wider resources than the shires. So too did Peter Wentworth. What has the appearance of style is often little more than embellishment. What we remark right up to the Civil War is neither character nor style but *capacity for business*.

The leading politician was a Court politician who had risen by virtue of early discerned talent, through having the right patrons. What was required was talent, in law, in finance, in organizing and diplomatic ability. The politician was a fiscal expert, like Empson, a negotiator on a grand scale like Wolsey, a man of business like Thomas Cromwell or William Cecil. He had talent before he had character or style. And of course not the vestige of charisma. Elizabeth, reviewing her troops at Tilbury under the threat of Spanish invasion or making her golden speech of reconciliation to her last Parliament, exhibited the peculiar Tudor authority. The prince was the lightning-conductor, the master of public policy and public relations: the immediate sanction of the politician.

Today we make a formal distinction, perhaps with increasing difficulty, between politician and bureaucrat, but in the sixteenth and seventeenth centuries all office-holders, whether in place through purchase, inheritance or ability, were personal servants of the king. Positions, it is true, were commonly franchises, held of right, remunerated by fees and gratuities from customers or other officials, or by defalcation. When the prince wanted an apple his servants took the tree. Office was not, therefore, very easily controlled—but exploitation was individual; there was no corporate bureaucratic power.[1]

[1] See G. E. Aylmer, *The king's servants: the civil service of Charles I, 1625–42*, London, 1961, chapters 2, 3, 4 and 7.

Yet 'he who has in his hands the execution of measures is in very truth the master of them...'.[1] All prerogative matters touching religion, foreign affairs and dynastic matters were ultimately the king's business, but secretaries of state, other officials of the royal household, might well have uninterrupted control over both the issues and the minutiae of domestic business for long periods.

There were exceptional leases of authority. Of Wolsey, Giustiniani, the Venetian ambassador, wrote that when he first arrived in England, Wolsey used to say to him 'His Majesty will do so and so'; subsequently by degrees he went on forgetting himself and commenced saying 'We shall do so and so'; in the end he had reached such a pitch that he said 'I shall do so and so.'[2] Yet Wolsey's power was revocable, and after his fall the Tudors were, in effect, the designers of their own policies, creating and acknowledging repositories of experience in their servants, subject to their influences, but remaining actively responsible and often making decisions without consulting ministers corporatively or individually. Neither Leicester nor Essex is a good analogue to Wolsey and we have to go forward to George Villiers, duke of Buckingham, to find a Court politician exercising the same influence within the prerogative and embellishing his ascendancy in the same way, and one who out of office was a like symbol of pride and corruption.

Thomas Cromwell has been seen as a creative man who carried out an administrative revolution setting up a bureaucracy which functioned independently of the royal will, as 'an autocrat as well as a bureaucrat in office, concerned with both the development of weapons of government and his own unrestricted use of them'.[3] Yet to the king he was a tool: a legal and financial officer of great competence and wide discretion to be discarded at will. To the old nobility he was little more than a financier. He took the odium for the despoliation of the monasteries while others established their fortunes. He was dismissed as soon as he bungled major business, the Lutheran *entente* and the Cleves marriage. In the end he was as isolated as Wolsey.

---

[1] Attributed to Sir Henry Taylor (author of *The statesman*, 1836) by Harold J. Laski, *Reflections on the constitution*, Manchester, 1951, p. 132.

[2] A. F. Pollard, *Wolsey*, London, 1953, p. 103.

[3] G. R. Elton, *The Tudor revolution in government*, Cambridge, 1953, p. 416.

The lesser men, the Petres, Paces, Wriothesleys and Sadlers, were little more than senior civil servants, voices of experience. They played safe, avoided religious or political commitment. Taxed by Wolsey with inserting his discretion in a certain matter, Pace, a secretary of Henry VIII, protested that he had done no more than obey the king's commandment.[1] There is a story by Robert Beale which underlines the reality of royal authority:

It is reported of King Henry 8 that when Sir William Petre at the first time he was a secretary, seemed to be dismayed for that the king crossed and blotted out many things in a writing which he had made, the king willed him not to take it in evil part, 'for it is I', said he, 'that made both Cromwell, Wriothesley and Paget good secretaries, and so must I do to thee'.[2]

'One of the remarkable features of Elizabeth's rule is the extent to which she kept both major and minor decisions in her own hands.'[3] No one would depreciate the extensive influence of that 'wise politic man', William Cecil, Elizabeth's sponsor and guard, who so successfully maintained the Protestant hierarchy in England. Yet Cecil, too, had 'the stoical realism' of the higher civil servant, a capacity for non-involvement which had already enabled him to serve not only Somerset and Northumberland but also Mary. Elizabeth employed his vigilance, his professional skill, but she was herself 'perfunctory about nothing'.[4]

Robert Cecil, James I's Lord Treasurer and Secretary of State, executant of government, domestic and foreign, pivotal and persistent, was primarily a royal factor who, while keeping the framework in repair, may be said to have developed, through cumulative attention to business, some modest 'policies'. 'Before God', said James, 'I count you the best servant ever I had, albeit you be but a beagle.'[5] James was remote, conducting government from racecourse and hunting-field, telling his Secretary how to reply, decisive. Cecil 'lies at home by the fire when all the good hounds are daily running on the fields'.[6] He had to work through those in

---

[1] *Idem, The Tudor constitution*, Cambridge, 1960, p. 120.
[2] *Ibid.* pp. 126–7.
[3] J. E. Neale, 'The magnanimity of Queen Elizabeth I', *The Listener*, 1 January 1959.
[4] 'Or to be precise, her officials could never rely on her being perfunctory...' J. E. Neale, 'The Elizabethan age', in *Essays in Elizabethan history*, London, 1958, p. 37.   [5] D. Harris Willson, *King James VI and I*, New York, 1956, p. 177.
[6] *Ibid.* p. 186.

immediate royal favour, know who was in, who was out, which gentleman of the bedchamber, remembrancer, or companion in the chase, focused power in the swollen disordered court.

The typical Court politician is the 'very Machiavel', the servant of power ranging widely in kind from Polonius to Webster's Bosola. There are rare exceptions like Essex who seek to captivate the populace rather than 'win the Queen'. But the end for Essex is not 'domestical greatness' but the scaffold after ignominious and futile rebellion. In Council, he was no match for the less prepossessing but better schooled Robert Cecil.

At Court the leading politician developed his own strength. Round him were auxiliaries, pensioners, servants and agents who invested in their master and rose and fell with him. From these he drew advice and intelligence. Wolsey sent his own agents abroad, so did Walsingham. The grandee's household was a training ground for new politicians. Wolsey was the protégé of Fox, Cromwell the protégé of Wolsey; and Essex rose under the patronage of Leicester. There is a vivid picture in Cavendish's biography of Wolsey of Cromwell weeping in the window of the great chamber of Wolsey's house at Esher because he 'was in disdain with most men for [his] master's sake'. He did not desert his master's cause; indeed, for his defence of Wolsey in Parliament subsequently, Cromwell 'was esteemed to be the most faithfullest servant to his master of all other...'. But Wolsey could no longer sponsor him, and it was virtually as a masterless man that Cromwell rode off to London and the Court, 'to make or mar'.

An established politician might well reach out beyond his camarilla at Court down to his shire, which, as Lord Lieutenant, as a patron of county or borough seats, he might partly or wholly dominate. A new man might buy land, build houses, enter into the commerce and government of his locality, and so become a figure eligible for politics.

Yet outside the king there was no persistent source of power. Wolsey knelt in the mud for royal favour. Even so it passed to members of his household, to Cromwell and the devious Gardiner, who had clear heads and as yet did not embarrass the Crown through having generated hatred at large. Without the king, Wolsey saw the future as a disaster which he could only forfend by giving up politics.

There were forces other than the royal will and pleasure with

which the leading politician had to treat. There were the am-
bassadors of foreign powers who might pay him pensions but
could also rock his position by marring his diplomacy. There was
the rival faction seeking to supplant him. Wolsey had to watch
Norfolk as Burghley watched Leicester and Robert Cecil. Within
his own household there might be enemies who would testify
against him.

The up-country nobility are slow to move and the people rarely
speak. The Court politician is mainly conscious of the obduracy
of the nation, the difficulty of governing men through an imperfect
administrative system, of seeing that instructions and orders are
followed. He informs himself through his agents of the attitudes
of notables, gentry and people. He may try to make an impression
on the popular imagination, through buildings, house furnishings,
clothes and horsemen, and knows that garbled versions of his
vices and virtues will circulate through the servants' quarters to
the crowds.

Usually the Court politician moves silently before the people;
his craft as a servant is evaluated by the king. He will sometimes
sound alarums on the safety of the realm, extol the magnificence
and beneficence of the prince. But he is not freely and publicly
committed. His rhetoric, when he has one, is devised mainly to
defend established things: he is a voice of the king. He may have
to do harsh things while the monarch smiles. Only when he goes
to the scaffold or dies in disfavour will he speak freely. Then,
while testifying to the overriding royal will, he is allowed to
describe his predicament.

Politics was the profession in which a man could most rapidly
acquire prestige, wealth and power. Prestige meant being talked
about in alehouses as well as country-houses, riding abroad at the
head of horsemen, men seeking preferment through one's offices
and influence. As for wealth, there were fees, annuities, messes,
wine, houses and beds and, more important, if he were a layman,
generous grants of land, perhaps patents and monopolies; if an
ecclesiastic, absentee preferments. Power consisted in being the
immediate channel of the royal will, as Lord Chancellor, Lord
Treasurer or Secretary of State.

The monarch appointed, dismissed, decided. Within that rule it
was possible for a leading politician to acquire lustre, to develop
what might be called a policy but which was really a method,

retrenchment, perhaps, or a particular kind of revenue-raising, or, more generally, an unrelenting attention to efficiency.[1] The factions thought chiefly in terms of organization and places and pleasing the prince. But the Court was not of one mind and the king had a choice of men and attitudes; he could range widely, and Charles I could even bring men like Thomas Wentworth and Falkland into executive positions.

Right up to the Civil War men were predisposed to serve the Crown. Even Raleigh, the rumoured republican, whose philosophy of history exhorted men to escape the bondage of the present, has come down to us as the great Elizabethan courtier who was executed after vainly trying to do James I a service. There was literary sustenance for independent political action, in the scriptures and ancient writers, in Calvinist and Jesuit political theory. The past of England provided precedents for bridling the king. Yet if you wanted to make politics you had to make it out of yourself. As Miss Veronica Wedgwood has said: 'There were no well-known banners, no catchwords, no organized programmes and very little tradition; men wrestled with their own problems and found their own solutions and a man's political convictions were a matter between himself and his own conscience.'[2]

Before he went into politics, approached the Court, the politician was a private man living in the ordered *patria*, the shires and boroughs of England. It was from this *patria* that the monarch drew serviceable talent, whether it was Villiers from his remote country-house or Thomas Wentworth from his rich and powerful one. Only the singular man would envisage an order different from that prevailing; only the most courageous would join others in common purpose, and seek an audience outside the Court.

It was possible for character to serve at Court. The best example is Thomas Wentworth. Wentworth acknowledged the grievances of the realm, opposed forced loans and Buckingham's foreign policy, but once grievances were redressed, as they were by the Petition of Right, he left the opposition and entered the service of Charles I. For he had the conservative's belief in government: he could not let business 'moulder upon his hands'. 'Thorough' is 'the resolute determination of going through with it...of dis-

---

[1] See Aylmer, *The king's servants*, pp. 10–12.
[2] C. V. Wedgwood, *Strafford*, London, 1935, p. 8.

regarding and over-riding the interested delays and evasions of those who made the public service an excuse for enriching themselves at the public expense, or the dry technical arguments of the lawyers which would hinder the accomplishment of schemes for the public good'.[1]

H. R. Trevor-Roper has said that Wentworth was 'a disaster in the mature politics of England'.[2] One may demur about the 'maturity' of Jacobean and Caroline politics but it is true that there is something out of joint about the release of all that pride, idealism and energy to sustain a régime of such doubtful worth. Here was the lion serving the fox, incorruptible rough character finding a bent at Court, indeed discovering independent power there.

More significant for the future is another politician, quite distinct from the man of affairs, who dissents from the Court. He is already clearly present in Elizabethan times. His base is in the House of Commons among those who jostle together to represent the communities of England. For the Reformation had given renewed authority to Parliament. Henry VIII had not carried out his religious changes by force but by laws made in Parliament— laws which had no precedent in content. If the Crown in Parliament could reframe the relationship between Church and State, what could it not do? Representing all and sundry, might not Parliament develop an initiative independent of monarch and advisers? As such usurpation became possible, a new kind of politician appeared, one who sought to control and shape the prerogative powers of the monarch and who addressed a (barely discernible) political nation outside the House.

The new politician was a rarity, for few wished to earn the stigma of disloyalty which protracted opposition might bring upon them. Moreover, there was always in the House a body of Privy Councillors who guided the assembly and plotted the legislative programme. They kept their ear to the ground and were forearmed to deal with recalcitrance; they were aided by a Speaker, formally elected by the House, but, in fact, a 'groomed man' expected to steer business in the royal interest.

The House does not, therefore, seem a likely place to breed dissenting politicians, yet, from the beginning to the end of her

---

[1] S. R. Gardiner, *History of England 1603–1642*, London, 1884, VIII, 67.

[2] H. R. Trevor-Roper, *Historical essays*, London, 1957, p. 192.

reign, Elizabeth was at odds with individuals and groups on one matter or another. In spite of a long succession of experienced managers, the business of 'staying' the House and preserving the mysteries of the prerogative became more and more difficult. Inside and outside the chamber, men of like mind clustered together and schemed to substitute their own right reason in matters religious for that of the sovereign.

Whether he wished to reconstruct the national church or abolish it, the Puritan challenged the order of things. He found truth in the scriptures and wished to make human behaviour and institutions conform with it. The words of the Bible gave him political hardihood. It was the answer of the wrathful Elihu in the book of Job which moved Peter Wentworth to dangerous words:

Behold, I am as the new wine which hath no vent and bursteth the new vessels in sunder. Therefore will I speak, that I may have a vent. I will open my lips and make answer. I will regard no manner of person, no man will I spare; for if I should go about to please men, I know not how soon my Maker will take me away.[1]

Peter Wentworth is an obscured English tribune. He was a Puritan when Puritanism was unpopular and has never been fully incorporated into the Whig story. For most historians of the Tudors are captivated in time by the masterfulness of the Tudor line and become as slavish in admiration of their will to power as their courtiers. Wentworth first showed courage in 1571 when he attacked Sir Humphrey Gilbert for carrying tales from the House of Commons to the queen. Five years later he delivered the great speech which was reported to the Courts of Europe.

We are told that this 'rude speech' was meditated for four years before 'he was bold and went forward', and certainly no more momentous statement was ever made in a Tudor Parliament. It is an open declaration of the fallibility and responsibility of princes, boldly delivered in the outworks of the Court itself—so uncompromising an attack that the Crown would not allow him to complete it.

Certain it is, Mr Speaker, that none is without fault: no, not our noble Queen. Since, then, her Majesty has committed great faults—yea, dangerous faults to herself and the State—love, even perfect love, void of dissimulation, will not suffer me to hide them to Her Majesty's

[1] See J. E. Neale, *Elizabeth I and her parliaments 1559–1581*, London, 1953, p. 318.

peril...It is a dangerous thing in a Prince to oppose or bend herself against her nobility and people, yea, against most loving and faithful nobility and people.

It is more than a standard indictment of evil counsellors and scant-born gentlemen who have wormed themselves into the confidence of the monarch. It is a direct moral condemnation of the lion and the fox.

Amongst other, Mr Speaker, two things do very great hurt in this place, of the which I do mean to speak. The one is a rumour which runneth about the House, and this it is: 'Take heed what you do. The Queen's Majesty liketh not of such a matter; whosoever prefereth it, she will be much offended with him....' The other is: sometimes a message is brought into the House, either of commanding or inhibiting, very injurious unto the freedom of speech and consultation. I would to God, Mr Speaker, that these two were buried in Hell: I mean rumours and messages.

These are three assertions which mark the advent of character in free politics. The first is Wentworth's insistence that men 'ought to proceed in every cause according to the matter, and not according to the prince's mind'. The second is that he will pass nothing until he understands what it is. There is no mystery which cannot be explored by reason, which can stand against human conviction. The third shows character feeling for an audience: 'for we are incorporated into this place to serve God and all England...'.

To whom is he speaking? Immediately, it is true that he may have had in mind powerful courtier politicians like Burghley and Walsingham who had some sympathy with his attitudes. And he himself did not despair of winning the queen for her own good. Years later he addressed to her directly a pamphlet on the succession and sought the aid of Burghley and Essex to get it into her hands.

But fundamentally he was speaking to the small segment of the population that was Puritan. Unlike many of the seventeenth-century constitutionalists he was no antiquarian. It was not to the historic liberties of Englishmen that he appealed but to the liberties of the Christian man. He spoke to the Commons but had little following there. The Commons themselves sent him to the Tower in 1576 and, during his three subsequent imprisonments by the

Crown, they did not stir a hand. Yet through the House he spoke at large. For here was a focus of the national life in which the worlds of action, religion, scholarship and politics were all represented, an assembly in which men were measured by their words, where 'meditated' speeches were recorded by diarists to percolate beyond the boundaries of the House through tavern, theatre, town house down to the great country-houses.

Mrs Wentworth declared that 'if the gentlemen of England were honest, there would be five hundred in prison for her husband's opinion'. Yet already character was speaking to the country and had found a precarious base. To Sir John Neale, Peter Wentworth is 'incorrigible',[1] 'pathetically at fault',[2] presumably because he differed from the queen. He was indeed a blemish 'on the body politic well-knit together'. He was one who rejected magnanimity and all the wise politic men who flourished in its shade.

Peter Wentworth is the precursor of the great dissentient politicians of the seventeenth century. It is not implied that men were speaking out for the first time. Individuals had spoken out throughout the whole of the medieval period. To brood on one's estates on bad lordship, feudal distortions and the iniquities of the king and his *familiares*, to come with grievances and a retinue to Court, camp or capital, to make the *diffidatio* and wage private war were within the conduct of the old politics. It is no Whig straining of the story to see the constitutional opposition of the seventeenth century as the heir of feudality. The difference is that the feudatories did not challenge the system. The new spokesmen do just this and they do so with a passion and commitment to cause that are new.

There is little agreement about why the old constitutional order was reshaped in the seventeenth century—unless it be that the old Whig interpretation which stressed the words and actions of parliamentarians, lawyers, and kings in the crucial phase of the English story of liberty is superficial. For this story is about what was said, and it is now widely held that words bear little relation to motivation or real goals. If seventeenth-century men spoke in religious, constitutional or legal terms, they were deceiving themselves. The issues were, in fact, economic or social.

---

[1] *Elizabeth I and her parliaments 1584–1601*, London, 1957, p. 255.
[2] *Ibid.* p. 265.

What happened is less of a narrative than it was, less of a debate and more of a process.[1]

Here indeed is a conflict between a decayed feudality, with an obsolete functionalist view of society, and the new commerce, resenting paternalist restrictions on the free play of economic enterprise and emphasizing individual rights, in chief those of property. The existing structure of society protects a dying political order. The gentry—a commercialized and Puritanized gentry—destroy this order so that they and not the Court and its hangers-on may shape the policy of the realm. This is a construction which predicates a gentry, politically negligible but economically ebullient. There is another which presents the gentry as equally negligible politically but economically frustrated to the point of blind and unconstructive rebellion. But, rich or poor, they are politically next to nothing and wish to become something.

A political order is sustained by dominant interests and ideas. If those interests and ideas change, the order will become archaic. Even so, political orders have great durability, and can tolerate great contradictions. It is difficult to set limits to the capacity to tolerate anomalies, or bear oppression. It may be, as Strafford believed, that 'the authority of a King is the keystone which closeth up the arch of order and government, which, once shaken, all the frame falls together in a confused heap of foundation and battlement'. But someone has to shake the frame. If the unjust order is to be torn up by the roots, men must be excited. And they are excited only by words, by absorbing dangerous ideas, submitting themselves to leadership. As the *Pseudo-Alcibiades* says, in De Jouvenel's mock-Platonic dialogue:

'Understand, Socrates, that men need and enjoy this stirring of the blood which occurs when I call them to action and make them confident of its outcome. When I lend them my imagination and they lend me their forces, then are we together a joyfully striding giant...'[2]

---

[1] There is some resistance to this hypercritical historiography. 'To say that men unconsciously acted primarily in their economic interests even though they thought in religious or moral terms is to get involved in a kind of historico-psychoanalytical mysticism.' Willson H. Coates, in 'An analysis of major conflicts in seventeenth-century England', *Conflict in Stuart England*, London, 1960, ed. W. A. Aiken and B. D. Henning, p. 33. Men fought and killed each other because they moralized on history and politics.

[2] B. de Jouvenel, *The pure theory of politics*, Cambridge, 1963, pp. 27–8.

For those who take to action, to unaccustomed political violence, for all '*hommes révoltés*', history is not just one damned thing after another, not a sempiternal cycle, but contains a meaning and a promise. If established relationships have to go, there must be a lucid appeal to past and future. Moreover, the dissidence must beat strongly enough for individuals to detach themselves from the existing order: there must be men who despise their fortune and are therefore able to make a stand. Yet the new tribune will need a political base to give his words resonance. He must have associates, a provincial retreat, or the shelter of some great and powerful men.

In his Ford Lectures, 1962,[1] Christopher Hill has described, with a nod to the 'revolutionist's handbook', the Genevan Bible ('you could brave the King of England, if you were obeying the orders of the King of Kings'), the secular, intellectual origins of the English Revolution. Into the vacuum left by the decay of traditional ideas comes the vision of a practical science which will relieve man's lot on earth, the Baconian method by which man will command nature. With it comes the new progressive conception of history to be found in Raleigh's *History of the World*. And, thirdly, there is Coke's adaptation of English law to the needs of a commercial civilization, and the potent historical myth which he constructed from the Year Books to enable God's Englishmen to identify and defend their liberties. There is a correlation, says Hill, between these ideas and political and religious radicalism. Bacon, Coke, and Raleigh, three unsuccessful Court politicians, all wrought more wisely than they knew, for their ideas were to be, 'together with the Puritan sense of destiny', the 'new ideological growing points for men who hitherto had existed only to be ruled'.

Hill sets up a rough, revolutionary syndrome grouping Puritanism, the new science, progress and parliamentarianism against neo-popery, traditional theology and royalism. Against sensuousness, courtly magnificence, rhetorical dogma and the internationalism of Counter-Reformation he ranges iconoclasm, austerity, introspection and insular patriotism. But in this impressive and moving clash of serried ideals and styles, both *eventful* and *eventmaking* men have still to give history a push.[1]

[1] Broadcast version in *The Listener*, 31 May–5 July 1962.
[2] A distinction made by Sidney Hook in *The hero in history*, London, 1945, chapter IX.

This is the notable thing about the dissentient politician, that he, as a private individual, came out of obscurity and publicly defied the Court, not as a rebel or outlaw but as a man claiming to have the country behind him. Country leaders had appeared in the time of Elizabeth, but until the last decade the forehanded Privy Council and the prestige of the queen had held them in check. In James's time Parliament turned in the hands of the Privy Councillors—there were now too few there. The Commons began to throw up its own leaders. Small groups began to accept guidance from forceful and eloquent men. The groups and leaders were periodically broken up by preferment at Court or in Council, yet in every Parliament there were knots of alienated men. Patriotic and dangerous, they read the Bible and Roman authors, cited parliamentary antiquities, became capable of conviction, were prepared to risk life for a cause.

The rancour of discontented men, city merchants and country-house radicals might turn to plot and sedition but what made conflict coherent was memorable language in Parliament or in the courts. Men of character found themselves striking attitudes, forming momentous sentences. The Commons provided both school and audience, and there is born a special kind of political heroism in which a gesture or phrase is sustained to the point of action and beyond. The powerful intellectual current of Puritanism bore many along, but many, said Hobbes, had read Latin and Greek authors and through them acquired anti-monarchical sentiments—and forgotten the blessings of peace. There is at work too the dangerous mimesis which Burke was to remark:

'I have often observed that on mimicking the looks or gestures of angry or placid or frighted or daring men, I have involuntarily found my mind turned to that passion whose appearance I endeavoured to imitate; nay, I am convinced it is hard to avoid it, though one strove to separate the passion from its correspondent gestures.'[1]

This is the dangerous beginning of style. Men looked into their own hearts to speak but there were some who made an art and an excitation out of it too. They were helped by their audience. 'The man who speaks to others and carries them to the actions he desires: there is the man who makes history. Yes, but there is one

---

[1] Edmund Burke, *A philosophical enquiry into the origin of our ideas of the sublime and beautiful*, IV, iv, quoted by Edgar Wind, *Art and anarchy*, London, 1963, p. 4.

who decided whether our "hero" shall indeed make history: it is the man spoken to.'[1] Through metaphor, Biblical and classical analogies, these simplifications of discourse, the audience escaped from the mundane present and made their response.

The spokesmen, the orators, knew that the counties had their eyes on them, that memorable speeches circulated in the country: 'Every man that sits have three powers, one of himself, and the country, and the whole realm after his coming.'[2] They were aware too that they were alone, that parliamentary assemblies had virtually ceased to function in the rest of Europe. 'We are entrusted for our country. If we lose our privileges, we betray it; if we give way to this, we lose our privileges...Let us not look upon ourselves only, but upon our posterity also.'[3]

Public words are measurable in terms of action, of life and limb: they are perilous. When arrested, Sir John Eliot had said that 'being now but a private man, he would not trouble himself to remember what he had either spoken or done as a public man'.[4] Private words are a man's own. During his impeachment, Strafford insisted that he should not be accountable for them:

If words spoken to friends, in familiar discourse, spoken in one's chamber, spoken at one's table, spoken in one's sick bed...if these things shall be brought against a man as treason, this, under favour, takes away the comfort of all human society...If these things be strained to take away life and honour it will be a silent world; a city will become an hermitage...[5]

What the dissentients wanted is not clear. It does not seem that either Coke or Eliot wanted to govern[6] and even Pym, while administratively creative and successful in organization, had no theory of state.[7] Some saw politics in terms of restoring the Elizabethan balance of Crown, Council and Parliament; others, more radically, wished to re-place medieval bridles on the prerogative: some, more rarely, conceived of a restored Anglo-Saxon golden age. They were not anti-monarchical as such; they merely sought to bring pristine virtue to a degenerate Court. They knew

[1] De Jouvenel, *Pure theory of politics*, p. 83.
[2] Cited in E. R. Forster, 'The procedure of the House of Commons against patents and monopolies', in *Conflict in Stuart England*, edited Aiken and Henning, p. 62.
[3] *Ibid.* p. 61.   [4] C. V. Wedgwood, *op. cit.* p. 80.
[5] *Ibid.* pp. 304–5.
[6] I. Deane Jones, *The English revolution*, London, 1931, p. 58.
[7] J. H. Hexter, *The reign of King Pym*, Cambridge, Mass. 1941, chapter x.

what they detested: the gilded bottlenecks of patronage; government control of trade; the men on the make at Court; the useless
pomp, the triviality, the masques, flambeaux and vices; the neo-
Catholicism which built bridges into despotic Europe; the traffic
with the Spanish enemy; and the instruments of religious conformity. They passed a moral judgment on the apparatus.

There is no organizing ideology or even constructive criticism[1]
but there is character. These are men not at all sure of the way they
are going or to what their public behaviour commits them. The
archetypal figure is, of course, Cromwell, poorly tailored, badly
shaven, with blood on his collar, 'the tyrant from the country'.
He came late to politics and arms but in the end was compulsively
absorbed in words and action. Marvell seized on the emergence of
heroic energy in one who might have lived out his life in rural
obscurity.

> And, if we would speak true,
> Much to the Man is due.
> Who, from his private Gardens, where
> He liv'd reserved and austere,
> As if his highest plot
> To plant the Bergamot,
> Could by industrious Valour, climbe
> To ruine the great Work of Time,
> And cast the Kingdome old
> Into another Mold.

But the exemplar is Sir John Eliot, the recruit to the Court
who was never absorbed into it, who broke on grounds of
principle with both the king and his own patron, the duke of
Buckingham. He stands outside.

Not in fidelity to constitutional arrangements, not in obedience to the
orders of a king or in obedience to the votes of a Parliament, lay the
secret of political capacity. The ideal statesman was to be the man who
had the open eye to discern his country's wants, the tongue to speak
freely the counsel which his mind had conceived, and the heart and
the resolution to suffer, if not to die, in the defence of his belief.[2]

Although, when in captivity, he moved towards the Puritan
position it was not the Genevan Bible that gave him hardihood.

---

[1] '"Success" by the Independents would have been a kind of decentralized anarchi-
cal gentry-republic, a Polish Diet. It is just as well that they failed.' Trevor-Roper,
Historical essays, pp. 203–4.
[2] Gardiner, *History of England 1603–1642*, London, 1884, VI, 104.

Yet his many citations of Roman writers served the same purpose: they made coherent the ragged world of politics. They took him further than could his own unaided gifts for political resistance.[1] He could widen and dignify an issue by making a metaphor. Buckingham became 'the Aeolus of the time' who loosed 'discordant winds', or Sejanus, the favourite of Tiberius.

Eliot's resistance ran in a broad, deep stream. He turned grievance into principle and seems to have had a sense that 'the ancient genius of this kingdom' was behind him, that there were thousands who would follow him. After the unsuccessful attempt by Charles I to manipulate the composition of the Parliament of 1626 he wrote:

So shallow are these rivulets of the court, that they think all wisdom like their murmur...But in this they deceive themselves...Great is the variety in a kingdom, both of knowledge and ability...This plots, that speaks, a third judges and discerns.

Some men, he says, are excellent,

yet appear not while their works are done by others...are content and happy to be shadowed in themselves...Yet against all, when necessity shall require, they will, and are ready to, stand forth.[2]

There is time and occasion for the right man.

There is a passage in *The Monarchy of Man* showing how character in politics must wrench itself from the felicities of private life:

Shall we forsake that sweetness? Shall we neglect that fatness of our peace (as the fig and olive said of old) for the public use and service? Yes! No difficulties may retard us...no exception is admitted to this rule; but where the greater good is extant, the duty there is absolute, without caution or respect...for the rule is *Officium non fructum sequi*, to observe the duty, not the benefit; to seek that end which is propounded in the general, not to propound an end and reason of our own. But dangers may be incident? It may betray our safeties and expose our fortunes, expose our liberties, expose our lives to hazard?...No danger, no hazard may deter us. The duty and office stand entire.[3]

Not all he did measured up to the rhetoric. To place integrity and the commands of conscience at the centre of public life is to invite a remorseless audit. Yet the posture became set; in his

---

[1] Cf. Hugh Ross Williamson, *Four Stuart portraits*, London, 1949, pp. 86–7.
[2] John Foster, *Sir John Eliot*, London, 1864, I, 433–4.
[3] Quoted by Williamson in *Four Stuart portraits*, pp. 83–4.

obduracy he suffered harsh and increasingly severe imprisonment which admitted no relaxation; had the temerity to see himself as a kind of Socrates, indicted for the crime of subjecting the established order to scrutiny; died for what character demanded.

Hampden was a man whom patriotism brought to the front, a man whose virtues might have otherwise been unknown.

He was certainly a person [wrote Sir Philip Warwick] of the greatest abilities of any of that party. He had great knowledge both in scholarship and in law. He was of a concise and significant language, yet the subtlest speaker of any man in the house...He was a man of a great and plentiful estate, and of great interest in his country and of a regular life...[1]

Wealth and connections were necessary supports, but the important thing was that, impelled by moral impulse, he emerged from the ruck and won 'popularity', the power to move and lead men.

He was rather of reputation in his own country than of public discourse or fame in the kingdom before the business of ship money; but then he grew the argument of all tongues, every man inquiring who and what he was, that durst at his own charge support the liberty and property of the kingdom and rescue his country from being made a prey to the Court.[2]

Clarendon, like Warwick, considered Hampden not unsubtle: 'he left his opinions with those from whom he pretended to learn and receive them'. Yet no one impressed Clarendon more as a man in command of himself, more deeply committed to act when the time was ripe, more sure of his 'popularity'. Here was 'a head to contrive, a tongue to persuade, and a hand to execute, any mischief'; his death in the field was 'a great deliverance to the nation'.

Pym, too, was character exercised in a political cause. He was deeply acquainted with the whole story; he had been in the Parliament of 'roaring boys' as far back as 1614 and knew what he hated: all those who had exercised personal power within the royal prerogative. He had early acquired 'popularity' in the country and, after the attempt to arrest the Five Members, the City was with him too. Forced into rebellion, he faced it

[1] *Memoirs of the reign of Charles I*, London, 1701, p. 240.
[2] Clarendon, *History of the rebellion*, Oxford, 1888, III, 62.

resolvedly. Before the Long Parliament he had said to Hyde that 'they must be of another temper than they were in the last Parliament; they must not only sweep the House clean below but must pull down all the cobwebs which hung in the tops and corners'.

But what there was besides courage was a great artificer of political action with sufficient eloquence: intrepid in securing the fall and death of Strafford, transferring power from monarch to Parliament, in designing war policy, providing war finance and securing the Solemn League and Covenant. He became virtual leader of the House, yet had no assured organization to command it. At his own peril he was the instigator; the gentry and the lawyers who had long brooded on their own now moved together. 'Whilst men gazed upon each other, looking who should begin, (much the greatest part having never before sat in Parliament) Mr Pym, a man of good reputation, but much better known afterward, who had been as long in those assemblies as any man then living, brake the ice...'[1] What common interest emerged was held together by his personal leadership of the middle group. Like Hampden he had only popular authority and with this he worked with moderated violence towards the redress of grievances. His manipulative and business ability was at the service of a cause.

The followings of the new politicians constituted independent sources of authority. Even if the minds of some, like Eliot, Wentworth and Coke, were impeded, as Hill suggests, so that they could not see their way forward towards a clear assertion of the right of Parliament to subordinate the king to the country's good,[2] even if character had little creativity, once the defiance was made there was no going back.

> The Mitre is down,
> And so is the Crown,
> And with them the coronet too...

The new politics was based upon the disobedience of private men in and through the powers of an autonomous Parliament, now seen as analogous within the state to the reasoning faculties in the human soul. Yet beyond reason lay conviction and the recalcitrant will. What had been ritualistic or conspiratorial is now achieved legitimately as political will inhabiting or usurping the

[1] Clarendon, *History of the Rebellion* I, 174.
[2] Christopher Hill, *The century of revolution*, Edinburgh, 1961, pp. 62–5.

prerogative. 'Cromwell', writes Irene Coltman, 'appeared to Clarendon as the expression of pure political talent as it could develop outside the restrains of order. His deeds were extraordinary: "He reduced three countries that hated him to complete submission and governed them by an army that wanted to be rid of him." And these fantastic things, thought Clarendon, were done for no other reason than that he wanted to do them.'[1]

The will might be wicked and, if it unified a crowd, dangerous too, but from now onwards those who command and those who obey are confronted with those who incite and those who follow. Trouble came when causes clashed and the monarchy, having become itself a cause, lost the power to mediate. Public peace was now perpetually in danger. One solution was to deprecate conviction and to set up Leviathan to ensure peace among men. In the same vein, Anthony Ascham maintained that men should reject all public causes, for there were no good ones.[2]

These extreme solutions were not adopted. The problem became one of practical wisdom, how to secure obedience from conceded diversity in society, how to increase consensus, reducing to mere verbal bellicosity the violence to which men fall victims. Something like the same problem faces African states today. Colonial authority is gone, tribal authority is decaying but still making faction. In such circumstances not all causes are admissible —certainly not those of foreign princes—and 'good old causes' may have to be driven under ground.

Conviction which had led to twenty years of civil war and usurpation had proved dangerous. Yet to banish moral impulse from politics because it bred violence was not feasible. What did prove possible after a century's turmoil was a cooling down of political enthusiasm, a narrowing of the political choice, so open and wide in the days of Leveller and Digger and Fifth Monarchy men. Thus the politician with a cause was admitted under scrutiny into politics. The divisions persisted but ran to the civilized and fruitful cleavage between Church and Chapel (the basic tension, thinks Kitson Clark, aesthetically, socially and intellectually in

---

[1] Irene Coltman, *Private men and public causes*, London, 1962, p. 76. This book contains a fine exposition of Clarendon's reasoned fears of unshackled political ambition. 'It [the Puritan conscience] liberated the political will and the unconfined freedom which the Puritans had claimed to be the opportunity for saintliness became the ground for soaring political aspiration.'

[2] *Ibid.* part III, 'Anthony Ascham and the low opinion of wounds'.

English life) and, after some unpropitious flares of violence, to the long uninterrupted fixtures between Whig and Tory. Moral impulse did not fade: the politics of England has been suffused with it ever since.

To Matthew Arnold the cultural clash was deplorable: 'On the one hand was the Royalist party, with its vices, its incurable delusions; on the other, the Puritans, with their temper, their false, old-Jewish mixture of politics with an ill-understood religion.'[1] In the Puritans there is unseemly energy. Their ideals were inadequate; the moral impulse which moved them should have been more carefully examined. Arnold prefers Falkland, that 'born constitutionalist', the 'hater of "exorbitances"' without righteousness. Beside Falkland, the unsuccessful moderator of conflict, 'the martyr of lucidity of mind and largeness of temper, in a strife of imperfect intelligences and tempers illiberal', the Puritans were indeed coarse and violent. Yet was not this energetic coarseness an essential part of the character that was necessary to breach the old order? Were the qualities which Arnold finds in 'the English nature', strength, boldness, self-assertion and instincts of resistance and independence, sufficient in themselves—without Puritan conviction—to secure freedom of person and property?

What could happen to public causes and Country virtue in a corrupted age after character had forced the door of the Court can be seen, forty years later, in the singular career and conduct of Anthony Ashley Cooper, earl of Shaftesbury, commonly regarded as the greatest *politician* of the seventeenth century.

Shaftesbury, it has been said, 'was educated in one revolution, presided over a second and was connected through his ideas and his friends with a third.'[2] At first sight, no one was more devious than he. He had left the royal for the parliamentary cause and much later joined with the Protector's enemies to bring the king into his own. Under Charles II he had been Chancellor of the Exchequer and then Lord Chancellor, had opposed the Clarendon Code and had supported the Dutch war. He was one of the dupes of the Secret Treaty of Dover, had broken with the Cabal and refused to be reconciled with the Court. In his last years he pre-

---

[1] Matthew Arnold, 'Falkland', in *Mixed essays*, London, 1880, p. 234.
[2] J. R. Tanner, *English constitutional conflicts of the seventeenth century*, Cambridge, 1948, p. 287.

sided over everything that was new and exciting in English politics; he made the House of Lords into a forum against the Crown, created the New Country party and the Green Ribbon Club. He raised such a stir that the Pension Parliament gave way to the 'mighty roaring Parliament' of 1679; he identified Monmouth, the king's natural son, as the Protestant successor. He then made the Popish Plot into a symbol of royal perfidy and promoted the Exclusion Bill until it came to sedition and the edge of civil war. Finally he was imprisoned for high treason, fled the country and died in exile.

'The multitude,' writes Macaulay, 'struck with admiration by a prosperity which, while everything else was continually changing, remained unchangeable, attributed to him a prescience almost miraculous, and likened him to the Hebrew statesman of whom it is written that his counsel was as if a man had inquired of the oracle of God.'[1] Yet while it is true that he had an eye for the rising interest, he was always much more than a weathercock politician. He was a bold man with no reverence for tradition, yet acutely aware of where he was in history.

> Our state artificer foresaw
> Which way the world began to draw...

Men responded to him. 'There is no simpler (or more important) phenomenon in human relations', writes De Jouvenel,[2] 'than that *A* moves *B*.' To predict who will move whom is difficult but it remains true that the *instigator*, the politician of intention and cause, must have this power to gather others around him in common action. Moreover, to move men he must know the *patria*. Of Shaftesbury Burnet wrote: 'His strength lay in the knowledge of England, and of all the considerable men in it. He understood well the size of their understandings, and their tempers.'[3] This was complementary to his 'particular talent to make others trust to his judgment, and depend on it'. Shaftesbury was a politician acutely aware of others and of what could be done through them.

Like Pym he was an instigator, making and seizing initiatives. Yet, as in Pym, character was overlaid by the craft of politics.

---

[1] *History of England*, London, 1913, I, 198.   [2] *Pure theory of politics*, p. 78.
[3] Osmund Airy (ed.): *Burnet's History of my own time*, part I, The reign of Charles the Second, I, Oxford, 1897, 173.

Having to work through others he became absorbed in organization. Like Pym he had the dangerous politics of the up-country
patriot, seeing the world from his Dorset manor-house. And, as
in Pym, his country virtue was not unalloyed. Like Pym, he knew
the force of city mob and mercantile pressure and achieved
'popularity'. When the Grand Jury acquitted him of treason, 'the
people fell a holloaing and shouting, the bells rung, bonfires were
made and such public rejoicing that never such an insolent defiance of authority was seen'. A medal was struck to celebrate the
occasion with, on one side, a bust of Shaftesbury inscribed
Antonio comiti de Shaftesbury and, on the other, a picture of the
Tower of London where he had lain imprisoned, with the sun
emerging from a cloud. But his enemies saw him as 'a man with
a long lean pale face with fiend's wings, and snakes twisted round
his body accompanied by several rebellious fanatical heads...'.[1]

  'There is', said J. R. Tanner, 'a much lower tone about the politics
of the Restoration period than had prevailed in the days of Hampden and Pym.'[2] Puritan earnestness[3] was lost under 'the external
coating of ceremony and refinement'; causes were irrelevant in
a 'polite world behaving like a troop of vicious children in its
impatience of seriousness and its contentment with anything at
at all in the shape of amusement', in a Court 'turning gladly from
the task of politics to the business of dissipation...'.[4]

  So too, G. M. Trevelyan:

The conduct of Whigs and Tories between 1678 and 1685 is so mad
and bad that it is a psychological puzzle to recognize any of the better
elements usually found in the English political character—humanity,
decency or common sense. Whigs and Tories act like the nervous and
hot-blooded factions of a South European race. They rant, scream,
bully, assassinate men by forms of law, study no interest but their own,
and betray even their own interest through sheer folly and passion.[5]

  There were two sources of authority. The first was the monarch.
Charles II was no *fainéant*. Faced with a Parliament, law courts and

---

[1] *DNB.*   [2] Tanner, *op. cit.* p. 219.
[3] Matthew Arnold thought that the Puritans had brought their eclipse upon themselves. 'So grossly imperfect, so false was the Puritan conception and presentation
of righteousness, so at war with the ancient and inbred integrity, piety, good
nature and good humour of the English people that it led straight to moral
anarchy, the profligacy of the Restoration.' 'Falkland' in *Mixed essays*, p. 227.
[4] Tanner, *loc. cit.* (from an untraced source).
[5] *The English revolution*, London, 1956, p. 37.

a local government system which worked practically independently of him, he found he could retain the reality of kingship
only by compromising with and perhaps by corrupting those who
worked the system. He might have defied his circumstances by
creating an intimidating standing army, but of all things Parliament, its anti-militarism sharpened by the Cromwellian experience,
would deny him this first. What he was able to do was to pursue
his own devious pro-French foreign policy and deceive both
ministers and Parliament. This policy, with its implication that
England should cease to be interested in the continental balance
of power and become a client state of France, could not be openly
avowed but had to be pursued along a tortuous route lined with
French gold, secret treaties and parliamentary prorogations. The
other centre of power was the self-confident Anglican Parliament,
heir of the accumulated authority of the Rump and Protectorate
assemblies and now mainly concerned with keeping an Anglican
clamp on the parishes of England, with suppressing the Dissenting
yeoman farmers, the small traders and old soldiers, through the
Clarendon Code. Parliament was royalist, yet it continually
thwarted the king, refused him arms, made nonsense of his policy
of religious toleration, broke three ministries. But it was corruptible by both the English and the French Courts. And it was because it was corruptible that both Protestantism and the liberties
of Englishmen seemed in peril.

A Marxist historian has seen the moment dramatically. It was
then that 'the figures passing down the country road—dissenting
farmer, brewer, clothier, shopkeeper, hawker, were amazed
to see the gates of the great park flung wide, not by servants
carrying broken meats from my lord's dinner to give to the indi-
gent, but by my lord himself, who in the urgent tones of a comrade
cried out: "Are you with me? If England is to be saved we must
unite together for the cause of liberty, the Protestant religion and
a new Parliament."'[1]

Shaftesbury had aristocratic zest and confidence. He knew the
value of his order: 'It is not only your concern', he said to his
fellow peers, 'that you maintain yourself in it; but it is the concern
of the poorest man that you keep your station.' Yet he was a
remarkable political entrepreneur: he mobilized the most robust
elements in the realm, aristocrats, squires, Dissenters, yeoman and

[1] Iris Morley, *A thousand lives*, London, 1954, p. 87.

tradesmen against a corrupt Court and Parliament; his political bases ranged from the West Country to Aldersgate, from Cheshire to Wapping.

To make a lasting style out of such desperate events in such sad and bad times was more than even he could manage. Yet up to the final catastrophe Shaftesbury's record was something of a political masterpiece. His organized opposition to the prerogative was the beginning of Whiggery, even if the Whigs have never fully received him; partly because he backed Monmouth as the Protestant successor instead of Orange; partly because the movement which he led included not only men of wealth and standing, Russells, Cavendishes and Delameres and the great squires of the West Country, but also the plotters, the disaffected in town and country, those in 'the gutters and backyards of courage'.[1]

To Bolingbroke, writing fifty years later,[2] the Exclusion crisis was something blown up by the Whigs to frighten the king but which, in the event, enabled Charles II to restore the political power of the Court by dividing what might have been a single, united Country party, the heir of seventy years of patriotic opposition politics. The Exclusion issue was an unnecessary prolongation of the political 'phrenzy' originating in 'the epidemical taint' of James I. 'It hath cost us a century to lose our wits and to recover them again.' Through the injurious partisanship of Whig and Tory, the nation had lost yet more of 'its primitive temper and integrity, . . . its old good manners, its old good humour, and its old good nature . . .'

The exclusion of James I was in fact achieved in 1688 with only a small part of the passion stirred by the first Whigs. In this temperate revolution there was at work neither Shaftesbury's *virtu* nor his organizing power. In these Shaftesbury outran not only his own century but the next. 'Nothing in the eighteenth century', writes the historian of the early Whigs, 'justified and demanded the discipline, organization, ruthlessness, and mass effort which, under Shaftesbury's leadership, made the first Whigs such a formidable force.'[3] Yet it seems that these men, like Pym and his associates, had no clear designs on the future; they merely wished to keep the institutions and liberties of England as they were by excluding a Catholic successor to the throne.[4]

---

[1] Morley, *A thousand lives.*   [2] 'A dissertation upon parties', *Works*, London, 1809, III.
[3] J. R. Jones, *The first Whigs*, Oxford, 1961, p. 212.   [4] *Ibid.* pp. 213–14.

In the eighteenth century there was constitutional peace and a persisting structure of politics: in the seventeenth century a protracted debate on fundamentals shook an unstable political framework. But with seventeenth-century passion there went a greater capacity for political mobilization. 'The first Whigs had necessarily to possess, or rather develop, the organization, cohesion, discipline, and mass appeal which made them a party, because of the intensity of the crisis through which they were living.'[1]

A nineteenth-century writer remarked Shaftesbury's modernity:

He resumes in himself not only all the more salient characteristics of his age of politics, but he prefigures some of the most striking traits of ours. In his single person he typifies all the passion and profligacy, all the reckless turbulence and insatiable ambition of the troubled times in which he lived, but those three most notable actors on the stage of later English politics—the modern demagogue, the modern party leader, and the modern Parliamentary debater—are in him foreshadowed also.[2]

> Of these false Achitophel was the first:
> A Name to all succeeding Ages curst.

To the springs of *ira et studium*, anger and enthusiasm, there were added powers of organization.

[1] *Ibid.* p. 212.   [2] H. D. Traill, *Shaftesbury*, London, 1886, p. 207.

3

THE ASSIMILATION
OF CHARACTER AND STYLE

For the durable truths of Whiggery which would mould a whole race
of politicians in the eighteenth century, including the Tories, one
would not go to Shaftesbury, the phrenetic man, but to the
pamphlets and aphorisms of his associate and friend in the Green
Ribbon Club and later his successful adversary in the great debate
over Exclusion, George Savile, marquis of Halifax. Halifax is
rightly the hero of both Macaulay and Trevelyan. The revolution
of 1688, writes Trevelyan, 'was a victory of moderation, a victory
not of Whig or Tory passions, but of the spirit and mentality of
Halifax the Trimmer'.[1] Halifax was one who 'hoped that God
would not lay it to his charge that he could not digest iron'. He
opposed all extremes: the Test Act and the attempt to exclude
James, duke of York from the throne; he was for Orange rather
than Monmouth, yet he sought to reconcile Monmouth and
Charles II; he sought to stay the foolhardy course of James. He
did not take the initiative in the Revolution of 1688 but helped
to establish it.

Halifax was a Country politician who came to bridge both
Court and Country and make a style out of it. As a courtier politician he was acceptable in turn to Charles II, James II and William
III. His great estates absorbed him but it was not his romantic
protests about country pleasures ('I confess I dream of the country,
as men do of small beer when they are in a fever...'; 'I grow
everyday fitter for a coal fire and a country parlour...') that
made him a Country politician. It was his deeply considered
patriotism:

Our Trimmer is far from idolatry in other things; in one thing only
he cometh [somewhat] near it; his country is in some degree his idol.
He doth not worship the sun because it is not peculiar to us; it rambleth
about the world, and is less kind to us than it is to other countries. But
for the earth of England, though perhaps inferior to that of many

[1] G. M. Trevelyan, *The English revolution*, London, 1956, p. 241.

[46]

places abroad, there is a divinity in it and he would rather die than see a spire of English grass trampled down by a foreign trespasser.[1]

Yet he distrusted the patriot with virtuous politics who would break up the unity of the country. He is an agnostic in causes, a sceptic about political passion:

Every party, when they find a maxim for their turn, they presently call it a *Fundamental*...no feather has been more blown about in the world than this word *Fundamental*...For all men would have the principle to be immovable which serves their use at the time.[2]

Halifax stands for political lenity: he disapproved of the political executions of Russell and Sidney. His is the politics of restraint, of dispute within safe limits with blunted weapons, within the consensus. To establish it there must be a secular settlement in which extremists are excluded. For the system, as Balfour maintained, over two centuries later, must be one in which men 'can safely afford to bicker; and [be] so sure of their own moderation that they are not dangerously disturbed by the never-ending din of political conflict'.[3]

It was always possible to come to terms with the enemy: '...our climate is a Trimmer between that part of the world where men are roasted, and the other where they are frozen...'[4] It was not an age in which men could follow 'the strict morality of better times'. Halifax was highly sceptical about the basic political division of the seventeenth century: 'The interest of the governors and the governed is in reality the same, but by mistakes on both sides it is generally very differing. He who is a courtier by trade, and the country gentleman who will be popular, right or wrong, help to keep up this unreasonable distinction.'[5]

It follows that for Halifax the nation is not divided into two camps. Whig and Tory are for him vulgar nicknames. Of them he says, 'Amongst all the engines of dissension there hath been none more powerful in all times than the fixing names upon one another of contumely and reproach...Such things ever begin in jest and end in blood and the same word which at first maketh

[1] 'The character of a trimmer' in H. C. Foxcroft, *The life and times of Sir George Savile, first Marquis of Halifax*, London, 1898, II, 335.

[2] 'Political thought and reflections', *ibid.* pp. 490–3.

[3] Introduction to W. Bagehot, *The English constitution*, 1928 (World's Classics), p. xxiv. [4] 'The character of a trimmer,' Foxcroft, *op. cit.* II, 342.

[5] 'Political thoughts and reflections', in Foxcroft, *op. cit.* p. 501.

the company merry groweth in time to a military signal to cut one another's throats.'[1] This was true enough of republican Whig and Divine Right Tory. Neither was to have authority after 1688. The Whigs changed their nature and forgot Shaftesbury. The Tories were only Jacobite when drunk.

'The angry buzz of a multitude is one of the bloodiest noises in the world.'[2] Shaftesbury stood for violence, emerging causes; Halifax for poise, some inactivity, consensus, a delimitation of politics, a minimization of rule. The politician must lose his zeal and work for prizes within a system. Who will govern? Both the privileged and the able. In the *Rough draught of a new model at sea* (a discussion of the relative merits of seamen risen from the ranks and gentlemen volunteers in the Fleet) he comes down in favour of the gentlemen provided that they 'restore themselves to a better opinion, both for morality and diligence':

To expect that quality alone should waft men up into places and employments is as unreasonable as to think that a ship, because it is carved and gilded, should be fit to go to sea without sails or tackling. But when a gentleman maketh no other use of his quality than to incite him the more to do his duty, it will give such a true and settled superiority as must destroy all competition from those that are below him.[3]

If men will follow the grain of history all will be well. 'Things tend naturally', he wrote to the stirring Dissenters, 'to what you would if you would let them alone, and not by an unseasonable activity lose the influence of your good star which promiseth you everything that is prosperous.'[4]

At this point of the argument [writes Butterfield] we are...introduced to an idea or to an inclination which became part of the political consciousness of the whigs and which—lurking perhaps in *obiter dicta*—was to become a recognizable element in the political judgments of the typical Englishman: the feeling that, apart from any action we may take in the present conjuncture, the world is changing, and history is moving forward on her own account; and we ourselves must reckon with this process and use it—must conceive ourselves as co-operating with history, leaning on events somewhat; not resting idly indeed, but lying in wait for opportunity.[5]

---

[1] 'Character of a trimmer' in Foxcroft, *op. cit.* p. 280.
[2] 'Political thoughts and reflections', in Foxcroft, *op. cit.* p. 501.
[3] Foxcroft, *op. cit.* p. 464.
[4] 'A letter to a dissenter', Foxcroft, *op. cit.* p. 377.
[5] *The Englishman and his history*, p. 89.

If it is true that eighteenth-century politicians co-operate with history in a way that their predecessors do not, it is Halifax who strikes their note.[1] Yet he was no quietist. Like the great Whigs he had both weight and nerve, even if he brought them down not against but on the side of history:

Jotham, of piercing wit and pregnant thought,
Endued by nature and by nature taught
To move assemblies, who but only tried
The worse awhile, then chose the better side;
Nor chose alone, but turned the balance too,
So much the weight of one brave man will do.

The new politicians of the seventeenth century had questioned the order: in the eighteenth century, new and old politicians worked within one. Rarely is the order challenged and it is not in jeopardy because it is given by the wisest of all revolutions. Constitutional conflict is rare; yet subtle inner transmutations imperceptibly produce the Cabinet system; and from the factions of the narrow political nation, there appear by the end of the century the lineaments of the two parties.

The trinity of politics was not Montesquieu's categories, legislature, executive and judiciary, but King, Lords and Commons, monarchy, aristocracy and people, in a balance which allowed men to live in liberty. The postulate was not the separation of powers but their necessary co-operation. And where conflict was imminent, men showed remarkable ingenuity for devising rules and practices to make assured and safe politics possible.

The Revolution settlement had prohibited certain actions of the Crown but had not defined its sphere of action. The laws which renewed and expanded the monarch's authority had to be passed in Parliament; the monarch could no longer suspend and dispense with them. All his servants now derived their powers from common or statute law. Yet the king still governed, was still responsible for administration, for the initiating and designing of policy, especially foreign policy, for making peace and war. And with him lay powers of appointment by which he could secure majorities in the House of Commons to support his ministries.

[1] Even when he declares that 'the best party is but a kind of a conspiracy against the rest of the nation'. For the eighteenth century did not legitimize 'the great parties' of the seventeenth century. See Harvey C. Mansfield, *Statesmanship and party government*, Chicago, 1965, chapter 1.

GCA

It was by offices, pensions, sinecures—'corruption'—that the king took the edge off the Commons' hostility. Without 'corruption' political achievements would have been small:

> Corruption does not demonstrate the strength of pro-government forces, but their weakness. Without it there would have been no living in a climate so unfavourable to strong administration as prevailed in the eighteenth-century commons; with it business could be carried on provided the policy and personnel of the ministry could appeal to the patriotism of country gentlemen or at least neutralize their anti-government bias.[1]

Thus, through patronage and patriotism, was the king's 'independency' assured. There were other means of control. The combined influence of Crown and Peers at election time—the influence of the Crown was relatively small—could secure a House predisposed to fall in with the policies of ministers. So close indeed were the familial or other ties between the peerage and the Commons that the House could be called 'a second-rate aristocracy' or 'a parcel of younger brothers'.

Government electioneering was invariably successful. There was no independent electorate capable of forcing the Commons into stances inimical to the royal interest. From 1716, elections were obligatory only every seven years and most Parliaments lasted six. Uninstructed from outside—and authorities as diverse as Hume, Blackstone and Burke approved this autonomy—and much managed from within, the Commons for well into the century had few issues to excite it. Except for a few sparks over occasional conformity, religion had ceased to engage attention. The dynasty was only fitfully and uncertainly challenged. There was no persistent dispute over the distribution of property among the classes. 'The House of Commons is become a mere quarter sessions where nothing is transacted but turnpikes and poor rates.'[2] The Septennial Act, although challenged from time to time, became an acceptable rule of the game. Most constitutional controversies were legal, over interpretations of existing rules, rather than on the formulation of new ones. A 'legalistic, propertied libertarian society'[3] sustained and admired the great institutional triad of King, Lords and Commons.

---

[1] J. Steven Watson, *The reign of George III*, Oxford, 1960, p. 9.
[2] Horace Walpole, quoted in R. Pares, *King George III and the politicians*, Oxford, 1953, p. 4.   [3] John Carswell, *The old cause*, London, 1954, p. 15.

By the middle of the eighteenth century Whig and Tory labels retained little meaning. 'Until the death of Anne whiggery descends like a torrent between narrow banks, gathering against obstacles till they are surmounted or swept aside. But on reaching the Georgian plain it slackens and spreads into many interlocking streams or stands in almost stagnant pools.'[1] 'All's Whiggery now': to be a politician was to be a Whig, one of those who enjoyed the inheritance of the Revolution (Halifax's kind of Whig, not Shaftesbury's).

'The two chief characteristics of the Tories', wrote Lord Hervey, 'originally were the maintenance of the prerogative of the Crown and the dignity of the Church; both of which they pretended were now become, if not by profession, at least by practice, much more the care of the Whigs.'[2] As many as a quarter of the members of Parliament in the 1740s might own the title Tory, but the general acceptance of the Protestant succession and the withering of Divine Right, even of non-resistance, had eroded the doctrinal basis of their politics. From 1714 the Whigs provided security for the whole political nation but they were to lose, like the Tories, real connection with their conspiratorial forebears. The extremists on both sides are excluded. There is a turning away from causes, from politicians who have 'worked the nation into a most unnatural ferment'.[3] Politics is the passion of the age, yet politics is once more dissociated from the imagination.

To nineteenth-century historians this was the antecedent political age: the eighteenth-century tribunes were the forerunners of their own Brights and Gladstones. It was, therefore, primarily to display the heroic 'public men' of the great crises that history was trenchantly epitomized. What was presumed was the primacy of the public forum and the public debate.

No one has chosen to deny that, in their own way, Chatham, Wilkes, Charles James Fox were all voices of freedom. Yet a race of more sedulous historians has examined the texture of eighteenth-century politics with great care; revealed the private behind the public realm; exhibited the patterns of local and familial interests in such overwhelming detail as to impair the old coherences. Political routes have been retraced and the simple postures which

---

[1] *Ibid.* p. 12.
[2] *Memoirs of the reign of George II*, ed. J. W. Croker, London, 1840, I, 4.
[3] Joseph Addison, *The Spectator*, no. 556, 18 June 1714.

convinced a less sceptical and less curious age have been complicated by intricate analyses of motive, disposition and interest. What replaces the forum is the mart for interests and preferment; what occupies the foreground now is the disreputable but system-sustaining persistency of the eighteenth-century political animal. The view is now the middle-range view—from the jungle path.

The biographies of the famous, in which, 'as in plays, the central figures act and speak, the others being mere dummies in the background, "citizens", "soldiers etc"',[1] are disparaged in favour of the history of the rank and file of 'the political nation'. 'We have written about Parliamentary leaders and great administrators, and more or less ignored those whom they led and with or through whom they had to do their work...'[2] There has been therefore much less emphasis on the issues of politics and the creative role of 'great' politicians. What we have recently learned much more about is the day-to-day activities and aspirations, the stock responses of lesser men. The 'political nation', examined in detail, becomes more than merely the possible sphere of attraction and force for great men. 'Our interests and requirements have changed and broadened, we want to know about the life of crowds, to hear symphonies and not arias...'[3]

The unusual continuing stability of the eighteenth century, the accretions of routine in a quiet time, have made it possible for historians to erect 'a structure of politics' or a system in which the stuff of politics (the origins and growth of issues, how they are resolved and by whom, the debates in Council and in Parliament) becomes merely the fuel consumed in the system rather than the medium in which unique political decisions are made. In the currently dominant historiography of the eighteenth century, deeds and narrative have retreated: the context is more important than the speaker. 'The *dramatis personae* are portrayed without that outer framework of ideas and purposes which affects political conduct...'[4] The politician fits unobtrusively into the simple yet dense pattern of Namier and his disciples—statesmanship is lost without a trace.

In the foreground were the leaders of political groups, the men

---

[1] Sir Lewis Namier, *Crossroads of power*, London, 1962, p. 1.
[2] *Ibid.* p. 2.   [3] *Ibid.*
[4] H. Butterfield, *George III and the historians*, London, 1957, p. 211.

who commanded followers, took a stand, were in or out of office. In office, they exercised, positively or negatively, the powers of the Crown, used such patronage or oratory as they had at their disposal to secure support on the floor. In so far as they dominated the king and called on forces which were extra-royal, they stood for a kind of autonomy or freedom. Out of office they were malcontents crying in the old way against the evil advisers of the Crown, the pliancy of the Commons, the sacrifice of British interests to an alien dynasty. Their tactics were to play on any lack of unity in the Cabinet, to attack any minister who monopolized power as 'a sole minister or prime minister'. There was, however, no recognized opposition; and those who did oppose did not hold out the prospect of an alternative government; they were merely group leaders who happened to be out of office and hoped to be absorbed into some future construction. Governments themselves were all coalitions and almost invariably a new one was a reconstruction, a replastering. There was seldom anything approaching a programme.

Below the leaders, in a sense below the level of politics, was a government administrative bloc, a hundred or two placemen holding offices of profit under the Crown. They were the Court party and whatever government was in power they supported it. They survived all attempts in the Commons to prune them by Place Acts—testimony in themselves to the felt necessity for honesty and character in politics. Some, the King's Friends, were virtually higher civil servants and, like their modern equivalents, served whoever was in power. Others, appointed by the minister himself and going out of office with him, were, in fact, spoilsmen. Most of the placemen held, at Court or in the royal household, offices which were virtually sinecures or performable by a deputy. They 'earned their bread' in the House of Commons by endorsing government measures and voting when asked. A few might provide oratorical or managerial services in the House. But whether their duties were heavy or light, they were endowed from royal revenues while seeking social status on the fringes of the Court.

The third group consisted of independent members and the country gentlemen 'attracted to the Crown but with no obligation to Ministers'. They formed a majority of the assembly, were commonly divided in outlook but would usually support the existing administration if only because persistent opposition was considered disloyal. They had strong views and independent judgment on foreign and economic affairs. Like the king they believed that there was a determinable patriotic line, a right policy. They were suspicious of the Court and its sedulous politicians. In this group the conscience of the nation was most alive, and from this centre of spirit and character dissident leading politicians of mind and passion might strike off sparks of real opposition, might even transcend the rules of the game. What the country gentleman lacked, however, was sustained attention to business.

Vertically penetrating these three layers of the political world were the 'connections' headed by notables from the great families, the Bedfords, Grenvilles, Rockinghams. When out of office, notables lost ground among the placemen; when in power, even the independents would swing towards them. For although political life had its centres beyond the Court, it was the monarch's favour that mobilized placemen and patriotism for the government. Sometimes the leading politicians were (as frequently in the early years of George III), little more than a façade behind which the administration entrenched itself. In default of royal policy they might well, like Walpole and Pitt, direct the affairs of the realm. Yet even these 'could not defy the strong, if incoherent, feeling of ordinary members about proper political behaviour. If once an administration was out of sympathy with the general sense of a proper constitutional course, its days would be few and difficult.'[1] And the monarch, too, who gave them authority and shored them up with his patronage, had his own strong preferences. Like the backbenchers, George III looked for men with honest intentions who could conceive the public interest.

What tendency there was for the efficient Cabinet to develop its own internal leadership and even, very dimly, a kind of collective responsibility arose partly out of royal preoccupation with Hanover, partly out of the habit of the royal advisers of meeting away from the royal presence. In such circumstances, a dominant will was likely to assert itself in Council; a common story to be devised in the anteroom to the Closet. More and more, the king left the politicians to deliberate on their own, appearing in person only at ceremonial Cabinets. More and more, the efficient Cabinets dealt with matters other than those referred to them by the

[1] Watson, *op. cit.* p. 66.

monarch; more and more they developed an independent initiative. Nevertheless, George III still saw his ministers separately and they still discussed with him only those matters which affected their departments. Each minister, Chatham insisted, retained his own independent access to the Crown. Even when a powerful will dominated it, the Cabinet was not a separate body standing over against the king, from whom, after all, and not from the legislature, it derived its executive authority. Seldom had the Cabinet the necessary unity to withstand the king: there were fissures and 'caves' within every ministry which he could widen or explore.

The monarchy had lost its divinity but was, as Bolingbroke clearly saw, all the more demonstrably above faction. Whether he was Walpole, Pitt, Bute or North, each minister had to capture the royal confidence. Walpole was indubitably a 'Court' minister; Pitt, who was not, was nevertheless intoxicated by 'the least peep into the Closet'; even the younger Pitt was the king's man and claimed no rights against the monarch.

Leading politicians in office therefore still lived precariously. Impeachment had fallen into disuse, dismissed politicians need no longer take cover, but ministers were still likely to be dispensed with when their policies proved barren. Only rarely, in great crises, would 'the people' rally to them. Provided that royal ministers were identifiable, i.e. that those who 'dictate[d] in private' were 'employed in public'[1] and that protracted disasters did not attend public policy, the Commons were unlikely to move. Moreover, it was accepted for most of the century that a minister should not be forced upon the Crown.

If politicians with public authority worked on such a narrow ledge, the absence of deeply divisive issues for three-quarters of a century prevented the opposition from drawing upon much more than the rancour of 'outs' for motive power. Opposition had no legitimacy; a 'formed opposition' was a body contending with public authority for power. A creative dissident politician might, in himself, have honour and respectability: faction or party[2] had not, nor could it, while it remained suspect in Parliament and at Court, provide him with an assured base.

---

[1] Earl of Harrington quoted by R. Pares, *King George III and the politicians*, p. 95.
[2] 'For faction is to party what the superlative is to the positive: party is a political evil, and faction is the worst of all parties,' Bolingbroke, 'The idea of a patriot king', *Works*, London, 1809, IV, 281.

Faction might possibly anchor itself to the 'reversionary interest' of the Prince of Wales, who could be presumed to be alienated from his father. Here was a prospect of faction becoming public authority, for would not the prince, when he came into his own, reward the faithful, choose his own ministers and dismiss his enemies? This, however, was not more than the familiar politics of all Courts.

A sounder anchorage for opposition, thought Burke, was in the legitimization of partisanship and party. He saw political virtue in 'the connections', the groupings in interest and amity round those heads of aristocratic houses who were deeply imbued with the sense of the country. These connections fostered friendship, possibly, but not necessarily, in pursuit of a cause; enabled men to become 'acquainted with each other's principles' and 'experienced in each other's talents'. And to 'the great oak' himself, the patron, capable of provoking a ministerial crisis, of 'storming the Closet', connection gave weight in the country, strength in Parliament and influence at Court.

This was a legitimate source of politicians: 'active men' of high quality in combination, under the leadership of those whose self-interest was most in harmony with the general good of society. As leaders, the landed aristocracy had many advantages: 'long possession of government; vast property; obligations of favours given and received; connexion of office; ties of blood, of alliance, of friendship...the name of Whig, dear to the majority of the people...'.[1]

Persons in your station of life ought [to] have long views [Burke wrote to the duke of Richmond]. You people of great families and hereditary trusts and fortunes, are not like such as I am, who, whatever we may be, by the rapidity of our growth and of the fruit we bear, flatter ourselves that, while we creep on the ground we belly into melons, that are exquisite for size and flavour, yet still we are but annual plants, that perish with our season, and leave no sort of traces behind us. You if you are what you ought to be are the great oaks that shade a country and perpetuate your benefits from generation to generation.[2]

Second, there was power based upon unusual ability and personal popularity. 'In fact,' writes Namier, 'personality, eloquence,

---

[1] Edmund Burke, 'Thoughts on the cause of the present discontents', *Works*, London, 1815, II, 238.

[2] *The correspondence of Edmund Burke*, ed. Lucy S. Sutherland, Cambridge, 1960, II, 377.

debating power, prestige, counted for more in the eighteenth-century House of Commons (which at all times contained a number of Members whose votes could be turned by the debate), than it does now...'[1] Yet to Burke this authority, this 'acquired consideration', was less durable than that based upon the character of honest men of substance and 'fixed influence'. It was founded in the unmoored ambition of men without roots in the permanent interests of the country. It was only safe if linked to connection, mediated through the established rule of those who trust each other and are trusted by the country.[2]

What Burke attacked was political power stemming from 'a plan of favouritism', faction ruling by the private favour of the Court against the general sense of the people. He would not admit that character could flourish in the shade of a monarch. The conduct of public men is best judged by the people. Burke rejected the dependent politician even if he were as able as Shelburne. *Thoughts on the cause of the present discontents* is more than a tract against Court politics: by implication it puts the Court out of politics.

George III had his own opinions: he despised 'connection' as selfish and dishonest. In his ministers, he sought both public purpose and ability. There was, however, he thought, hardly an honest man in the whole political nation. At the outset of his reign Bute was, it seems, his substitute for politicians of uncertain fidelity and corrupt motives. And those who rallied to the king commonly considered that they were saving him from the Whigs. For the Whigs had grown fat. It was the former liberators, still shot through with the faded threads of the old cause but long preoccupied with dividing the spoils and long corrupted, who now constituted an *ancien régime*. What might renovate the realm was an honestly served kingly power.

Honour, honesty, character, however obscured or ill-found, are therefore subjects of the story for both George III and Burke. 'We must', thought Burke, 'be tainted with a malignity truly diabolical, to believe all the world to be equally wicked and corrupt.'[3] It is significant that the country gentlemen would respond

---

[1] *The structure of politics at the accession of George III*, p. 7.
[2] On the relation between the *novi homines*, the politicians who acquired fame through public service, and those who represented established interests, see Mansfield, *Statesmanship and party government*, chapters 7, 8 and 9.
[3] 'Thoughts on the cause of the present discontents', *Works*, II, 261.

to honesty and patriotic leadership from any quarter. Discernment
about political virtue, about who was capable of giving sound
government, was their business. On the whole, they preferred
men of prudence to 'those confounded men of genius'.[1]

'Constitute government how you please,' said Burke, 'infinitely
the greater part of it must depend upon the exercise of the powers
which are left at large to the prudence and uprightness of ministers
of state.'[2] And further:

When, therefore, the abettors of the new system tell us, that between
them and their opposers there is nothing but a struggle for power, and
that therefore we are no-ways concerned in it; we must tell those who
have the impudence to insult us in this manner, that, of all things, we
ought to be most concerned, who and what sort of men they are
that hold the trust of every thing that is dear to us.[3]

'To govern according to the sense and agreeably to the interests
of the people is a great and glorious object of government.' The
heart of the political nation hardly beat beyond Whitehall, Westminster, the fashionable clubs and eating-houses, the racecourse,
the great mercantile centres, the country-houses and the country
towns. Its most lively manifestation was at election time in the
counties or in the few boroughs with wide electorates. Outside
Parliament there was a lively world of pamphlets, broadsheets,
weekly and even thrice-weekly newspapers which formulated
issues and disseminated ideas. There was, Burke estimated, a
general public of about four hundred thousand, and towards the
end of the century it had become common for segments of this
public to associate for political ends.

Burke 'reduced the role of the people in politics to that of
uttering cries of distress, whose interpretation and remedy was
a matter for a sanhedrin of skilled legislators...'.[4] But the
very invocation of the 'people' implied dimly that there was
a wider purpose than those of the factions and interests and that
political conduct at critical moments had to be justified in Parliament in the light of this purpose.

Somewhere beyond this were the passions of a populace, which
commemorated and vilified the great by ballad and rumour and
would believe almost anything, could see in the substitution of
an Excise for a Customs duty the advent of 'slavery and wooden

[1] Watson, *The reign of George III*, p. 404.   [2] 'Thoughts', *Works*, II, 260.
[3] *Ibid.* p. 261.   [4] Pares, *George III and the politicians*, p. 43.

shoes', would lynch the unfortunate Porteous for firing on the mob and, in the Gordon Riots, turn the representations of the Protestant Association into nights of murder and arson.

But neither 'people' nor 'populace' had any renovating powers as yet and, within the system, the practical counterpoise to the Court was to be found in the aristocracy, for whom the Whig principle still stood for liberty, and the country gentry, who looked for the indubitable patriotic line.

Here, then, were possibilities for sophisticated politics: the acceptance of circumscribed dissidence, political lenity (little impeachment or proscription) and the 'virtual' representation of known interests. 'The problem was to give cohesion to society by compromise, to find the routine for a quiet time, to teach contending leaders when to strive and when to cease their strife in order to achieve the common good.'[1] On a stable social base were developed a regulated competition for office and an acceptable process for distributing rewards among those who did service. 'Service is obligation; obligation implies return.' Here too was a system which discreetly but perceptibly opened up the prerogative and permitted politicians to create traditions of initiation and appeal; a system which lived on restricted responses, depended on restraint.

This was humane, civilized and realistic politics. Yet, as Burke saw, it must be constantly vivified by the interest of 'active men'. The virtue, judgment and prudence of those in office must mirror the virtue, judgment and prudence of the people. Good men must combine in party to infuse principles which could not come from the Court bent upon management, upon 'disjointing the natural strength of the kingdom'.[2] Individual character and style in politics could only be kept up by legitimating party, the 'formed opposition' aspiring to become public authority, not the great fierce party of the seventeenth century but the parliamentary group adhering to principle and prudently competing in the public eye. If party did not exist, Burke had to create it. It alone could produce 'generous contention for power' on 'manly and honourable maxims'.[3]

---

[1] W. T. Laprade, *Public opinion and politics in eighteenth-century England*, New York, 1936, p. 15.
[2] 'Thoughts on the cause of the present discontents', *Works* , ii, 247.
[3] *Ibid.* p. 336.

On this base there is constituted a hierarchy of politicians (and political values) not yet effaced in England: the Court favourite; the political manager; 'the man of genius'; the man of character with the weight of the country behind him. For Burke the order is an ascending one and his values were to prevail.

The Court favourite survives in Bute, who taught George III to despise 'the great politicians' of the Whig tribe. He 'has a good person, fine legs, and a theatrical air of the greatest importance,' said Lord Waldegrave.[1] Yet this 'fine showy man' had neither administrative nor parliamentary ability (he had to rely for parliamentary majorities upon Henry Fox). His hopes of private power behind the throne were illusory. The mechanics of management were too much for him.

The managers who now straddle Parliament and the Court must also be able to contend in public and maintain their credit with the political nation. There are those who are thoroughly at home and pull all the levers to hand. In their different ways Wharton, Walpole, Newcastle, Henry Fox and North successively fall into this category. They have no standards outside the system in which they operate. They are devotees of the game for its own sake.

Contrasted with these are the rarer politicians who either, like Chatham, seek to transmute political conditions through some inner vision of passion, or seek to re-interpret and therefore change them, like Bolingbroke, Charles James Fox, or, in more extravagant ways, Wilkes and Lord George Gordon.

Burke came out against style which seemed merely to cloak egotism. Pitt sought 'to keep hovering in the air, over all the parties, and to souse down where the prey may prove best'. Burke preferred the 'unbought grace' of those habituated to hold in trust for the country to 'the operations of fancy, inclination and will' in the affairs of government.

To be bred in a place of estimation; to see nothing low and sordid from one's infancy; to be taught to respect one's self; to be habituated to the censorial inspection of the public eye; to look early to public opinion; to stand upon such elevated ground as to be enabled to take a large view of the widespread and infinitely diversified combinations of men and affairs in a large society; to have leisure to read, to reflect, to converse...these are the circumstances of men,

[1] *Memoirs 1754–58*, London, 1821, p. 38.

that form what I should call a *natural* aristocracy, without which there is no nation.[1]

The *self-interest* of men so nurtured was more in accord with the general good than the self-interest of others. Such men were prudent, trained for government and had (as Pitt himself said) 'weight and credit in the nation'. Burke expected more from public men who could recommend themselves through the opinion of the nation than from those who, like himself, had risen from obscurity. Horace Walpole called him 'a very indifferent politician' and he was fully aware of his own deficiencies as a practical statesman. Although a thinker in metaphors and, as an orator, like Fox 'luminous to the last', Burke did not consider that oratory was a qualification for office-holding and admired rather Rockingham's 'peculiar, persuasive and conciliatory manner in talking over public business.'[2]

Walpole was one of the managers who did well out of the Whig liberation. 'His face', wrote Bolingbroke in *The Craftsman*, 'was bronzed over with a glare of confidence.' He understood, said Lord Hervey, the fluctuation of human affairs, never built on certainty and so, instead of worrying about the possible, 'always applied himself to the present occurrence, studying and generally hitting upon the properest method to improve what was favourable, and the best expedient to extricate himself out of what was difficult'.[3] Industrious, loyal and without sensibility, Walpole's formidable quality was his attention to business. There are few problems, he wrote to Pelham, 'that cannot be surmounted if properly and resolutely engaged in...It is a pity that you have not time, for time and address have often carried things that met at the first onset with great reluctance.'[4] This is a copybook heading for a Court politician.

Yet Walpole was also a master of parliamentary business, of ready argument. He had, thought Chesterfield, an extraordinary talent for persuading, using men. 'A hearty kind of frankness, which sometimes seemed impudent, made people think that he

[1] 'Appeal from the new to the old Whigs', *Works*, VI, 217–18. Burke, of course, also included 'the opulent merchants and manufacturers, the substantial yeomanry,' in 'the natural strength of the kingdom'.
[2] Burke, *Correspondence*, II, 411.
[3] John Morley, *Walpole*, London, 1889, p. 115.
[4] *Ibid.* p. 114.

let them into his secrets, whilst the impoliteness of his manners seemed to attest his sincerity.' He became both indispensable and predictable within the system erected on the new political stability. Burke considered him an honourable man and Morley insisted that he 'was the least unscrupulous of the men of that time, the most straightforward, bold, and open, and the least addicted to scheming and cabal'.[1] The 'corruption' was secondary.

Walpole had, thought Burke, no style. 'A careless, coarse and overfamiliar style of discourse, without sufficient attention to persons or occasions, and an almost total want of political decorum, were the errors by which he was most hurt in public opinion.'[2] Bolingbroke's animus does not seriously weaken the validity of his general criticism. For him Walpole was 'the cunning minister'. A wise minister should rise above mere cunning, should consider 'his administration as a single day in the great year of government; but as a day that is affected by those which went before and that must affect those which are to follow'. Walpole saw and was concerned to see no further 'than his personal interests and the support of his administration require'. And Morley had to admit that despite his skill, his grasp of the facts of public business, 'the world will never place Walpole in the highest rank of those who have governed men, for in the world's final estimate character goes farther than act, imagination than utility and its leaders strike us as much by what they were as by what they did'.[3]

It is now the fashion to praise Newcastle, but there is little more to his forty years of boroughmongering than the assiduity of the mole. The majorities which he so fussily provided may have prevented the Commons from falling into anarchy, and from this he obliquely acquires virtue; but the demerit of Newcastle lies precisely in his having, like bee or ant, only functional importance within 'the structure of politics'. Unlike Walpole, who has still popular fame as 'the first prime minister', as the exponent of lenity, *quieta non movere* and hardboiled attentive politics, the most compulsive of the managers has been perhaps justly forgotten.

English political dualism was already taking root in the long Walpole years. Its characteristics were the recognition of honest dissidence, generosity, allowing the enemy to live within the gates. It could survive only with self-restraint on both sides.

---

[1] Morley, *Walpole*, p. 120.   [2] *Ibid.* p. 114.   [3] *Ibid.* p. 114.

There was not much eloquence in an Eton collar about Shippen (his school was Stockport Grammar School)—the leader of the constitutional opposition. He spoke, it was said, 'with his glove before his mouth'. Yet his politics were angular enough. Member of the October Club, leader of the high-flying Tories, he was a Jacobite both when Jacobitism was dangerous and when it became futile. He challenged the long Parliaments of the Septennial Act and standing armies, proposed the reduction of the civil list and lamented that the king was a stranger to our language and our constitution. For public intrepidity he went to the Tower, but somehow his politics, unlike those of Bolingbroke, never ran to conspiracy, and he was not involved in either the '15 or the Atterbury Plot. He kept within the system. And so we have some of the earliest testimonials from the Leader of the Ins to the Leader of the Outs and back again:

'I will not say', declared Walpole, 'who is corrupt but I will say who is not, and that is Shippen.'

'Robin and I are two honest men,' said Shippen (on another occasion), 'he is for King George and I for King James but those men in long cravats only desire places under one or the other.'

Henry St John, Viscount Bolingbroke is the first stylist in the Tory succession and Tory stylists, although rare, last a long time. His Toryism is agnostic, the kind that persists by divesting itself of ideological encumbrances like Divine Right, refuses to enter into futile engagements with the past. It is also patriotic, an appeal to a pristine Englishry. Tories have a predilection for government, yet Bolingbroke made his mark not so much as an office-holder (although it should be noticed that he was the negotiator of Utrecht, surely one of the most successful of all treaties), but as the organizer of opposition to Whig oligarchy and corruption, as the anti-minister with ideas under the Georges. The epitaph composed by himself commemorates not success in office but set purpose in adversity.

> Here lies Henry St John,
> In the reign of Queen Anne
> Secretary at War, Secretary of State and
> Viscount Bolingbroke
> In the days of King George I and King George II
> Something more and better.
> His attachment to Queen Anne

Exposed him to a long and severe persecution;
He bore it with firmness of mind.
The latter part of his time he spent at home
The enemy of no national party
The friend of no faction;
Distinguished under the cloud of a proscription
Never entirely taken off
By zeal to maintain the liberty
And restore the ancient prosperity
Of Great Britain[1]...

This restless unfinished man is interesting because he anticipates some of the traits least appreciated in English politics. For he is the highly articulate, *overfluent* politician. He is the 'brilliant failure', like Carteret and Lord Randolph Churchill; one of 'the first-class brains' kept out of office by mediocrity; 'the spruce gentleman who had made the set speech [and] would never improve',[2] yet one who was loved by the House of Commons because he could 'show it game'. He is 'the posture-master' ('Of all the characters in our history', says Morley, 'Bolingbroke must be pronounced to be most of a charlatan; of all the writing in our literature, his is the hollowest, the flashiest, the most insincere.'[3]) He is the libertine, the hard drinker who lives with Miss Gumley, 'the most expensive demi-rep of the kingdom'; the extravagant who has 'run naked through the park in a fit of intoxication'. But the prism holds more: the attentive statesman who plods 'whole days and nights like the lowest clerk in an office'; the highly accomplished political analyst who gives 'a system of conduct' to the opposition to Walpole; the politician-*littérateur* who, like Disraeli, epitomizes history to invoke the free Englishman.

He is also the sportsman who knows his hounds by name: the man of letters who periodically retires like Halifax and Charles James Fox into rural solitude. He is one of those who 'cannot pass unperceived through a country. If they retire from the world, their splendour accompanies them, and enlightens even the ob-

---

[1] Balancing this lapidary assurance, there is also the defensive irony in a letter to Swift (who, like Pope, thought Bolingbroke a very great man indeed): 'Might not my life be entitled much more properly a what-d'ye-call-it than a farce? Some comedy, a great deal of tragedy and the whole interspersed with scenes of Harlequin, Scaramouche, and Dr. Baloardo...' (noted in Richard Faber, *Beaconsfield and Bolingbroke*, London, 1961, p. 55).

[2] *DNB*.   [3] Morley, *op. cit.* pp. 79–80.

scurity of their retreat. If they take a part in public life, the effect is never indifferent.'[1]

Bolingbroke had more than the manners, the attitudes of an aristocrat—he also sought the renovation of the titled order so that they might truly serve the realm.[2] But he had no firm connection, indeed despised it, and is better seen as a man of style seeking fame and popularity, yet at the same time demanding the mobilization of ability for national ends. History and politics existed in order that he might make a gesture. In exile and in opposition, he had time to fashion his principles; he sought classical models but they did not school his passions. Reflection, 'unlike the demon of Socrates, whispered so softly, that very often I heard him not, in the hurry of those passions by which I was transported.'[3] Behind the calm *nil admirari*, he burned for political distinction. Yet all that 'fiery imagination' could not make up for lack of ballast—'the weight', the sober public purpose, the talent for trimming which kept men like Walpole and North in office for so long. Nevertheless, he had the insight to realize that whether or not politicians had 'brilliance' or 'weight', 'the true interest of England' would be attended to by 'honest country gentlemen' elected by the political nation.

Highly publicized adversity produced in Bolingbroke, not character, 'the virtue of hard times', but a style, a set of words committing him to a policy and a programme that would influence Chatham, Shelburne and Disraeli. Character was lost in the years before 1715; not even among the Tories did he ever recover it. All he could do, in the long years of exclusion from taking a direct part in politics, was to develop an eloquence in which he could transcend his own nature.

Moral resolution is self-consciously shaped and schooled for a purpose:

We must not proceed, in forming the moral character, as a statuary proceeds in forming a statue, who works sometimes on the face, sometimes on one part, and sometimes on another: but we must proceed, and it is in our power to proceed, as nature does in forming a flower, an animal, or any other of her productions...'She throws

---

[1] 'On the spirit of patriotism', *Works*, IV, 190.
[2] On the sense in which Bolingbroke's politics were aristocratic, cf. Mansfield, *op. cit.* pp. 74–7, and Isaac Kramnick, 'An Augustan reply to Locke', *Political Science Quarterly*, LXXXII, no. 4 (December 1967).
[3] 'Of the true use of retirement and study', *Works*, IV, 173.

out altogether, and at once, the whole system of every being, and the rudiments of all the parts'... Just so our Patriot King must be a patriot from the first. He must be such in resolution, before he grows such in practice.[1]

Bolingbroke took up too many diverse themes: Toryism, the philosophy of Locke (if not his political theory), Machiavellianism (with reservations, not the least of which was that his prince had not merely to pretent to virtue; he must really possess it), the persistence of an original 'free Gothic constitution' in England, and political Anglicanism: 'There can hardly be a spectacle in English history more nauseating than this of a profligate deist pleading for the destruction of nonconformity in the name of the Established Church.'[2] In power he was for resolute, overriding government, for Queen, Church and the gentlemen of England: out of power and in exile, he advocated mixed government, reflecting a balance of estates and classes, yet giving a tempered authority to a patriot king. At the same time he saw the free monarch as 'a sort of standing miracle' who would transform the sentiments and the lives of men, end 'corruption'.

'He was in a false position through life,' says Leslie Stephen in the *Dictionary of National Biography*; Bolingbroke's ethical tone, his principles, were, it is said, the product of his exclusion. In power he would have been as wicked as the Whigs. But it is not enough to say that Bolingbroke held out the prospect of ordered patriotic government, strenuous public spirit, merely because he could not get his feet in the political trough. Political ethics always depend upon those who do not get their feet in, those who are out of favour. Bolingbroke could speak freely and honestly because he was excluded. It was his belief that, in his corrupted times, ability and integrity had their home in the opposition. Only when he was out of power could the politician develop the character or style that would sustain him in office. Style had to be practised beforehand. 'It is something to desire to appear a patriot, and the desire of having it is a step towards deserving it, because it is a motive the more to deserve it.'[3]

To nineteenth-century Liberals, Pitt the elder was the pre-eminent man of the mid-eighteenth century because he transcended

---

[1] 'The idea of a patriot king', *Works*, IV, 265.
[2] D. G. James, *The life of reason*, London, 1949, p. 188.
[3] 'The idea of a patriot king', *Works*, IV, 248.

the politics of his time, because he was manifestly a hero, perhaps even a saint. 'Had he lived four centuries earlier, miracles would have taken place at his tomb.'[1] His power lay in the force of his incandescent words. 'His invectives', wrote Chesterfield, 'were terrible, and uttered with such energy of diction and stern dignity of action and countenance, that he intimidated those who were the most willing and the best able to encounter him; their arms fell out of their hands...' His largely unrecorded rhetoric was confined to Parliament but there he made himself a figure in the country—with the eye that could 'cut a diamond', the black velvet, the bandages, the huge boot. His name and presence excited men in the streets but he never spoke to a large popular audience and was indeed hostile to popular pressures on Parliament. Yet 'in him', said Lecky, 'the people for the first time felt their power'.[2]

He spoke for the liberties of Englishmen during the Wilkesite controversy and during the American War of Independence but his most powerful words were for commerce, for Empire, for England. It was the citizens of London and other commercial centres, contemptuous of the other members of Parliament, who 'rained gold boxes upon him'. He has come down as the 'Great Commoner' not because he championed parliamentary power—indeed he retained the seventeenth-century belief that there were certain things it could not do—but because he could really move it; could effectively change votes. Pitt was great because of independent authority, given by unique oratorical and histrionic talents.

He was, wrote Macaulay, 'an actor in the closet, an actor at Council, an actor in parliament; and even in private society he could not lay aside his theatrical tones and attitudes'. Yet the politician who, said Chesterfield, 'set out with acting the patriot' *became* the patriot; his stance committed him to action. And with this went a contempt for what was prescribed, what had been done before: 'Talk not of precedents...to search in all the flaws of antiquity with a curious mischief—to run into every offensive crevice and to wind, meander and spin some silky line, entangling our plain sense and defacing those clearly delineated ideas which

[1] C. Grant Robertson, *Chatham and the British Empire*, London, 1946, p. 182. Or, in the words of an anonymous contemporary writer, 'modern degeneracy had not reached him...there was in this man something that could create, subvert, or reform'.

[2] W. E. Lecky, *A history of England in the eighteenth century*, London, 1883, II, 516.

should be fixed on every man's mind and should direct his conduct...'tis insupportable...'

Pitt chose 'commonsense' but it was a peculiarly relentless commonsense. From his early days as a *frondeur* of Cobham's Cubs to his establishment as a man of destiny of the 1760s and 1770s, he was always a dangerous man. 'I am resolved', he said, 'to be in earnest for the public and shall be a *scarecrow of violence* to the gentle warblers of the grove, the moderate Whigs and temperate statesmen.'

He was as fierce as Bolingbroke in his rejection of the conventions of the game: 'unattached to any party I am, and wish to be, entirely single'. He aimed to carry on government by public opinion alone. He therefore exploited no 'connections' and detached himself from those he had, even from the reversionary interest at Leicester House. Even George III was eventually impressed by Pitt's freedom from connections. His ministry in 1766 was Burke's famous 'tessellated pavement', deliberately constructed from all groups to emphasize its national basis. He also ostentatiously rejected the working principle of Whiggery that 'those who dedicate their time and fortunes to the service of government should be entitled to a share of the rewards that are in its disposal'.[1] And with independence went ineptitude on the backstairs. He could conceive and direct a grand design, he could not work with colleagues; he could not moderate the confidence which he had in his own judgment.

He had not a wide enough appeal or a sufficiently uninformed audience to be called a demagogue. He spoke to a House which was knowledgeable and circumspect about its own interests. What gave him stature was his independency, the knowledge that he spoke 'free from stipulations' and acted 'upon the best convictions'. No one knew better than Pitt that the successful statesman had to exploit the prerogative. The very vigour of his policies, the *numen* of his personality, tended to deprive the monarch of initiative, to impersonalize him. That was Pitt's real achievement in the Whig story.

The elder Pitt did not play to the rules; as patriot, as the 'scarecrow of violence', he conjured politics out of the recesses of his personality. But he spoke mainly to his associates. More significant among the leading politicians as a portent of the nineteenth cen-

[1] In the words of a Whig in 1757, Robertson, *op. cit.* p. 17.

tury, more than the younger Pitt despite his lasting impress upon the office of Prime Minister, was Charles James Fox, 'our first great statesman' [says G. O. Trevelyan] 'of the modern school'.[1] Although he deepens the lode of English politics and breaks ground for both Bright and Gladstone, Fox strikes back into native dissidence, infusing moribund Whiggery with feeling and style.

Although he became heir to what could be retained from the great revolutionary tradition of the seventeenth century, and was in that role greatly to widen the arena of politics, Fox began as one of the King's Friends, a courtier politician angling for jobs in North's administration. 'From childhood', we learn, 'he was courted for his gaiety, originality and genius.'[2] 'The enemies of promise' were around him from the beginning and made the most of his Etonian eloquence (he was, in fact, a debater rather than orator), quickness of apprehension and hard, bold wit.

In the early days, 'the people' meant little to Fox. Indeed he was intent on insulating Parliament from popular influences, doubting if the people could ever really know their own interests. He opposed the publication of Commons debates and spoke vigorously against Wilkes. He stood for a kind of closed politics determinable by parliamentary majorities, and followed, in a hard and emphatic way, the line of his father, Henry Fox, a notorious maker of majorities.

This artificial precocious politics came to an end when he fell under the spell of Burke in 1774. It seems that his political sensibility was first really awakened by the American War and the consequent loosing of discontent with both the monarchical initiative and the close oligarchical Commons. As the war progressed he came to see the issues in large constitutional terms. Both English and American liberties were threatened by the assertion of executive authority in America.

Until then personally irresponsible, he now became the searcher for purpose and the gatherer of causes, the advocate of wider participation (well short of democracy) in public life. Sometimes the stance was that of Chatham, sometimes that of Burke. Fox took things up, both causes and opportunities. He was quick and articulate. George III, a fair judge of political 'weight', thought him without any principle 'of common honour or honesty'. He could be indiscriminately prehensile. He took up

---

[1] *The early history of Charles James Fox*, London, 1881, p. 1.   [2] *DNB*.

not only the cause of Keppel, the Benares charges against Warren Hastings, triennial Parliaments, 'economical reform' and religious liberty; he also supported the reversionary interest of the Prince of Wales, struck up a bargain to share power with his old adversary Lord North and unwhiggishly defended the Crown against Parliament in the Regency crisis of 1788–9.

Fox is then primarily the protagonist of causes, laying his foundations, as Burke advised him in 1777, 'deep in public opinion'. He needed an audience and for a time he found one among the disquieted country gentlemen and freeholders who, towards the end of the American War, had sought to impress the sense of the people on the government, by petitioning Parliament, through the establishment of 'associations' in the counties. They were anti-Court, for 'economical reform' which would destroy the royal 'interest' in politics, and for peace with America. Above all (like Fox) they were concerned with 'the true cause of those misfortunes which have reduced this once flourishing empire to a state which words cannot describe'.

The county associations hoped to set up a central representative body at Westminster, which might well usurp the position of the House of Commons long corrupted by the Court. Fox, chairman of the Westminster committee, quickly became through his superb sense of audience 'the idol of the people'. He now set himself to catch the swell of popular opinion, 'to conform to the sentiments, and in some degree even to the prejudices of the people'. But the new cause foundered in the blind, popular violence of the Gordon riots. The country gentlemen drew back even as Fox fought and won the great uncertain popular constituency of Westminster.

Fox was in fact not to come to power as the Man of the People but first as 'the captive Prince' of the Rockingham Whigs, those men whom Burke had seen as blessed 'with honest, disinterested intentions, plentiful fortunes, assured rank, and quiet homes'; and secondly in the 'unnatural junction' with North which seemed a studied affront to public opinion. This seriously damaged Fox's public 'character', even though he thought that he was, in all consistency, striking a blow at the Court. (He had previously rashly rejected partnership with the heir of Chatham, the brilliant but charmless Shelburne, who advocated non-partisan reforming government, because even if he were in tune with the best thought of his age, he seemed to Fox yet another royal instrument without the sense of the people behind him.) It was not Fox, despite another personal triumph in the Westminster constituency, who carried public opinion in 1784, but Pitt and George III.

But it is not for office that Fox is remembered even though he shone in the few months that he had. What he showed was that a politician could thrive in adversity—that it was possible for a great politician to do no more than criticize public authority. When Pitt the younger, like Bute, saved the king from the politicians and entered upon eighteen years of power, Fox went into the wilderness and refused to be reconciled. He stuck to his principles even at the expense of office. He gathered friends about him and bound them to him with ties of affection. Clad in buff and blue (the colours he gave to the reforming Whigs), deliberately ill-kempt, he became the well-beloved, the symbol of generous feeling and spirited resistance for all who were in opposition. And with this went the bottle, gaming, cricket and partridge-shooting —the publicized habits of the Man of the People who was also the Man of Pleasure; long retreats from politics (from 1797 to 1802 he was hardly ever in Parliament) and austere but obtrusive reading of the classics.[1] Yet despite his protracted absences, politics was his vocation. Under the libertarianism we can plainly see the committed public man of the nineteenth century. He is to the nineteenth century what Halifax was to the eighteenth.

Fox became identified with all liberal causes, of the *sans-culotte*, the Hindu, the negro. Of these the most remarkable was his sustained welcome of the French Revolution: 'How much the greatest event it is that has ever happened in the world! and how much the best!' Even when in a hopeless minority during the war against revolutionary France, Fox showed that principles need not be disavowed merely because they endangered national unity. He took opposition to limits not conceived practical before. Moreover, although as 'the Man of the People in Liberty Hall' he had the feel of the popular audience, and wished the people 'to consider their own weight and consequence in the state', Fox never really took 'the political battle outside the Parliamentary forum'.[2] He remained a parliamentary politician.

Popular politics were generated because he felt that every man must be incorporated within the state, must believe 'that he is

---

[1] See Carswell, *op. cit.* chapters XVI–XXI. [2] *Ibid.* p. 349.

fighting for himself and not for another; that it is his own cause, his own safety, his own concern, his own dignity on the face of the earth, and his own interest on the identical soil which he has to maintain'. Perhaps his greatest achievement was not merely to legitimate party but through the art of his personality to make opposition illustrious during both the American and French wars. Thus he gave partisanship, duality in politics, the place which Burke had claimed for it but could not ensure.

Fox attained honesty in politics because, as he himself said, his vanity was greater than his ambition. In 1778 he wrote to Fitzpatrick:

With respect to my own share, I can only say that people flatter me that I continue to gain, rather than lose, my credit as an orator; and *I am so convinced that this is all that I shall ever gain (unless I chose to become the meanest of men) that I never think of any other object of ambition.*

I am certainly ambitious by nature, but I really have, or think I have, totally subdued that passion. I have still as much vanity as ever, which is a happier passion by far; because great reputation I think I may acquire and keep, great situation I *never* can acquire, nor if acquired, keep without making sacrifices that I never will make.[1]

Vanity gave him principles and a desire to excel but it is sensibility and qualities of the heart, not vanity or brilliance, which distinguish Fox. Bolingbroke was brilliant, vain but heartless, and too clever by half. So too was the deviser of the unfortunate American revenues, Charles Townshend, with his conscious and demonstrated superiority over others, his exhibitionist 'champagne' oratory, his gifts of imagination and analysis, his firm resolution 'to act the part of a man of business and a man of honour; to be decided by things and not men; to have no party; to *follow no* leader...'. It is of Townshend that Namier writes: 'Poverty of heart warped even his judgment: too much preoccupied with his own person, he did not enter into the feelings of other men, lacked intuitive awareness, and so would misjudge situations.'[2] Fox was never in danger of falling into such political solipsism. There is balance and realism in his words:

'I love idleness so much and so dearly, that I have hardly the heart to say a word against it; but something is due to one's station in life, something to friendship, something to the country.'

[1] Quoted in Edward Lascelles, *The life of Charles James Fox*, London, 1936, p. 74.
[2] Namier, *Crossroads of power*, p. 203.

4

PLATFORM POLITICIANS

Fox was at the source of a tradition in which the leading politicians of the nineteenth century would create their own fields of attraction on the platform as well as in Parliament. There would be overtones too of Wesley and Whitefield and sometimes of Wilkes. Wilkes had fewer progeny than one might expect. Yet he had had a real following, and a real power among the unenfranchised London populace; 'he was the sole unrivalled idol of the people, who lavished on him all in their power to bestow, as if willing to prove that in England it was possible for an individual to be great and important through them alone'.[1] Some recognized in him a symbol of their own discontent and deprivation; some, their passion to re-order the garbled liberties of Englishmen. He had started something and was borne along. There were intimations of a new popular impulse in the Gordon riots too, but still preponderant was the old and almost constitutional lord-of-misrule violence of the mob.

Writing at the end of the nineteenth century, John Morley, remembering apparently only Daniel O'Connell, could say that 'the agitator has not been a very common personage in English history'.[2] If this is so, and it is certainly true that fewer effective popular leaders were thrown up than might be expected, it was hardly because of lack of opportunity. For in Britain, in normal times, petitioning, public meetings, broadsheets were allowed on a scale unknown in most of Europe. Men like Cartwright, Place and Cobbett may not have wanted to dislodge very much but they were all Radical agitators in the sense that they wished to shake off parasitic growths upon the Constitution. Whether artisans or men of substance, they wished to end Old Corruption, to purge the executive and regenerate the legislature. And in these ends they had, at least before the French Revolution, the gentry of England with them. For the Radicals, Parliamentary Reform

---

[1] Weston MSS, *Parliamentary Papers*, XLIV (1885), 413, quoted in H. Jephson, *The platform*, London, 1892, I, 48.
[2] J. Morley, *Life of Cobden*, London, 1881, I, 192.

became a cause, a panacea, a cure for even 'bread and blood' riots. It was against Cobbett's 'Thing', and not against a class that they contended. 'The enemy of the reformers was not an aristocratic estate, nor the entire agrarian capitalist class, but a secondary complex of predatory interests.'[1]

There was talk of French theories and examples by men like Paine, Priestley and Price or the Cato Street Conspirators, but those who spoke to the populace rarely did so in a consistently anti-parliamentary way. Burdett fought and won notable elections at Westminster. Orator Hunt had a tricoloured flag and a cap of liberty at Spa Fields in 1816, but all he was doing at Peterloo, when the yeomanry got out of hand, was advocating Parliamentary Reform. Bright saw him elected to Parliament in 1830. Cobbett used all his energies to direct men's attention away from violence to Parliamentary Reform and even the Chartists sought their millennium in parliamentary terms. Nevertheless, it was a matter of redeeming rather than merely of adjusting existing institutions. It was intended that the People should enter and transform Parliament.

To those who ruled, and, in particular, to Lord Liverpool, 'the very last who, in the strict sense of the word, can be said to have governed England',[2] such aspirations were alarming enough. For to him 'the labouring people were not susceptible of political life, except in the politics of loyalty and obedience'.[3] Those who had a stake in the country, in land and commerce, were the rightful holders of power, 'independent of any qualification of merit or fitness for its exercise',[4] holding in trust for and presiding pragmatically over a society of contending interests. Until the new Toryism of the 1820s and the Whig triumph of 1830, the dominant Tory politicians such as Liverpool and Eldon learned their politics according to the prescription of Stendhal's Duchess Sanseverina, as one would learn whist: 'Believe or don't believe the things that are taught to you, *but never raise any objections.*'

What characterized the old Toryism of Liverpool was firm administration in the interests of public order and more willing-

---

[1] E. P. Thompson, 'The peculiarities of the English' in Ralph Miliband and John Saville (eds.), *The socialist register*, London, 1965, p. 324.
[2] C. D. Yonge, *Life of Lord Liverpool*, London, 1868, I, 3–4.
[3] R. J. White, *Waterloo to Peterloo*, London, 1957, p. 103.
[4] C. P. Villiers in 1836, quoted in Norman Gash, *Reaction and reconstruction in English politics 1832–1852*, Oxford, 1965, p. 138.

ness to court unpopularity than the Whigs. What distinguished the new Toryism which Peel was to lead was greater efficiency and greater willingness to go along with their times. Yet to Disraeli, both the school of Liverpool and the school of Peel were *administrative,* not *political,* Tories.

The Whigs were Whigs by inheritance. In their eyes the Reform Bill of 1832, which they never wished to repeat, was a timely renewal of the framework of government which they had helped to create in 1688. They were supposed to have opinions but these were difficult to define. They sought popularity but did not want popular rule. They stood for the People and would bow to popular opinion but claimed that the function of their thousand families was to produce leadership, to break the shock of change. Yet this is what they did not do. Neither Melbourne nor Lord John Russell had sufficient energy. Neither provided the persistent leadership that was required. Both compared ill with Peel, the fully equipped Tory leader.

There were politicians on the fringes of Whiggery and Toryism who, impelled by Dissenting, Evangelical and perhaps Benthamite convictions, sought to change the order of things, but little was achieved without the concurrence of the men who ruled and they were mainly concerned with keeping the administration going. Yet, with the exception of Peel and his school among the Tories and Palmerston among the Whigs, the custodians were not good administrators. They were not open to ideas unless very forcefully expressed. This did not mean that the Whigs were not at times considerable legislators (especially in the 1830s). Yet, when a Factory Act, a New Poor Law or Municipal Reform cracked the surface, it was merely a necessary concession made at the appropriate time to pressures that could be resisted no longer. (True, there was a something more positive about Grey's introduction of the Reform Bill.)

But if they were safe because they were squeezable, they were safer because they did not respond over-readily to the squeeze. They could retain their influence—by preserving the sort of régime in which their influence could effectively be felt—only if resistance was habitual and concession occasional. Concessions were represented as contributions to the greater glory of Whiggery. But too much concession would be self-destructive.[1]

[1] Donald Southgate, *The passing of the Whigs*, London, 1962, p. 194.

There were, as Matthew Arnold later pointed out, whole classes of men who had acquired nobility of character, freedom from vulgarity, 'by habitual dealing with great things'. Of these, the exemplar must be John Charles Spencer, Viscount Althorp, third Earl Spencer, who would post all night after a sitting in the House of Commons to hunt with the Pytchley. The only subject upon which he was known to have spoken 'with eagerness and almost with passion' was prize-fighting. 'A shy, awkward, and ill-grounded boy', he had been drawn from Toryism and rural pursuits by the young Whigs of Cambridge and an unlikely admiration for Charles James Fox. In the Commons he read the *Debates* thoroughly and studied works on trade and law. He spoke with 'the advanced men', with Whitbread, Mackintosh, Romilly and Brougham, supported Catholic Emancipation and Parliamentary Reform. He joined Grey's ministry only when it was clear that a ministry could not be formed without him and, 'having consented to be a member, he then selected for himself to Grey's surprise, the post of chancellor of the exchequer and leader of the House of Commons, as being, in spite of his inexperience, the position in which he could be of the greatest use'.[1] He became, it was said, the best Leader of the House that any party ever had.

After the passing of the Reform Bill of 1832, Sir Henry Hardinge said 'it was Althorp carried the Bill, his fine temper did it'. There was apparently no resisting his influence in the Commons. Yet he always found speech-making difficult, and said that he went down to the House as if to his execution. Entering politics, he thought, was the great fault of his life which he must expiate. 'The best picture of him', says J. A. Hamilton, the author of the excellent sketch in the *DNB*, 'is one painted by Richard Ansdell about 1841, called "A scene at Wiseton", in which he figures with his stewards, his herdsman Wagstaff, his bull Wiseton, and his dog Bruce.' His was a triumph of probity, 'of a man', said Lord Holland, 'who acts on all matters with a scrupulous, deliberate and inflexible regard to his public duty and private conscience'.

The ideal character [said Stanley Baldwin[2]] is a harmony of many virtues, and it is a tradition amongst us to give to truthfulness the position of the cardinal virtue. Hence, for example, the curious power of Lord Althorp, who was known to have said to the House of

---

[1] *DNB.*
[2] *On England*, London, 1926, p. 85.

Commons, 'I know this to be right. I cannot remember why—but you may take it that it is so,' and they believed him.

The traditional leadership kept its hold because it had for so long successfully directed the affairs of the nation, because it had achieved accord with 'the people', as Brougham defined them, 'the middle classes...those hundreds and thousands of respectable persons—the most numerous and by far the most wealthy order in the community'.[1] Especially important, too, had been the sympathy, long sustained, between the aristocracy and 'the populace'—a rapport which did not exist in continental countries, even in France, where the common people were more highly civilized. The populace might now be alienated in their dark satanic mills and the rulers might well need, as Macaulay insisted, the middle class to mediate for them at critical moments with the 'mob', but it was still true that the Englishman did not deeply resent a lord.[2] Not so much because of 'deference' but because there was a common national tradition, because the many as well as the few had long had a stake in the liberties of Englishmen. All orders of society had been involved; the nobility could claim to have contributed, by timely insurgencies, and the populace, by riot and tumult, as much to the liberties of Englishmen as the 'inner light', rationalism and self-reliance of the middle classes. Aristocracy, middle classes and populace all had a share in the achievement of 1832. But the leadership was now faced with problems of an industrialized society, which by education, training and experience they were not equipped to solve. Here were 'social facts' for which middle-class business sense, Evangelical or Dissenting vision, were more appropriate than the restrained gestures of aristocratic statesmanship. 'Presence' was not enough.

Democracy, said Matthew Arnold, was trying to affirm its essence and so too must the *state* if English society were to achieve that ordered power in which all could play a full part.[3] The existing custodians of power would doubtless contrive to adapt with

---

[1] Southgate, *Passing of the Whigs*, p. 22.
[2] Such resentment as he harboured was, it seems, primarily at the level of fantasy provided by aristocratic villainy in Victorian popular novels and melodrama. In life men respected the quality then identified, according to Kitson Clark, as 'bottom': the character, the spirit which served the nobility so well in war, sport and politics. See G. Kitson Clark, *An expanding society: Britain 1830–1860*, Melbourne, 1967, pp. 17–20.
[3] Matthew Arnold, 'Democracy' in *Mixed essays*, London, 1800, *passim*.

caution the old political tradition, would recruit the political élite from a wider circle than the thousand or two established families; would use the skill and energy and knowledge of the new professional and business classes, but these would not be enough. They were neither willing to enlarge the political nation after 1832 nor to invoke the authority of the state. Power should still go with rank and property. And the expanded electorate wanted very little—abolition of tithes and Church rates, economical administration, low taxes and modest industrial reforms and so on— which could not be granted. The task of government was to concede to the new interests their modest due.

With this the Radicals were not in agreement. They saw themselves as conduits for the will of the people, catching the great upswellings of opinion among a sturdy and rational electorate. For them the numerical majority should be dominant and they would willingly have extirpated special interests. Within Parliament the Radicals had little unity. But in the country, the Anti-Corn Law League was a model of successful popular agitation and Chartism had both moral power and a programme with a national resonance. Statesmen were coming out of seclusion: the public meeting and the peripatetic speaker were becoming more familiar. Yet during the fifteen or sixteen years after the collapse of Chartism 'there was no great Platform campaign to compel a Government to adopt a particular policy, or to make some special concession to popular wishes...'.[1] Up to 1867 popular discontents were dredged neither deeply nor persistently by the leading politicians.

The literature of social re-organization was in flood but Saint-Simon, Comte, Owen and Fourier had little influence on the English debate. Utilitarianism was a method rather than a dogma,[2] Evangelicalism and Dissent, climates for individual heroic energy —so too was the pervasive influence of Carlyle. Even the *novi homines*, the leading politicians whose origins were outside the

---

[1] Jephson, *The platform*, ii, 423.

[2] The influence of Benthamism upon statesmen and administrators is difficult to trace. 'In fact, as Dr MacDonagh has pointed out, a great deal of administrative and legislative development was the result of the empirical actions and hard-bought experience of a number of officials, many of whom had probably never heard of Bentham, but on whom public demands had imposed novel and very difficult tasks.' G. Kitson Clark, *The making of Victorian England*, London, 1965, p. 19.

ruling class, Disraeli, Bright, Cobden and Gladstone, were without comprehensive theory—even Disraeli had not so much a theory as an abridgement of history to show him the ground on which he stood. Yet all of them created political worlds; they were not merely administrators or custodians of the administration giving way when necessary to dominant ideas outside themselves. They were powers in their own right, unprepared 'to bow before any wisdom whose mouth is loud enough'.[1] Of the new men the most notable administrative athlete was Gladstone and it is significant that, up to 1860, he was politically the most indeterminate. He took a long time to find his ground.

Much of the major legislation, the Factory Acts, the Public Health legislation, the rationalized Poor Law, the beginnings of state responsibility for education, the emancipation of slaves, owed little to either new or old leading politicians. The politician's task was characteristically one of adoption, not of initiation. Indeed, apart from Catholic Emancipation and the Repeal of the Corn Laws, those for whom politics was vocation or avocation had little to their credit in this classical period of parliamentary government. The initiative and stimulus of peculiarly committed individuals like Chadwick, Southwood Smith, Oastler and Shaftesbury came from outside, with waves of opinion achieving particular majorities for particular ends. But not very often; the relatively small political nation after 1832 had little appetite for reform outside their immediate interests. The old undisciplined House of Commons was therefore rarely stirred by popular impulse. It was no Athenian assembly in which the demagogue could there and then commit the polity to action.

Yet the Commons had long been the locus of power, the centre of the nation's deliberations and, since the very modest injection of democracy in 1832, had acquired a freedom, on the one hand, from the influence of the monarch, who no longer found it discreet or practicable to involve herself overtly in politics, and, on the other, from that of the House of Lords, which had received no comparable popular impetus and was losing political weight. Government business was only just beginning to monopolize time on the floor. The Cabinet, still owing immediate responsibility to the House, hardly looked over its head to public opinion outside. And within the House, 'ministers and followers alike were

---

[1] C. H. Sisson, *The spirit of British administration*, London, 1959, p. 23.

apt to claim the right of individual judgement and to follow their conscience, their interest, or their responsibilities'.[1]

Vulnerable cabinets, a national assembly which educated the nation, a soporific House of Lords as an emblem of stability, a dignified monarchy to make government intelligible to the many: these constituted a system in which the only doubtful elements were the constituencies. There, providentially, acquiescence in the given leadership, concern for private business and a continuing rascality—'the electorate was far more wicked than the candidates'[2]—served to insulate the higher political world. Bagehot was to have forebodings about a new politics in which the parties would 'bid for the support of the working man'.[3] But as yet the country was preserved from the perils of democracy, from a polyarchy of appetitive constituencies, by acquiescence or trust in the available politicians. At most the constituencies 'were competent to decide an issue selected by the higher classes, but they were incompetent to do more'.[4] Politics were not made out of the desires of the people: the people had merely to 'judge decently of the questions which drift down to it, and are brought before it'.[5] *Good* government, said Robert Lowe, was the aim and 'we may violate any law of symmetry, equality or distributive justice in providing the proper machinery'.[6]

'It does not appear to me', wrote Lecky, 'that the world has ever seen a better Constitution than England enjoyed between the Reform Bill of 1832 and the Reform Bill of 1867.'[7] Yet it flourished in a period when the decisions which confronted statesmen were relatively simple. There was tacit agreement to limit the orbit of politics in order that the game be played with decorum. From Peel's death in 1851 until 1867 expediency was the keynote. Bagehot was well content to live in anti-reforming times. Bright was not, but writing to John Bigelow, the American diplomatist in 1863, he conceded the persisting strength of the structure:

Our system consists of these great families, with great landed properties; of the State Church, which is almost entirely in their hands and devoted to their interests; and of the large class chiefly derived from the territorial ranks who fill the best offices under the Government, and in all

---

[1] Gash, *op. cit.* p. 125.
[2] Asa Briggs, *Victorian people*, London, 1954 (citing Trollope), p. 111.
[3] Introduction to *The English constitution*, London, 1929, p. xxii.
[4] *Ibid.* p. xv.   [5] *Ibid*, p. xix.   [6] Southgate, *Passing of the Whigs*, p. 302.
[7] *Democracy and liberty*, London, 1899, I, 21.

the services of the State. In the House of Commons a large proportion of the members, more than one-third of them I think, are directly connected with members of the House of Lords, and thus the whole thing is so interwoven that it makes a fabric so strong that probably only some great convulsion will ever break through it.

The path to power and influence was still largely one of insinuation, of winning the favour of the great. Disraeli had to work through Bentinck and Stanley as he had, in a sense, worked through Lord John Manners and George Smythe in his Young England phase. Cobden's success hinged upon his conquest of the mind of Peel—himself an *assimilado* to the ruling class.

What was remarkable in this golden age of Parliament was the paucity of the domestic issues—at least up to the quickening of the Parliamentary Reform movement in the 1860s. Yet the Whigs were in power most of the time and it was from them rather than the Tories that innovation of political theme and vocabulary might be expected. 'When out of office', said Roebuck, 'they are demagogues: in power they become exclusive oligarchs.' This is apt enough, but Roebuck himself, a patriotic Radical, became as preoccupied with the effective deployment of British power, efficient military administration, whether of the Crimean War or of an Afghanistan campaign, as with domestic issues.

Certainly much of Bright's best oratory was on foreign and not home affairs. His themes were Ireland, India and the Crimean War. At home he was concerned with Church rates, reduction of taxation and a changed land law (an epilogue to the Corn Law agitation). Domestically it does not seem as though he wanted more than a free and fair field in which the energy of Dissenting Englishmen could make its mark. Matthew Arnold might deplore this kind of political operating, the unworthiness of its objects and the mechanical way in which they were pursued. Freedom from Church rates, to marry one's deceased wife's sister was not enough. But for Bright there was 'nothing that is so much worth discussing as politics'.

At another level, in 1856, Gladstone found that 'the pain and strain of public life is multiplied daily by the want of a clear and firm ground upon which visibly to act'. Yet he shared the earnest belief of Thomas Arnold that 'the great work of government' was 'the highest earthly desire of the ripened mind'[1] and

---

[1] Quoted in Asa Briggs, *The age of improvement*, London, 1959, p. 411.

continued: 'The desire for office is the desire of ardent minds for a larger space and scope within which to serve the country, and for access to the command of that powerful machinery for information and practice, which the public departments supply.'

English historiography had celebrated documents, Magna Carta or the Petition of Right, rather than men. Even Cromwell and Chatham had been subsumed into a process, a history of the impersonal, the slow solidification of precedents. It was difficult for the personal to break through this tough constitutional integument. Even in this romantic phase, political leaders in England were not required to turn the course of history but to make pragmatic decisions in the light of larger purposes. Bagehot tells us that 'the leading statesmen in a free country have great momentary power. They settle the conversation of mankind. It is they who, by a great speech or two, determine what shall be said and what shall be written for long after.'[1] Even so, he admitted that Bright and Gladstone were the only men of their time whose eloquence changed men's votes. It was not a politics which denied the emergence of gifted men with an insight into the needs of their times but it did demand intelligence and close argument as well as force and romantic effusion. The great speeches of the period—Disraeli's on the state of Ireland or Bright's on the Crimean War—were triumphs in an assembly not easily impressed.

Liberty had no novel apocalyptic mask in Britain—there had been no reception of Mazzini, no need for it. Middle and working classes would cheer Kossuth but their enthusiasm was for *less happy* realms rightly struggling to be free. Romantic orators were commonly Irish like Feargus O'Connor, Smith O'Brien and Thomas Meagher. There was no question of an ancient dynasty crumbling 'at the breath of the people', of a youthful England 'springing from the old, like the moth from the chrysalis; this glowing life arising in the midst of death...'.[2] England was a country of ancient liberties, obscured and lost, perhaps, under Norman yoke, Reformation profiteers, enclosing landlords, and textile manufacturers, but ultimately redeemable within the span of her own history.

An English hero-politician had to work hard at his craft as a

---

[1] *The English constitution*, p. xix.

[2] *Life and writings of Mazzini*, quoted in John Morley's 'Liberalism and Reaction' in *Oracles on men and government, Works*, xv, London, 1921, 108.

Parliament-man needed 'connexion' as well as a popular audience. Yet Palmerston, who had these and more—he provided the administrative skill and leadership that Melbourne and Russell never had—has never fitted into the Liberal pantheon. Not all that hard desk-work, capacity for decision-making, Civis Britannicus speechifying, deeds and gestures with gunboats, ironclads and martello towers made him into a lasting hero. Even for the businessmen, the fierce Dissenters, the country gentlemen, he was the embodiment of what Disraeli called 'the national idea', rather than a hero. In spite of his belief that every country must have its Glorious Revolution and enjoy the Rule of Law, in spite of his belligerence abroad to spread these benefits, his principles were suspect. He had no *gravitas*.

Disraeli, the exotic fully assimilated into the English tradition, was a prodigy rather than a hero. There was too much of 'Shylock' and 'Old Clothes' in the constituencies for him to hope to impose himself on the political nation. Although no man was quicker to recognize Agitation as 'that new principle and power' in the constitution which might ultimately absorb all, he himself could not draw upon the new source of political strength; '...none of his success was due to demagogy; he made no "pilgrimages of passion" among the electorate'.[1] He was therefore obliged to make politics out of his own sensibility and out of the study:

Born in a library and trained from early childhood by learned men who did not share the passions and prejudices of our political and social life, I had imbibed on some subjects conclusions different from those which generally prevail, and especially with reference to the history of our own country. How an oligarchy had been substituted for a kingdom, and a narrow-minded and bigoted fanaticism flourished in the name of religious liberty...But what most attracted my musing, even as a boy, was the elements of our political parties, and the strange mystification by which that which was national in its constitution had become odious, and that which was exclusive was presented as popular.

He was the *littérateur* who wished to do the great deed. 'Poetry is the safety valve of my passions but I wish to act what I write.'

His response to liberalism is set out in Monypenny's inventory of his political stock-in-trade: 'a sincere and ardent patriotism, genuine popular sympathies, a strong and apparently instinctive

[1] W. F. Monypenny and G. E. Buckle, *Life of Disraeli*, London, 1929, II, 1505–6.

antipathy to Whiggery, and an hereditary disposition to Toryism derived from his father with an imaginative interest in its romantic aspects that was native to himself'.[1] The language of his pamphlets, novels and speeches is characteristically that of the eighteenth century as when he contended against 'that rapacious, tyrannical and incapable faction', or when he came before the electors of Marylebone and claimed he was 'supported by neither of the aristocratic parties...an independent member of society who had no interest, either direct or indirect, in corruption or misgovernment, and as one of a family untainted by the receipt of public money'. Into an old and forgotten Toryism he breathed romantic energy in order to achieve what Isaac D'Israeli called 'a positive *name* and a *being* in the great political world...a *perfect style*'. He was the fabricated politician.

He admired the Tory gentry but, like Bolingbroke, maintained a 'vigilant and meditative independence'. He was a Tory, but had to be a Tory with a difference. Like Bolingbroke he sought to make politics more than it is. He moved it on to a higher plane 'to raise the sentiments of the people', not through abstract ideas but through the concrete past. And yet of that past, again like Bolingbroke, he was the moralist rather than the historian. He let his free imagination play round the constructions of others. It was this imagination which evoked 'the idea of a free monarchy, established on fundamental laws, itself the apex of a vast pile of municipal and local government, ruling an educated people, represented by a free and intellectual press'.

He proclaimed his political ambiguity: 'I am neither Whig nor Tory. My politics are described by one word, and that word is England.' He asserted, too, that the conduct and opinions of politicians at different times in their career must not be 'too curiously contrasted in a free and aspiring country. The people have their passions, and it is even the duty of public men occasionally to adopt sentiments with which they do not sympathise, because the people must have leaders.' It was this flexibility plus tactical opportunism which made men like Sir James Graham and, later, Salisbury insist that he had no principles. Yet over the whole of his political life there is a deeper consistency and a clearer understanding of the predicament and potentialities of England than in any other leading statesman.

[1] Monypenny and Buckle, *Disraeli* I, 214.

He was always handicapped by the fact that his political rise was also a social rise. 'Bookworms', says Lady Montfort in *Endymion*, 'do not make Chancellors of State. You must become acquainted with the great actors in the great scene. There is nothing like personal knowledge of the individuals who control the high affairs...' Disraeli had to infuse ideas into men who, to Arnold, were never vulgar or ignoble but had 'a not very quick or open intelligence'. For the party chosen by Disraeli, the Tory party, was in the 1840s almost bereft of ideas, lingering on under the *magni nominis umbra* of the Duke of Wellington, made up of gentlemen who in matters of politics went along 'with their families'. They had, as Disraeli said, tried to substitute 'the fulfilment of the duties of office for the performance of the functions of government; and to maintain this negative system by the mere influence of property, reputable private conduct, and what are called good connexions'.

Disraeli's achievement was a triumph of intelligence and energy in the beginning of the democratic era. He won eminence 'in fair and open Parliamentary fight'[1] and, without strain, made the necessary social ascent. He had no charisma; his invocation of Monarchy and People and objurgation of oligarchy became mechanical over the years. He was not capable of striking the chords of moral impulse in the British people—he thought Gladstone's drenching rhetoric highly dangerous. His virtue was that he reminded men 'that the whole history of England might have been different'.[2] He clarified choice and responsibility for choice in an age in which Britain could still choose. At a time when distinctions between the parties were not clear he insisted on making them. Moreover he did so with the clarity of a detached intellectual in a party not inclined to examine their political opinions 'like a philosopher or a political adventurer'. His gift was the gift of the imagination tempered by irony: through it he brought to English politics a tension which the Constitution could tolerate. For although he liked 'to be oracular and to ignore the other side', he was always, 'we may be certain, perfectly conscious of its existence'.[3]

Disraeli wished to create a truly *political* Toryism and this becomes clearer if, for a moment, we compare him with Peel. Peel

[1] *Ibid.* II, 1505.   [2] *Ibid.* I, 694.
[3] *Loc. cit.*

was a great Parliament-man, not the less because he was broken
by Parliament; he was also a remarkable administrator, a model
Prime Minister whose surveillance of the departments has not
been rivalled since. Although inducted into the old Toryism in
the Napoleonic period and always insistent on maintaining
existing institutions and keeping public order—even in the 1830s
and 1840s he feared the approach of revolution—he became a
practical reformer, of the criminal law, of the police, of economic
policy, and showed that he had the nerve for political action. No
one had greater sincerity in politics than he; no one was more
likely to be convinced by the facts: facts persuaded him to accept
Catholic Emancipation, the repeal of the Test Acts and the end of
the Corn Laws. He had the liberal virtue of being able to enter
into the minds of others. 'He kept tight hold', says Kitson Clark,
'of the ordinary Tory difficulties and arguments, for he took them
seriously...But he also took seriously the arguments of his
adversaries; he was not simply content with parrying them; he
was sensitive to the moral challenge behind them...'[1]

Peel feared democracy but was not timorous. Just before
entering upon his great 1841–6 ministry he declared: 'If I
exercise power it shall be upon my conception—perhaps imperfect
—perhaps mistaken—but my sincere conception of public duty.'
He was a masterful man whose good intent was accepted. When
he died men wept in the streets. And yet he had few ideas and
those few unexamined. 'The powers of a first-rate man and the
creed of a second-rate man,' said Bagehot. He educated administrators but had no mind or taste for the creative generalizations
which might have animated his party. For him 'the tone of
England' was 'that great compound of folly, weakness, prejudice,
wrong feeling, right feeling, obstinacy, and newspaper paragraphs
which is called public opinion'... He had no memorable words
to give it meaning.

It may seem strange to include Cobden among the leading
politicians of the mid-nineteenth century. He never held political
office; indeed refused it. Nevertheless, he had the Hegelian
requirements for a political hero; he was a thinking man who had
an insight into the requirements of the times—an ability to seize
on those things that were ripe for development and moralize on
them after that brief fermentation of which Morley has written:

[1] G. Kitson Clark, *Peel*, London, 1936, p. 47.

A great wave of humanity, of benevolence, of desire for improvement
—a great wave of social sentiment, in short,—poured itself among all
who had the faculty of large and disinterested thinking. The political
spirit was abroad in its most comprehensive sense, the desire of
strengthening society by adapting it to better intellectual ideals, and
enriching it from new resources of moral power.[1]

It was a world away from 'the aristocratic philosophy of tread-
mills, gibbets and the thirty-nine Acts of Parliament "for the
shooting of partridges alone"....'.[2]

Politics was Cobden's vocation; his business interests suffered
considerably because of his absorption in public life. For him,
politics meant the bending of power to the larger purposes implicit in society. 'When the newspaper was unfolded in the
morning, that furnished him and his friends or his guests with the
topics for the day. Events all over the world were deliberately
discussed in relation to wide and definite general principles; their
bearings were worked out in the light of what Cobden conceived
to be the great economical and social movements of the world.'[3]
His success consisted in his infusing the Manchester capitalists
with ideas and giving them a consciousness of their own power.
He made Radicalism effective by associating it with the successful
campaigning of the Anti-Corn Law League. He himself had intellectual influence rather than power. And his triumphs were
secured by capturing the minds of those who held office, particularly Peel and Gladstone. *The Times* newspaper would call him
and Bright the Gracchi of Rochdale but he had little demagogic
afflatus. He regretted the violations of 'good taste and kind feeling'
in orations, the temptations to play on the emotions of his
audience. In fact he had 'a style that seldom went beyond the
vigorous and animated conversation of a bright and companion-
able spirit'.[4]

Although Cobden believed that 'a moral and religious spirit'
could be infused into political topics, his appeal was to reason.
Orators like Lamartine, he said, were of the '*genus sentimentalist*',
who might mouth about international rights but 'was just as
ready as king or kaiser to march an army into Italy...'. And to
Bright he wrote in 1859: 'I sometimes doubt whether you would
not have done more wisely to rely on your House of Commons

[1] J. Morley, *Life of Cobden*, 1, 91.   [2] *Ibid.* p. 92.
[3] *Ibid.* 11, 478.   [4] *Ibid.* 1, 197.

influence, and been more shy of the Stump. Your greatest power is in the House. In quiet times, there is no influence to be had from without, and if we fell into evil days of turbulence, and suffering and agitation, less scrupulous leaders would carry off the masses. You are not the less qualified to take your true place, from having shown that you are an outside, as well as an inside, leader. But I have an opinion that if you intend to follow politics and not eschew office, you must in future be more exclusively a House of Commons Man.' There is not much of the 'Boanerges of Liberalism' in these words.

Indeed Cobden was aware that there was no tinder to be set alight among the people on domestic matters, that the Anti-Corn Law League itself had flourished because of this absence of competing issues. The 1850s had shown that much more enthusiasm could be generated for Palmerstonian wars than for free trade and financial reforms. A Liberal party based upon principles and with a clear-cut programme, with its motive power in Lancashire and Yorkshire, was slow to emerge. More and more Cobden became convinced that practical political ends could only be achieved through acceptance of the persisting political power of the Church and Aristocracy. His interest in Parliamentary Reform dwindled: there was too much popular ignorance on such important matters as financial reform, colonial government and the land question, for universal suffrage to be other than dangerous. The people were distinguished by the inadequacy of their desires and the absence of even the rudiments of effective political organization. He knew as well as Matthew Arnold that what the populace wanted was 'their beer, their gin and their fun' rather than the rights of man, but his advocacy of the temperance cause as the starting point on the road to 'decent self-possession and courteous manners' showed just how much more practical he was than Arnold.

Cobden's victory, the ending of the Corn Laws, had been achieved through an appeal to public opinion. But when he and Bright turned from moralizing an economic issue to moralizing issues of war and foreign policy in the 1850s they found that neither the political middle class nor the Radical movement would follow them, and that the Dissenters themselves were divided. Their indictment of war as the proclivity of a predatory aristocratic class, as an activity which devoured resources which should be used for other ends, was brilliantly sustained and became part of an anti-militarist tradition upon which Radicals have rung the changes ever since. Yet Cobden's hold upon his audience became uncertain—the Crimean War was highly popular—and for his last great single-handed feat, the negotiation of the Free Trade Treaty with France, he cultivated the established centres of power, Napoleon III, Rouher and Gladstone, as any good Fabian would. So much so that members of Parliament alleged that Britain was merely registering the decrees of a foreign despot.

Cobden was the most creative politician of his time, 'the real author of the middle-class Liberalism which dominated England for more than a generation'.[1] His greatness lay in his conviction that industry and commerce could be solvents of international conflict and domestic tension, and in 'the persevering labour' which he applied to the business of political agitation as a teacher of politics who respected his audience. As Bagehot said, there had never been anyone like Mr Cobden before. Here was middle-class conscience and competence at work in politics.

Disraeli made politics out of his own sensibility; Cobden, out of the overwhelming arguments of political economy. Bright was the tribune of Dissent. Evangelicals were probably more committed to causes than the Dissenters but they worked within the Anglican Church and were not sufficiently alienated from the political order to produce major Radical politicians. But Dissenters were at once numerous enough and estranged enough to sustain them. Originally Dissent had meant Congregationalists but, by the eighteenth century, it compassed Presbyterians and Baptists as well.[2] The Methodists too, although not in schism until 1784 and credited by Élie Halévy with having saved England from revolution—Disraeli could still call them 'a preserve of the Tory Party'— slowly became possessed of political ideas. Dissenters were to the fore in nearly all the agitations of the day, canvassing for the end of the Corn Laws under Cobden and Bright, seeking the Ten Hour day, advocating national responsibility for education[3] and through the temperance movement releasing moral energy among the people.

'My abode', said Cobden, 'is near the Great Western Station,

---

[1] Monypenny and Buckle, *Disraeli*, I, 503.
[2] E. Routley, *English religious dissent*, Cambridge, 1960, p. 8.
[3] *Ibid.* p. 166.

Paddington.' He did not care for the rigorous and damp climate of Lancashire. Bright of Greenbank, Cronkeyshaw Common, Rochdale was quintessentially Lancashire. Quaker Schools, the Rechabites, the Rochdale Literary and Philosophical Societies, the Bible Society and the Temperance Society made him.[1] It was a world in which Church rates were a constant reminder of 'the iron hoof, the mental thraldom of a hireling State priesthood', in which landlords were titled felons, where public life was the club and the chapel, and where trade and manufacture were forces of redemption. He began with Church rates: 'Men of Rochdale, do your duty. You know what becomes you! Maintain the great principles you profess to hold dear; unite with me in the firm resolve that under no possible circumstances will you ever pay a Church rate.' His Hebraism was leavened by a deep reading of the English classics; his audience widened and eventually he was to arouse the political consciousness of the working class as a whole. Palmerston might call Bright 'the honourable and reverend gentleman', but in 1859 he kept him out of his Cabinet, not because of his sectarianism but because he roused class antagonisms.

Bright was never a creative politician. He played on existing discontents and often found, as Cobden noticed, very little to say that he had not said before. In the 1850s the stuff of his politics, the extension of free trade, reduction of taxation, a cheap foreign policy, aroused less fervour than Palmerston's panache and 'the blood-red blossom of war'. Manchester burned him in effigy and rejected him at the election of 1857. He had to move to Birmingham to find a following of working and middle classes who would sustain him.

One cannot read his collected speeches today without being impressed by the consuming earnestness which united speaker and audience.[2] Here was one of the most persistent attempts 'to measure the exercise of political power by the ordinary man's sense of right and wrong'.[3] It presumed a fund of moral power in the

[1] Briggs, *Victorian people*, p. 215.
[2] 'He always looked exactly the same mixture of strength and simplicity. When speaking on the platform he came straight up to the edge, never hiding behind a desk. He once said to a speaker who showed a desire to conceal himself, at least partially, behind a row of flower pots—"No man can move an audience that does not see his boots." You saw Bright from head to heel and every syllable as it fell from his lips reached your ear.' R. Barry O'Brien, *John Bright, a monograph*, London, 1910, pp. xi–xii.
[3] Lord Eustace Percy, *The heresy of democracy*, London, 1954, p. 167.

people and faith in representative institutions. Of Bright, Gladstone said that he 'elevated political life' and 'bequeathed to his country the character of a statesman, which can be made the subject not only of admiration and of gratitude but of reverential contemplation'. But there were defects of sensibility. For just as Lloyd George was to claim in 1911 that he was doing the work of the 'Man of Nazareth', so Bright asserted that in enacting the Corn Laws 'we have put Holy Writ into an Act of Parliament'.

He also bequeathed to succeeding Radicals their characteristic hostility to soldiers, governors, establishments and the imperial theme generally. He was not a pacifist but insisted that wars be grounded in justice:

I believe [he said] if this country, seventy years ago, had adopted the principle of non-intervention in every case where her interests were not directly and obviously assailed, that she would have been saved from much of the pauperism and brutal crimes by which our Government and people have alike been disgraced. This country might have been a garden, every dwelling might have been of marble, and every person who treads its soil might have been sufficiently educated. We should indeed have had less of military glory. We might have had neither Trafalgar nor Waterloo; but we should have set the high example of a Christian nation, free in its institutions, courteous and just in its conduct towards all foreign States, and resting its policy on the unchangeable foundation of Christian morality.

Bright's arguments for Parliamentary Reform were simple. His constant theme was the anomaly of a new English society sustained by industry, and yet still retaining an old territorial political structure based upon the land. The balance of the Constitution must be restored by the admission of the people. This was about as far as his pursuit of general causes would take him. He had no model in mind: 'to confer the franchise is only to give to every man a key by which, if he is wise, he may unlock the treasures which are open to a well-governed people'. The Reform Act of 1832 had allowed two aristocratic factions to continue a casual, uninformed kind of government, to wage with no great efficiency wars which were unnecessary to a nation which, unencumbered, could 'produce more than is produced by any other nation of similar numbers on the face of the globe'. Strangely enough, he believed that a popularly elected Parliament would reduce taxes and seek economies. All our subsequent political experience has proved him wrong; nothing has blunted the financial conscience of the nation more effectively than universal suffrage.

To achieve an immediate good Cobden advocated recognition of aristocratic power. Bright's likening of the great territorial families who had ruled England since the Revolution of 1688 to 'jackals of the desert' following their prey, and his indictment of the principle of the balance of power and solicitude for the liberties of Europe as merely providing 'a gigantic system of out-door relief for the aristocracy of Great Britain', drew laughter from his Birmingham audience, but they made it certain that he would have to wait for a place in a Palmerston Liberal Cabinet. Yet it is doubtful if Bright really wanted office[1] and Sir James Graham, for one, thought it wrong that men who greatly influenced opinion should not bear a portion of the responsibilities of executive government. He was certainly no administrator. When he went to the Board of Trade in 1868 at the age of fifty-seven, 'it was rather late in life to begin work at the head of a great Government department. He had a great distaste, and almost an incapacity for wading through a bundle of official papers. It was said in the office that he did not know how to untie the tape which held them together.'[2]

Bright's peak was in the 1860s when the American Civil War—one war of which he approved—and the quickening of the Parliamentary Reform movement established him as the leading popular politician. For him the Northern states of the United States with their free church, free schools, free land (no primogeniture) and a free career for the humblest child born in the land, were a vast area for creative human energy. He was vulnerable to large and simple notions. 'I see one vast confederation stretching from the frozen North in unbroken line to the glowing South, and from the wild billows of the Atlantic westward to the calmer waters of the Pacific main,—and I see one people, and one language, and one law, and one faith, and, over all that wide continent, the home of freedom and a refuge for the oppressed of every race and of every clime.' In contrast the old order in England was played out: 'Let us try the nation.' He spoke at the right time. For once middle and working classes were excited

---

[1] 'It was his business to inveigh against evils and perhaps there is no easier business.' Trollope, quoted in Briggs, *Victorian people* p. 209.

[2] G. J. Shaw Lefevre quoted in O'Brien, *op. cit.* p. 217.

about the same things; in 1866 the railings of Hyde Park gave way before the London crowds. Great outdoor meetings were held in all the large cities; in the evenings Bright filled the town halls. And in the Commons he fought the last great oratorical duels with Robert Lowe, who with his 'Botany Bay view of his countrymen' insisted that in the end democracy would corrupt, take the virtue out of the British 'mixed' system of government.

As long as Palmerston lived and the rulers of England held out against Parliamentary Reform, Bright and his audiences provided a slow-rising political yeast. The end was simple: a piece of legislation to extend the franchise. He and his most penetrating critic agreed that it was not good 'to live in a society of superiors ...to be heavily over-shadowed, to be profoundly insignificant...'.[1] Give men the vote and they will gain in status. There was more to it than that. Break the monopoly of the political classes, those who by heredity, tradition and experience had governed for the people for so long, and a new kind of politics would be possible. The old device of government would remain but through it the people would be able to pursue rational ends. Bright did not need to know the topography of the promised land; it was sufficient to say that the emerging political order was a phase in the story of liberty. On what would happen to the old saving dualism of Tories and Whigs, their rules of the game, on the implications of numerical majority rule, Bright said little that was explicit. He assumed that the populace would become attracted to the old political institutions, that force and argument would not replace discussion.

'When a man speaks to you, he is not speaking solely for himself. He is inevitably speaking for others.'[2] So Bright for a short period embodied the protean ideas of democracy and liberalism. Yet his role was more modest than those of Kossuth, Lamartine, Garibaldi or Lincoln. Lassalle, whom 'the hot-blooded Rhinelanders received...like a God',[3] was more exciting than Bright. The Gladstone ministry from 1868 to 1874 achieved most of what he desired: the end of Church rates, the disestablishment of the Irish Church, the entry of Dissenters into universities, the end of the purchase of commissions in the Army, the beginnings of a

[1] Matthew Arnold, *Mixed essays*, pp. 10–11.
[2] Albert Camus, *Resistance, rebellion and death*, London, 1961, p. 170.
[3] R. Michels, *Political parties*, New York, 1959, p. 64.

national education system. The way was clear for men of principle and energy to seek the general good in a milieu of competition and self-help.

At the same time as Bright was assuming the leadership of the working and middle classes, Gladstone felt within him 'the rebellious unspoken word'. 'I will not be old. The horizon enlarges, the sky shifts around me,' he wrote. 'It is an age of shocks; a discipline so strong, so manifold, so rapid and so whirling that only when it is at an end, if then, can I hope to comprehend it.'[1] For some time it had been possible that the most able of the new men—Gladstone was on the periphery of the ruling class, not of it —would join John Bright as the voice of the middle classes. Palmerston foretold 'strange doings' when his young colleague got his place, yet it was a difficult transition from the young man steeped in early Christian theology, with his deep respect for ancient ways, authority and old Whiggery, who emphasized good government and only modest reforms, to Clarendon's 'audacious innovator with an insatiable desire for popularity', 'the people's William', the popular politician of Midlothian.

Like Disraeli he took politics very seriously, wished to do the great deed, but unlike Disraeli he was slow in making a political map for himself. Yet when he devoted himself to a particular issue none doubted his power. 'On the Succession bill the whole cabinet was against him. He delivered to us much the same speech as he made in the House of Commons. At its close we were all convinced.'[2] His sphere was the Commons and 'he conquered the House because he was saturated with a subject and its arguments, because he could state and enforce his case'. This abiding faith in discussion and rhetoric, this devotion to the dialectic of Parliament, are fundamental. 'I have lived now for many years in the midst of the hottest and noisiest of its workshops,' he declared, 'and have seen that amidst the clatter and the din a ceaseless labour is going on; stubborn matter is reduced to obedience, and the brute powers of society like the fire, air, water and mineral of nature are, with clamour indeed but also with might, educated and shaped into the most refined and regular forms of usefulness for man.'

[1] J. Morley, *Life of Gladstone*, London, 1908, 1, 543, quoted in Briggs, *Victorian people*, p. 237.
[2] Lord Aberdeen, 1856, in Morley, *op. cit.* 1, 345.

Religion and the private life competed with politics but the fascination which the public realm had for him comes out in a conversation with Sir James Graham in 1846. Graham was 'weary of labour at thirteen or fourteen hours a day, and of the intolerable abuse to which he was obliged to submit; but his habits were formed in the House of Commons and for it, and he was desirous to continue there as an independent gentleman, taking part from time to time in public business as he might find occasion, and giving his leisure to his family and to books'. But Gladstone could not conceive 'that men who have played a great part, who have swayed the great moving forces of the state, who have led the House of Commons and given the tone to public policy, can at their will remain there, but renounce the consequences of their remaining, and refuse to fulfil what must fall to them in some contingency of public affairs'.[1]

From Peel he had learned the sober business of statecraft: 'on no account to try to deal with a question before it is ripe; never to go to the length of submitting a difference between two departments to the prime minister before the case is exhausted and complete; never to press a proposal forward beyond the particular stage at which it has arrived'.[2] Under-Secretary for War and Colonies at twenty-six, Cabinet Minister at thirty-three, he rejoiced in the work in hand and was content to do notable things within the existing pattern.

Yet for Cobden, Gladstone was the only member of Palmerston's Cabinet not afraid to let his heart rule his head. Active moral impulse had taken him in many directions. In the political and judicial processes, and in the prisons of Naples, Gladstone saw 'illegality, the fountain-head of cruelty and baseness and every other vice'. For Gladstone, writes Morley, the Crimean War was at its outset 'the vindication of the public law of Europe against a wanton disturber'.[3] Yet against the China War of 1857 he called up 'that justice which binds man to man; which is older than Christianity, because it was in the world before Christianity; which is broader than Christianity, because it extends to the world beyond Christianity...'.

The assiduity of his intellect was generally admitted. 'His first principles are rarely ours; we may often think them obscure—sometimes incomplete—occasionally quite false; but we cannot

---

[1] *Ibid.* p. 218.   [2] *Ibid.* p. 199.   [3] *Ibid.* p. 359.

deny that they are the result of distinct thought with disciplined faculties upon adequate *data*, of a careful and dispassionate consideration of all the objections which occurred, whether easy or insuperable, trifling or severe.'[1] The political world 'could not understand him: they never knew what he would do next...'. Intellect, respect for facts, had made him a Peelite free-trader; conservative affinities kept him a member of the Carlton Club.

His political ambiguity began to dissolve in 1859 when he entered Palmerston's Liberal Cabinet as Chancellor of the Exchequer mainly because of moral sympathy with the Russell–Palmerston pro-Italian foreign policy. The time had come for the determination of his political stance and from 1860 the coiled power within him is released. Two struggles within the Palmerston government brought him into the ambience of Cobden and Bright. The first was over the cost of Palmerston's armaments and the second over the passing of the Paper Duties Bill. The catalyst in the retrenchment issue was Cobden, whose clarity and consistency of mind captured Gladstone. Gladstone was aware that he needed fresh sources of knowledge. Previously his 'first promptings of inward instinct [had been] to seek advice from persons in the same situation of the same habits of mind and political training and connections'.[2] Cobden supported him on armaments and he reciprocated by encouraging the steps towards a free trade treaty with France.

Bright, too, was a point of power, a portent of change:

The men [he wrote to Gladstone] whose minds are full of the tradition of the last century, your *chief* and your *foreign minister* [Palmerston and Russell] will still cling to the past, and will seek to model the present upon it—but the past is well nigh really past, and a new policy and a wiser and higher morality are sighed for by the best of our people, and there is a prevalent feeling that *you* are destined to guide that wiser policy and teach that higher morality.[3]

The conjunction with Cobden and Bright at the minimal level of Free Trade, retrenchment and anti-imperialism was of the highest importance. Gladstone began 'to learn his creed of his time', to sink roots into the Radical and Dissenting earth, even if

[1] W. Bagehot, 'Oxford', in *Works and life*, i, ed. Mrs Russell Barrington, London, 1915, 164.
[2] W. E. Williams, *The rise of Gladstone to the leadership of the Liberal party*, Cambridge, 1934, p. 34.   [3] *Ibid*. pp. 47–8.

he was neither Radical nor Dissenter. An uneasy member of Palmerston's Cabinet, he cut back the military estimates and began to question the traditional foreign policy of England.

The Paper Duties measure not only propelled Gladstone towards Liberalism; it also helped to create his audience of the future. The stamp duties on newspapers had gone and now, when the remaining taxes on knowledge, the paper duties, were removed, a long-unsatisfied hunger for political news could be met. For a short period the editors

wrote for men who were genuinely interested in politics. No one can open the files of any English provincial newspaper between 1860 and 1890 without being struck by the character of the news. Foreign policy was discussed with a detail which a university class would now find overpowering; the clauses of treaties and bills were printed. This is true of provincial papers published in industrial towns, where the circulation could not depend on a leisured or a cultured class.[1]

Even the Speaker of the House of Commons praised the penny newspapers in 1864 and Bright asserted that 'in quality of writing, in elevated and moral tone, in the industry with which facts and news are collected and offered to the people...the newspapers which are sold at a penny will bear comparison with any of their dearer neighbours...'.[2]

Public men were now fully revealed by a reverent press to the newly enfranchised or the about-to-be enfranchised. These yearned for political leadership and proved highly susceptible to Gladstone's overwhelming righteousness, to his large and splendid evocation of the themes of the moment. He was to announce in 1864 that 'every man who is not presumably incapacitated by some consideration of personal unfitness or political danger, is morally entitled to come within the pale of the Constitution'. In 1862 the people of Newcastle had astonished him with the warmth of their reception. When, ejected from Oxford, he moved to the North to represent South Lancashire he inherited Bright's audience, and within that regional support the political pertinacity of the Nonconformists would sustain him to the end. 'No sixteenth-century reformer wielded more power over his adherents or roused more savage hatred in the haunts of

[1] *Ibid.* pp. 4–5.
[2] John Bright, *Selected speeches*, London, 1907 (Everyman), p. 261.

privilege than did the leader of the Liberal party. His followers in Manchester, or in Bradford or in Wrexham, became zealots with all the paraphernalia of a religion. They had their priest, and if the oracle was sometimes perplexing, it only served to intensify the blind adherence.'[1]

In later years, the trivia of his life would be popular knowledge, his home become the centre of pilgrimages. But well before Gladstone's beatification, the new political classes glowed in what Lecky called his 'moral incandescence'. He did not instruct, he had not Cobden's art in reducing a subject to its elements. He edified, expounded the 'oughts' of duty, honour, human dignity and God as no leading politician has done since. And all with the passion, the *ira et studium*, which is the politician's element. 'No other great politician so habitually steeped his politics in emotion, and this was one great cause of his wide popular influence.'[2] This passion was in his parliamentary oratory too. When he spoke to the Reform Bill of 1867, 'it seemed as if the souls of all the compound householders in England had entered into him'.[3]

It was the new popular audience which made Gladstone. On the platform he proved the greatest persuader of his time. And it was not debate that he initiated there so much as conviction, an undetailed ardour. Bagehot's era of 'government by discussion' —among gentlemen—proved short-lived. At the public meeting, 'a wholly new vein of political opinion and intelligence'[4] may well have been opened but those who came were usually of one heart and soul. The judgments which they passed on the old political order were derived, as much as anything, from prevailing religious sentiments.

To the crowd Gladstone gave the power of judgment but little more. ('It is written in legible characters, and with a pen of iron, on the rock of human destiny, that within the domain of practical politics the people must in the main be passive.') He had little sympathy with or understanding of what Radicals or Dissenters wanted, yet they recognized 'in the ring of his voice, in his choice of words, in the sanctions to which he appealed, the same spirit as that which possessed them'.[5] In his first ministry from 1868 to

---

[1] Williams, *op. cit.* p. 4.   [2] W. E. H. Lecky, *Democracy and liberty*, London, 1899, I, xxx.
[3] *Ibid.* p. xxxiii.   [4] Jephson, *The platform*, II, 561.
[5] G. Kitson Clark, Introduction to R. T. Shannon, *Gladstone and the Bulgarian agitation 1876*, London, 1963, p. xxii.

1874, he lost his rapport with these emergent groups and, having lost it and seeing no great liberal issue in sight likely to restore it, he retired from the Liberal leadership.

What brought him back was the Bulgarian atrocities of 1876. At the outset Gladstone was the reluctant agitator. Yet because of tremendous style and prestige he inevitably came to the front. His detestation of power and coercion as such, his insistence on an exact congruence of political and private morality, had a peculiarly wide appeal. He staked a claim which seemed highly appropriate at a time when religion still penetrated deeply into public life, when moral progress was accepted as a fact, to British moral leadership in the world—a claim intermittently asserted ever since. It has been well said that at this time 'he was moving not from right to left in the conventional manner, but rather into a lofty station of his own, remote from the main political course'[1]—a puzzle to his own Whig colleagues and to some of the harder-headed Radicals, and an exasperation to the Tories. Yet it was this independent moral power which changed the history of the Liberal party, turning it away from specific radical measures to the denunciation of Beaconsfieldism, to the cause of Ireland, to internal divisions on imperialism.

Moreover, Gladstone remained, even if persuasive, a gentleman, believing in the necessity of a leisured ruling class, prepared to respect the Whigs and give them their place in a unified Liberal party. In his Cabinet of 1880, great offices went to the Whigs and he preferred to be succeeded in the leadership of the Liberal party not by Chamberlain, the man of measures and organization, but by Hartington, the great Whig who once said that he could not understand what Gladstone meant in private conversation. What Gladstone therefore provided, and largely through the 'gift or habit of words, vast, nebulous and resonant',[2] was 'continuity between the old party system, with all the parliamentary techniques it had developed and all the experience it had garnered, and the activities of the new classes who demanded a position of their own in politics'.[3]

Force and passion united with a quite extraordinary capacity to study detail. And yet no one knew where he was going. To friends

---

[1] Shannon, *Gladstone and the Bulgarian agitation*, p. 11.
[2] G. M. Young, *Victorian essays*, Oxford, 1962, p. 87.
[3] Kitson Clark in Shannon, *op. cit.* p. xxii.

and enemies it seemed that he could, at the touch of events, bend the whole of his tremendous gifts and apparatus of argument in the way he wished. He endowed political choice with moment and drama. And yet the choice which he made was often not a clear one. For he could remain anchored to Whiggery while making gestures towards equal opportunity and social mobility. Built into promises were saving clauses, pledges to the past. There were limits to his vision.

Out from the classic and well-charted waters of Free Trade, Free Contract, and Free Competition, he never pushed an adventurous prow. He was a late, half-hearted convert to the ballot: to free education he was never wholly converted. With those two movements which were gathering force through all the second half of his life, Socialism and Imperialism, movements over which the far less stable genius of Disraeli shot rays of fantastic light, he was utterly out of sympathy.[1]

An expanding market, a retrenching administration, and peace would solve all, even the problem of labour.

Lecky saw Gladstone as a barometer of the political weather.

It is a truth which should never be forgotten, that in the field of politics the spirit of servility and sycophancy no longer shows itself in the adulation of kings and nobles. Faithful to its old instinct of grovelling at the feet of power, it now carries its homage to another shrine. The men who, in former ages, would have sought by Byzantine flattery to win power through the favour of an emperor or a prince, will now be found declaiming on platforms about the iniquity of privilege, extolling the matchless wisdom and nobility of the masses...[2]

Yet if an inventory were made of the legislation of Gladstone's Cabinets or the causes he espoused, very little would fall into the vote-catching category. His first ministry alienated interests in every sphere in which it made law or policy. Throughout his political life, his opposition to heavy armaments and imperial expansion often ran clean contrary to the climates of opinion even in his own centres of support; his comminations of cruelties and wrongs in Naples and Armenia were spontaneous and his campaign against the Bashi-Bazouks was launched when Radicals tended to be anti-Russian.

Even the casuistry, traceable in origin to his early Tractarian

---

[1] Young, *Victorian essays*, p. 100.
[2] Lecky, *op. cit.* 1, 30.

period, the syntactical devices which enabled him to bear the consequences of his own rhetoric, were testimonies to his own high responsibility. He needed those ambiguities to preserve his own inner freedom of action. He knew that he had not the gift of prophecy. Or conversely, sometimes, as with Newman, 'the mind moved and the internal decision was taken some time before it was announced, and the apparent dissimulation during the interval was in each case attributed to policy or duplicity'.[1]

There was in Gladstone none of the iron mastery of history and its ways attributed to continental political heroes like Bismarck. 'The whole of my public and exoteric life', he wrote later in his career, 'has been shaped as to its ends for me, scarcely rough hewn by me.'[2] He was not one of history's commanding officers who, having the favour of prince or people, can plot the future with cold sagacity. But even Lecky had to admit his indomitable courage: 'He had every kind of courage...the courage that never feared to face a hostile audience, to lead a forlorn hope, to defend a desperate cause, to assume a great weight of responsibility—the fatal courage which did not hesitate to commit his party by his own imperious will to new and untried policies.'[3]

---

[1] David Knowles, *The historian and character*, Cambridge, 1964, p. 10.
[2] Shannon, *op. cit.* p. 274.   [3] Lecky, *op. cit.* p. xxxiv.

5
THE MANTLE OF ELIJAH

Gladstone [wrote Graham Wallas] could step on to the platform of a great meeting with the same sense of consecration to the purposes of Providence with which he had knelt that morning at the eucharist. The management of his splendid voice, the well-graced movement of his body and features, the skill with which 'the old Parliamentary hand' (as he was proud to call himself) made twenty thousand people feel that his sonorous phrases expressed their varying aspirations, *while he yet left himself free* [my italics]; in these things Gladstone had no more sense of unreality than had Disraeli in his calculated audacities, or Lassalle in the gestures which he used to rehearse before his mirror.[1]

In this age of hope, adulation went to the man whose oratorical power and strength of conviction were outstanding. Even Michels conceded that before organization had transformed the leading politician into an oligarch, before popularity had made him a 'celebrity', he had 'been pushed forward by a clearer vision, by a profounder sentiment, and by a more ardent desire for the general good'.[2] There he stood, noble in vision and sentiment, reflecting in his outer personality the transformation of his times, sensing the desires of the people before they did themselves. What he could do for the common cause, no one else could do as well. And the virtue of the people recognized the virtue of the leader.

Marvellous was the impress which these men made on the Platform. By prodigious labour and self-sacrifice, by the constant reiteration of the highest and noblest truths of political morality, and by the high-toned example which they set, they weaned the rougher elements of society to constitutional courses; they instilled great political principles into their minds, and set them an example of what the Platform ought to be, and how, with it, to win an apparently hopeless cause.[3]

Yet it was not necessary for the popular leader to catch the on-coming tide. To G. J. Holyoake, Bright was only marginally

[1] *The great society*, London, 1914, p. 320.
[2] R. Michels, *Political parties*, New York, 1959, p. 206.
[3] Jephson, *The platform*, II, 597.

'better than the better sort of Tories';[1] Bradlaugh, whom the young Tom Mann thought 'the foremost platform man in Britain' would have nothing to do with Trade Unionism or Socialism. Gladstone had no belief in social organization. What the tribune offered was words, to alleviate the frustration and pain of social change and individual misfortune.

There was a gap between these large and generous words and what could be done. The promises of the new politics were to be more clearly 'seen through' on the continent (notably by Italians), where the academic mind was already dismissing democratic animation as a mere passing phase. For a short period the people would prostrate themselves before the Stentor of 'liberty', 'progress', or 'humanity'. But the words were illusory, merely embellished a hoax, built the myth by which an élite rose to power. 'Freedom' was a word whose exposition enabled vigorous and ambitious individuals to pose at the centre of action, to impose their personality on their day and age. All the masses responded to was 'oratorical gifts as such, beauty and strength of voice, suppleness of mind, badinage'.[2]

Similar criticism, less systematic and less trenchant, circulated in Britain too, but here it contended with a tradition (established at least since the eighteenth century) that politics was a sphere in which character, intelligence and sensibility might be freely and honourably exercised. The great politician acted in an *existing* tradition of confidence which he might reinforce but did not create. He did this neither by truckling to his audience nor by deceiving them, but by giving order and sequence to barely formulated desires. Both words and deeds were like the actions of Pericles' famous men 'woven into the stuff of other men's lives'.

Jephson was impressed by the sheer moral reverberations. 'The people, with their growing power, have risen to their increased responsibilities; far wider knowledge is displayed at their meetings than formerly; a far higher moral tone is apparent; a more discriminating judgment; quicker intelligence...'[3] The English leading politician, encouraged to audacious oratory, did not always put in qualifying clauses. But because there was already in

---

[1] *Sixty years of an agitator's life*, 3rd edition, London, 1903, II, 272. 'He was always for the Crown, the Bible, and the Constitution as much as any Conservative' (p. 275).   [2] Michels, *op. cit.* p. 71.
[3] *The platform*, II, 599.

existence a system grounded upon consent and subject to popular control, because within it power was accessible to those who developed the discourse of politics (which was not the case in many other countries where the political intelligentsia constituted an alienated enclave), the debate, in spite of claptrap on the platform and orotundities in editorial columns, remained, if not very profound, relatively close to the subject, to what was possible. In Britain, even the opposition, says Michels, had strategical talent rather than theoretical profundity.

What Whigs, tentative Liberals and Tories all feared was Jack Cade. 'It cannot be denied', wrote W. H. Mallock, 'that there is such a thing as the malignant democrat, who, having full sagacity to see, or at least to suspect, that the measures he proposes may be either ruinous or delusive, is yet prepared to do and dare anything by which he personally may contrive to raise himself. . .'[1] The others, the genuine Utopians and 'the accidental Radicals', were not so dangerous. But were the people when 'their more vehement champions' addressed them able to consider their character, birth, history and motives? This indeed was the great fear of the nineteenth century, that the new voters would be taken in by 'malignant democrats'.

Following Bright, Bradlaugh, 'with his thunderous consecutiveness and accumulated power of statement',[2] proved that a great Radical agitator could easily acquire celebrity in the quickening politics of the 1870s. 'One man with right on his side, against the hosts of wrong', with self-schooled intellect and commanding physique, could, even if he refused to identify himself with the working class, hardly concerned himself with social reorganization and propagated the secularist truths of the French Enlightenment of the *previous* century, win unqualified support from the working classes, make many Radicals and republicans. Bradlaugh was a splendid figure: Shaw said of him that if he had been an archbishop he would have been 'a more tremendous archbishop than had ever been seen in this country'.[3]

There was little doubt that the tribune, inveighing against evils, could hold his special audience. What was perhaps doubtful was the maintenance of rapport between the responsible leading

---

[1] *The nineteenth century*, November 1880.
[2] G. J. Holyoake, 'Appreciations' in Bradlaugh Centenary Committee, *Champion of liberty*, London, 1933, p. 35.   [3] *Ibid.* p. 49.

politician with his base in Parliament and in party and the people at large. Measures were necessary and could be accepted but beyond them what was wanted was continuity of men. Bagehot, for example, had maintained that as long as expectations in statesmanship were conditioned by the old Constitution, all would be well. Leading politicians, like Joseph Chamberlain and Lord Randolph Churchill, who made a mark in Parliament and on the platform were therefore precarious bridges between the old and the new conditions. They bore the heat of the day when what was ' outside Parliament seem[ed]. . .to be fast mounting, nay to have already mounted, to an importance much exceeding what is inside.'[1]

'The future of Democracy,' wrote G. C. Brodrick, 'mainly depends on the willingness of the omnipotent people to be led by highly trained and conscientious statesmen, on the future supply of such leaders, and on their willingness to serve the people upon such terms as Democracy will accept.'[2] Like Palmerston, Gladstone worried about what would happen when he was gone:

If I were in a dying condition, I confess, I should have one great apprehension in my mind—what I conceive to be the great danger to my country. It is not Ireland. That difficulty will be solved. It is not the character of future measures. The good sense of the people will take care of those. It is the *men* of the future—personalities of the stamp of Randolph Churchill and Chamberlain.[3]

If there were years in which the continuity of British political leadership seemed to falter, they were surely 1885 and 1886. Issues which had coursed along separate affluents suddenly converged in a narrow and perilous channel. There were two general elections with a substantially expanded and unpredictable electorate, three new governments. In a period of high political excitement during which the single-purpose Irish party seemed capable of bending the two historic parties to its will, the last of the Whigs lodged themselves with the Tories and left the Liberals preoccupied with Ireland. Although the crises were followed in great detail in both the popular and higher journalism, and the politicians plumbed and excited popular feelings at mass rallies, it was in Parliament

---

[1] Morley, *Gladstone*, II, 182, Gladstone to Lord Rosebery, September 1880.
[2] *The nineteenth century*, November 1883.
[3] R. R. James, *Lord Randolph Churchill* London, 1959, p. 257.

that the fates of both the Salisbury and Gladstone governments were in the end decided. Of the great debate on Home Rule in May 1886, J. L. Garvin has written: 'It moved upon a higher level of argument and appeal than has been reached since then, though nearly half a century has passed. Most eminent speakers excelled themselves; Hartington attained a massive force and dignity never forgotten by those who heard him...Chamberlain became a much more potent figure at Westminster than before.'[1]

Hartington, who refused the Prime Ministership of England three times, and was deeply appreciated both for his transparent honesty and his 'weight' in the country by leading politicians as different as Gladstone and Balfour, represented the best of the old Whiggery. Chamberlain was a portent—'so deeply the originator of the modern kind of politics,' says J. A. Spender.[2] Like Bright, Chamberlain was an emergent Dissenter; as a Unitarian, even a Dissenter from Dissent. As a youth he had rejoiced in the triumphs of Free Trade and identified himself with the movement to end Nonconformist civil disabilities. But his mind had been fired, as Bright's was not, by the journalism which hailed the liberal revolutions on the continent and he took up, like his mentor and associate Dr R. W. Dale, the Birmingham divine, a Palmerstonian briskness in foreign affairs.

But this would lie dormant. What was significant in his early politics had nothing to do with Palmerston. At the outset he was the politician of the franchise, of the extra-parliamentary association, of causes. But the causes were too narrow. Both the chairmanship of the Birmingham United Kingdom Alliance, which advocated civic control of the liquor trade, and of the executive of the National Education League, which battled against Anglican domination of primary education, he found too restricted in scope. The politics of Dissent gave way to general politics.[3] As the most famous municipal politician of his day, he wanted Birmingham to be an example to the nation. But the real sign of a new breath of principle was his sponsoring as an urban politician of the cause of the voteless and landless labourers. To Free Education and Free Schools he added Free Land.

Even more distinctive was his political base. He was not the

---

[1] *Life of Joseph Chamberlain*, London, 1933, II, 235.
[2] *The public life*, I, 80.
[3] Garvin, *Joseph Chamberlain*, I, 147–8.

first of the leading politicians of the nineteenth century to draw his strength from the provinces. Bright had symbolized the industry and energy first of the North and then of the Midlands. Yet he had never entrenched himself. Not only was Chamberlain the master of Birmingham municipal politics, the leader of the School Board; he also had available a political machine which gave him a local redoubt that no other leading politician could match.

The Liberal caucus in Birmingham not only rationalized procedures for choosing candidates at elections, marshalling the Liberal vote and capturing municipal and parliamentary seats; it also mobilized political energy and gave the great city of Birmingham a distinctive political personality, rallied large audiences responsive and sympathetic to the Radical tribune. Here was something which persisted between elections, held the continuous loyalty of the voluntary workers. Moreover, the caucus gave a model to other cities and when, one year after Chamberlain entered Parliament, the system was confederated in 1877 in the National Liberal Federation, it provided not the single-cause pressure, so typical of early and mid-nineteenth-century politics, but a general, yet concerted, Radical extra-parliamentary force which threatened to oust the established parliamentary leadership of the party.

The machine did good work for the Liberals in 1880 and it was as lord of the caucus that Chamberlain forced his way into Gladstone's Cabinet in 1880 after only four years in Parliament. But Chamberlain not only used the caucus; he beat it. When he left the Liberal party in 1886, Birmingham followed him into the Unionist camp. 'Burke had to leave Bristol, Bright to leave Manchester, Morley to leave Newcastle. Not so Chamberlain. When a day of disruption comes; when Gladstone who blessed the birth, and Schnadhorst who nourished the growth, of the original Caucus, hope to use it against its author, Chamberlain will be too much for it and them.'[1]

Office as such never meant much to Chamberlain. When he discovered that most of his colleagues were antagonistic to social reform, he insisted that the Cabinet's 'corporate existence' should not override the independent representative character of its members. Although a more effective administrator than Bright

[1] *Ibid.* p. 265.

and with a good legislative record at the Board of Trade, he was quite prepared to leave office and fight for either his Radical programme or the franchise. With a faithful staff in Birmingham, a compact group of Radical supporters in Parliament, more direct contacts with the Press than most of his colleagues, he knew there was no need for him to work modestly within the old Liberalism. With Dilke and Morley as his lieutenants, he could see his constructive Radicalism irresistibly borne forward—on the shoulders of an enlarged electorate mobilized by a Radical caucus.

He identified the enemy. Like Wilkes, he was fighting those in possession. He knew the value of ready pugnacity; he fought not only the old gang of his party and those 'acred up to the eyes and consolled up to the chin' but also his Tory analogue, Lord Randolph Churchill, who had also sensed the power outside the House and was busily engaged in catching Radical straws in the wind.

Chamberlain had no fine sensibility. His political theory was naive: 'If you will go back to the early history of our social system you will find that...every man was born into the world with natural rights, with a right to a share in the great inheritance of the community, with a right to a part of the land of his birth.' But to dispossessed Scottish crofters or to landless labourers his words pointed the moral effectively enough. And *The radical programme* of 1883 which, two years later, became 'The Unauthorized Programme' was, says Garvin, 'one of the best briefs for a fighting party that ever was compiled'.[1] It was concrete and practical; most of its objectives, free primary education, graduated taxation, manhood suffrage, payment of members, were substantially achieved in the next generation. Those that were not, such as Home Rule all round and complete disestablishment of State Churches, have at least remained politically practicable.

The Tories chose to regard him as a flaming Jacobin but there was nothing utopian about him. He pushed specific measures. What disturbed both Tories and Whigs was his political strategy of first exciting public opinion on a particular issue, including his remedy in a programme endorsed by caucus, and then firmly using the majority on the floor of the House to give it legislative form.[2] To Lord Salisbury, for example, who considered that if a

[1] Garvin, *Joseph Chamberlain*, p. 546.
[2] G. M. Young, *Victorian England: Portrait of an age*, Oxford, 1936, p. 135.

matter were contentious it was not ripe for legislation, all this was highly heretical.

The press projected him as 'the Robespierre of the caucus', the 'Brummagen Girondist', and sometimes his words were in character:

Lord Salisbury constitutes himself the spokesman of a class—of the class to which he himself belongs, who toil not neither do they spin, whose fortunes, as in his case, have originated by grants made in times gone by for the services which courtiers rendered kings, and have since grown and increased while they have slept by levying an increased share on all that other men have done by toil and labour to add to the general wealth and prosperity of the country...

It was an unusual experience for an audience to hear a Cabinet Minister say: 'We are told that this country is the paradise of the rich; it should be our task to see that it does not become the purgatory of the poor.' No wonder that the working classes in town and country seethed with excitement in theatres and public halls from Edinburgh to Trowbridge as he went on his oratorical way in 1885.

G. M. Young does not include Chamberlain among those late Victorian politicians from whose speeches and writings 'a sound body of political philosophy might still be extracted'.[1] Disraeli thought his language 'coarse and commonplace abuse such as you might expect from the cad of an omnibus'; *The Times* newspaper called it 'Billingsgate'. He disseminated words and ideas among audiences which did not handle them easily. As he told Gladstone: 'Popular government is inconsistent with the reticence which official etiquette formerly imposed on speakers and which was easily borne as long as the electorate was a comparatively small and privileged class, and the necessity of consulting it at meetings infrequent and limited. Now the platform has become one of the most powerful and indispensable instruments of Government...'

At the time he seemed 'the man of the future'. Today his 'new conceptions of public duty, new developments of social enterprise, new estimates of the natural obligations of the members of the community to one another'[2] are easily under-assessed. Chamberlain had courage and audacity: twice he took his political life in

[1] *Ibid.* p. 137.
[2] Preface to *The radical programme*, London, 1885, p. vi.

his own hands and on each occasion he was possibly damning his chances of the premiership. He lived for politics and sold out of business to devote his life to his causes. He welcomed the coming of the professional politician. 'I should like to know,' he said, 'why politics are the only business which must be left to amateurs.' Yet his professionalism in no way implied brokerage or facing both ways. Like Chatham, to whom Garvin likens him in 'imperious instinct and trenchancy of decision',[1] he neglected connection, was always prepared to pit the whole of his powers against the politics of men whom he thought mistaken. He was alive to opportunity; he knew that Gladstonianism was running into the sands and considered that the Conservatives whom he joined, however good at administration, were merely 'painstaking scholars' who learned 'by rote not by heart'. Concerned with the making of decisions rather than with who made them, he could not subordinate himself to group or party. As a conduit from the old politics into the new, he had to be strenuously egotistic. His style paid the penalty in briskness, coarseness and too little scruple:

The man who passed at two strides from the policy of 'ransom' to the bosom of the Conservative Party had not the kind of *character* required in a Liberal leader. The Liberal Party must be led with rectitude, with sincerity of purpose, if it is to remain worthy of the allegiance of true Liberals. When Gladstone gravitated to Liberalism after setting out in life as a high Conservative, all men knew that it was in virtue of his moral bias... Who could say so of the conversion of Chamberlain? He was of another species.[2]

Randolph Churchill, one of Burke's 'turbulent discontented men of quality'—the sort of aristocrat who in other cultures gets himself precariously involved in conspiracy and sansculottism— was perhaps more alarming than Chamberlain. There is much about him that is unattractive: his pursuit of 'the glittering prizes', ill manners and cultivation of shallow political realism. When Lord Salisbury condemned 'the temptation, strong to many politicians, to attempt to gain the victory by bringing into the Lobby men whose principles were divergent and whose combined forces therefore could not lead to any wholesome victory', Lord

---

[1] Garvin, *Joseph Chamberlain*, I, 88.
[2] J. M. Robertson, *Mr Lloyd George and liberalism*, London, 1923, pp. 21–2.

Randolph observed that, while such moralizing might come well from country gentry, 'discriminations between wholesome and unwholesome victories are idle and impracticable. Obtain the victory, know how to follow it up and leave the wholesomeness or unwholesomeness to critics.'[1]

He had an excessive contempt for middle-class Conservative worthies—R. A. Cross, the Lancashire businessman, and W. H. Smith, were 'Marshall and Snelgrove'. Cross, 'thinking that he might propitiate this terrible young man' on one occasion passed some information to him in the House. 'Randolph stopped speaking, and looked at it carefully, holding the paper with a dainty repugnance between finger and thumb. "A pretty thing affairs have come to in the House of Commons", he observed pleasantly, "when we have amendments passed around on dirty little bits of paper." '[2]

His aristocratic background and fox-hunting high spirits were secondary. He was, in fact, a man of ability, a careerist like Bolingbroke, and he sought to acquire a style quickly. There was not much sign of a cause in the early days. Instead, there was a phrase and mood-catching celerity. With the little knot of Fourth Party *frondeurs* he made the long-harboured Tory resentment of Gladstone's rectitude and omniscience articulate. On the platform he gave the crowds bright, exciting and personalized politics. He exploited the growing tensions between Whig and Liberal and between Radical and Liberal, the new passion in the politics of Ireland and about the 'condition of England'.

Churchill took his cues well: he was as fiercely anti-imperialist as Wilfrid Scawen Blunt during 'the bondholders war' in Egypt; in spite of Irish sympathies, he sought to pin Home Rule firmly to Gladstone in 1886 and unscrupulously play the 'Orange card'. 'After all,' he wrote to Labouchere, 'if the G.O.M. goes a mucker, it may be a good thing for everybody. He has always disturbed the equilibrium of the parties and done no good to any one except himself.'

The first cue came during the protracted attempts to keep the atheist Bradlaugh out of the House of Commons. This enabled him by a gross oversimplification to associate the Liberals with 'atheism, disloyalty and immorality'. 'The Bradlaugh case was

---

[1] Winston Spencer Churchill, *Lord Randolph Churchill* (1907), London, 1951, p. 185.
[2] James, *Lord Randolph Churchill*, p. 87.

inexhaustible in scenes and sensations... whenever it occupied the stage the Government was powerless.'[1] From then onwards there was danger in the dandiacal politics of the Fourth Party.

The second cue was from Disraeli although there is little sign that there was a similar intelligence or sensibility at work. He found 'Trust the People' a better card than 'Throne and Altar'; 'in the main he simply allowed himself to become intoxicated by the ease and fluency with which he found himself able to propound his ill-digested ideas and by the effect they had upon uneducated audiences'.[2]

More important than the actual elements of his 'Tory Democracy', comprising a Radical programme not very different from that of Chamberlain—Churchill once professed that he had not much time for political thinking—was the central proposition 'that the Conservative Party was willing and thoroughly competent to deal with the needs of democracy and the multiplying problems of modern life',[3] and secondly that the Tories could produce a popular leader, one 'upon whom the mantle of Elijah has descended'. Indeed, without a leader 'who fears not to meet and knows how to sway immense masses of the working classes and who either by his genius or his eloquence, or by all the varied influences of an ancient name, can 'move the hearts of households''', the Conservatives would be beaten from the start. Salisbury might have the first claim to such leadership but the implication was, of course, that it would revert to Lord Randolph.

In Parliament, he proved to be a master of debate and, with his associates, severely hampered Gladstone's second administration. From the causeless politics of the Fourth Party he moved to the public platform and there expounded in high style whatever ideas were to hand and whatever issues were worth exploiting. It has never been difficult to condemn Liberal governments for not sustaining Liberal principles, i.e. for not sustaining in office what is a highly elevated state of mind. It was therefore easy for Churchill to invoke the 'Peace, Retrenchment and Reform' of Bright and Cobden against a Liberal government resorting to coercion in Ireland and military intervention in Egypt. For a Tory supporter of established institutions, of monarchy, Lords and Church, he

[1] Churchill, *Lord Randolph Churchill*, p. 112.
[2] Chilston, *Chief Whip*, London, 1961, p. 29.
[3] Churchill, *Lord Randolph Churchill*, p. 230.

could show remarkable sympathy with the revolutionaries (on the good liberal ground that 'suffering situations' justified what they did):

The revolution of Arabi was the movement of a nation; like all revolutions, it had its good side and its bad; you must never for purposes of practical politics, criticize too minutely the origin, authors, or the course of revolutions. Would you undo, if you could, the Revolution of 1688 which drove the Stuarts from the throne, because of the intrigues of the nobles and of the clergy? Would you undo the French Revolution because of the Reign of Terror?...You know you would not; you know that those revolutions were justified by atrocious Governments.

From the very beginning he revealed a remarkable talent for caricaturing the great politicians of his day (paying back Chamberlain in his own coin). On Gladstone:

For the purposes of recreation he has selected the felling of trees; and we may usefully remark that his amusements, like his politics, are essentially destructive. Every afternoon the whole world is invited to assist at the crashing fall of some beech or elm or oak. The forest laments, in order that Mr Gladstone may perspire, and full accounts are forwarded by special correspondents to every daily paper every recurring morning.

As for vituperation, he claimed that it was expected of him. 'But, to tell the truth,' writes his son, 'he responded to the public demand with inexhaustible generosity.'[1] In his extremely violent election address of June 1886, he went far beyond raillery in his unfrocking of Gladstone:

The negotiator of the *Alabama* arbitration, the hero of the Transvaal surrender, the perpetrator of the bombardment of Alexandria, the decimator of the struggling Soudan tribes, the betrayer of Khartoum, the person guilty of the death of Gordon, the patentee of the Penjdeh shame now stands before the country all alone, rejected by a democratic House of Commons.

In return 'he was drawn as pygmy, a pug dog, a gnat, a wasp, a ribald and vicious monkey, so habitually, that nearly everyone, who had not seen him in the flesh, believed that his physical proportions were far below the common standards of humanity...'.[2]

[1] *Ibid.* p. 216.
[2] *Ibid.*

Provocation was politics. Before going down in 1884 to Birmingham, that great Liberal and Radical stronghold, he 'sounded a trumpet-call of defiance'[1] from Woodstock in which he referred to 'the savage animosity' in Mr Bright's speeches, 'the grinding monopolies of Mr Chamberlain' and 'the dark and evil deeds of Mr Schnadhorst'. Whigs and Old Tories disliked him; Whigs because he was seeking the kind of 'popularity' which they thought was theirs; the Old Tories, because they disliked such popularity and such language, doubted his soundness. Hartington, the man with weight in the country, said that Churchill was 'vile, contumacious and lying'[2]: Salisbury observed that 'the Mahdi pretends to be half mad, but is very sane in reality; Randolph occupies exactly the converse position'. But Churchill proved that a Tory leader could get working-class support, that Tory democracy, 'necessarily a compromise (perilously near a paradox in the eyes of a partisan) between widely different forces and ideas',[3] could be given life. It is indeed the Tory working man who has made the Conservative party the normal governing party since 1885.

In seeking to displace the self-selected Central Committee of the Conservative party by the Council of the National Union, a body which was elected and could claim to be responsible to the rank and file of the party, he was, like Chamberlain, trying to institutionalize a truly democratic leadership. Like Chamberlain, he failed to oust the old leadership with its parliamentary base. Yet Churchill became a separate force within the party, with which Salisbury, not a very good judge of character, had to negotiate (Salisbury thought that, in some way, Churchill kept the party in touch with popular opinion). His success was such that after only five years in politics and never having held any office at all, he was able to force Northcote, the Conservative Leader in the Commons, into the Lords and a year later, at the age of thirty-seven, to assume both the House Leadership and the Chancellorship of the Exchequer.

The famous resignation when he failed to get his way in Cabinet on the Service estimates was a miscalculation. Withdrawal, resignation, awkwardness, he had always found profitable, and

---

[1] Churchill, *Lord Randolph Churchill*, p. 225.
[2] Captain O'Shea called on him, on Lord Randolph's behalf, to demand satisfaction. Hartington apologized. James, *op. cit.* p. 107.
[3] Churchill, *Lord Randolph Churchill*, p. 763.

most notably when, in 1884, he had resigned from the chairmanship of the National Union to be triumphantly swept back again.[1]
But this time there was no appeal beyond his colleagues and
Salisbury was glad to get rid of 'the boil on his neck'. Churchill
had risen in notoriety and cut himself off from the club.
Now 'the whole Cabinet was groaning and creaking from the
wayward and uncontrolled language of one member'.[2]

His platform reputation was not so quickly extinguished. There,
like Chamberlain, he had put facile words into circulation: 'the
Moloch of Midlothian', 'the pinchbeck Robespierre', 'the old
man in a hurry', 'Ulster will fight and Ulster will be right'. He had
horrified the Carlton Club and worried the middle classes: but to
the working classes he remained, with his bulging eyes and
gutteral delivery, an entertainment, 'a gentleman pugilist of
politics'.

'There is no more hopeless condition in which a popularly
governed state can be plunged', said the marquis of Salisbury
from a public platform in Sheffield in July 1884, 'than when its
policy is decided by demonstrations held in the streets of the
metropolis.' He rejected other trends that he discerned in the new
politics. In an early review essay on Pitt and Castlereagh,[3] he had
condemned politicians 'living only in and for the House of
Commons, moving in an atmosphere of constant intrigue, accustomed to look upon oratory as a mode of angling for popular
support and upon political professions as only baits of more or
less attractiveness...'. The statesman should do what was right
and care for neither popularity nor unpopularity. He had praised
the character of the younger Pitt, 'his lofty and inflexible spirit',
his dedication to his country. 'Since his first entry into the world
he had been absolutely hers. For her he had foregone the enjoy-
ments of youth, the ties of family, the hope of fortune. For three
and twenty years his mind had moulded her institutions, and
shaped her destiny.'

As early as 1860 he had not hesitated to attack Disraeli for the
'flexible' and 'shameless' parliamentary tactics by which he had
been able to entice into the same lobby 'a happy family of proud

[1] R. C. K. Ensor *England 1870–1914*, Oxford, 1944, p. 175.
[2] Lord George Hamilton, quoted in Chilston, *op. cit.* p. 99.
[3] Quoted in A. L. Kennedy, *Salisbury 1830–1903*, London, 1953, pp. 38–40.

old Tories and foaming Radicals, martial squires jealous of their country's honour, and manufacturers who had written it off their books as an unmarketable commodity... '. Gladstone's stratagem over the Paper Duties Bill in 1861 was, he considered, 'worthy rather of an attorney than a statesman', words which then carried great offence in Parliament and which he refused to withdraw. His condemnation of Disraeli's opportunism in legislating for Parliamentary Reform was unequivocal:

> Our theory of Government is, that on each side of the House there should be men supporting definite opinions, and that what they have supported in opposition they should adhere to in office; and that everyone should know, from the fact of their being in office, that those particular opinions will be supported. If you reverse that, and declare that no matter what a man has supported in opposition, the moment he gets into office it shall be open to him to reverse and repudiate it all, you practically destroy the whole basis on which our form of Government rests, and you make the House of Commons a mere scrambling place for office...

The early Salisbury is a political Ishmaelite,[1] hostile to composite majorities, to feeble convictions and to the belief that 'office' was the sole object of politics. He was to learn that there are occasions when these strict standards may have to be lowered simply because politicians must achieve office and when in office have to take particular decisions in circumstances which do not admit a strict separation between their intrinsic and effective merits.[2] During the San Stefano crisis of 1878, he found it necessary to tell a lie in order that personal candour might not involve him in 'a public breach of trust'.[3] Yet no man stood more consistently for the conservation of spiritual capital, for what honesty there was in politics.

For there was 'a stiffer and less corrupted morality out-of-doors'. Yet it was not to be found on the platform. Upon the crowd he was as severe as Le Bon:

> Passion is fostered equally by the two main characteristics of the democratic sovereign—ignorance and numbers. A profound argument must

---

[1] His own description. Lady Gwendolen Cecil (in what is surely one of the best of all English political biographies, *The Life of Robert Marquis of Salisbury*, London, 1921, I, 123), considers it over-emphatic.

[2] See discussion of the theme of moral elevation in politics in Maurice Cowling, *Mill and liberalism*, Cambridge, 1963, chapter 6. Salisbury's 'elevation of sentiment' differed, of course, from Mill's.   [3] Kennedy, *Salisbury 1830–1903*, p. 119.

commend itself to each man's individual reason and derives no aid from the congregation of numbers. But an emotion will shoot electrically through a crowd which might have appealed to each man by himself in vain. Thus it is always difficult to commend a far-sighted, passionless policy to a large assembly; perfectly impossible, if it consist of men whose minds are unused to thought and undisciplined by study.

After 1867 he accepted democracy but thought that the prospects for civilized politics were poor. The professionals, 'good electioneers, clever wire-pullers, smart men to coin the largest gain out of any popular sentiment of the day', were blind to patriotism and honour. He hated agitators: 'There are rewards which can only be obtained by men who excite the public mind, and devise means of persuading one set of persons that they are deeply injured by another...The invention and exasperation of controversies lead those who are successful in such arts to place, and honour and power.' The substance of agitation, the incessant demands of the have-nots upon the haves, 'eats out', he thought, 'the common sentiments and mutual sympathies which combine classes into a patriotic state'.

Salisbury would not have private theatricals at Hatfield House because they nurtured insincerity. He was for a sober and attentive politics; he discountenanced 'that enthusiastic temper which leads men to overhunt a beaten enemy, to drive a good cause to excess, to swear allegiance to a formula, or to pursue an impracticable ideal...'. He suspected style. When his father, the second marquis, reproached him for attacking the policy of Disraeli, he replied, 'I have merely put in print what all the country gentlemen were saying in private.'

Salisbury was never a jingo and was always highly critical of 'tariffs of insolence' in foreign affairs. Yet despite his sobriety, his practical bias, he had 'a nervous passionate temper'.[1] Imagination as well as character had been developed in isolation. No leading English politician better exemplifies J. S. Mill's creative solitary: 'It is not good for man to be kept perforce at all time in the presence of his species. A world from which solitude is extirpated is a very poor ideal. Solitude, in the sense of being often alone, is essential to any depth of meditation or of character...'.[2] The least

---

[1] Cecil, *op. cit.* I, 114.
[2] J. S. Mill, *Principles of political economy*, ed. W. J. Ashley, London, 1909, p. 750.

gregarious of politicians, Salisbury was the least dependent upon expert advice fed to him from outside. In 1877 he wrote to Lord Lytton: 'No lesson seems to be so deeply inculcated by the experience of life as that you never should trust experts. If you believe the doctors, nothing is wholesome: if you believe the theologians, nothing is innocent: if you believe the soldiers, nothing is safe. They all require to have their strong wine diluted by a very large admixture of insipid common sense.'

It has been said that in Salisbury an old kind of English politics, the statesmanship of the land, reached its culmination.[1] He posited a hierarchical society in which the well-to-do were responsible for the less fortunate. Such a society would provide justice so long as the privileged met their responsibilities. He did not consider that power could pass in any real sense to the people, who, indeed, 'as an acting, deciding, accessible authority are a myth'.

He thought the poor no worse, no better, than other men. But given political power, the power to tax, even English workmen, though happily free from Parisian fanaticism, would be hardly likely to resist the opportunity of pillaging the rest of the community. Moreover 'the rule' of the many would be transitory.

'If there is any lesson which a general survey of history teaches us, it is that the preponderance of power in a State seldom remains in the same hands for any length of time. But the doctrine that all States have been and are intending to entrust this preponderance finally to the multitude is one that cannot be supported by any evidence whatever.' Whatever is prescribed, 'the multitude will always have leaders among them and those leaders not selected by themselves'. This is his iron law of oligarchy. Men will be fortunate if they can acquiesce in the authority of 'natural leaders' advantaged by wealth, birth, intellectual power and culture. For these men alone have it in them to ensure probity and to give the business of state the attention it deserves. Moreover, echoing Burke, 'they occupy a position of sufficient prominence among their neighbours to feel that their course is closely watched, and they belong to a class among whom a failure in honour is mercilessly dealt with'. If checked by opinion and constitutional forms, they have a rightful pre-eminence. Such men will see that action goes along with words.

Palmerston said that Salisbury never lost an opportunity of

[1] Kennedy, *Salisbury 1830–1903*, p. 5.

doing or saying an unhandsome thing. But with angularity, passion and literary power that pushed him to excess, there went high responsibility (because of his profound Christian beliefs, hardly felt), prudence and humility. Only the human character of ruler and ruled redeemed the world of politics. 'A character for unselfish honesty is the only secure passport to the confidence of the English people.' And among the ruled, 'peace and good will not be the result of some clever contrivance which men by much debating and many experiments may hope to hit upon. If they attain it [at] all it will be by rooting out the selfishness which good fortune nurtures, and the recklessness which springs from misery.'[1]

This is the politics of limited participation, urged when enlarged political participation was the leading theme. No one knew better than Salisbury how difficult is candour for a Conservative of his kind on a public platform. Yet, largely because of Liberal dissensions, he dominated English affairs for most of the last fifteen years of the nineteenth century. He, too, did some public haranguing and found that his own carefully prepared and deliberate words got a fair hearing even from those who did not like what he said.

The wider the participation in politics the more rapid would be the disintegration of the language of politics. Salisbury had always cared for the use of political words.

There is no science [he had written in 1865] in which the wholesome ordeal of definition is more needed than in politics. So little of exact reasoning and so much of *ad captandum* declamation is employed in political discussions, that words are of much more importance in it than thoughts. The man who can discover a phrase by which the desired argument or assertion is hinted, without being formally laid down, does far more for his cause than the keenest reasoner...A deceptive word or phrase does not seem to convey an argument and disarms antagonism, while the trouble of analysing the arguments contained indisposes the hearer for scrutiny.

There is a close congruence between these views on political participation and language and those of T. S. Eliot some eighty years later: 'We may assume, I think, that in a society so articulated the practice of politics and an active interest in public affairs would not be the business of everybody, or of everybody to the same degree; and that not everybody should concern himself, except at

[1] *Ibid.* p. 74.

moments of crisis, with the conduct of the nation as a whole.'
Moreover, 'in a healthily *stratified* society, public affairs would be
a responsibility not equally borne; a greater responsibility would
be inherited by those who inherited special advantages, and in
whom self-interest, and interest for the sake of their families ("a
stake in the country") should cohere with public spirit'.[1]

Such stratification would mean a cultivated ruling class to speci-
alize in the reception of political ideas. However much such ideas
conflict, 'the practical politician must handle them with as much
deference as if they were the constructions of informed sagacity,
the intuitions of genius, or the accumulated wisdom of the ages'.[2]
A small and critical public would secure restraint in the use of
words. Politics would thus be confined to persuasion and deliberation among those who knew something about it. Reason could
dwell quietly at its task without conceding too much to appetite.

Like his great ancestors William and Robert Cecil, the third
marquis of Salisbury was an attentive politician, technically well
equipped for the business of politics and diplomacy. But what
made him great was the combination of knowledge of the details
with a fashioning statesmanship. As well as *attention*, there was
intention,[3] grounded in imagination. Of this happy combination in
Salisbury of the power to conceive with the power to execute,
A. L. Kennedy has written: 'Instinct and skilled craftsmanship
were combined in him in the highest and rarest degree—the flash
of inspiration, followed by immersion in detail, an instinct that
could survive prolonged calculations; a policy swiftly visioned
and steadily elaborated.'[4] And because intention was economically
stated in words upon which men could rely (unlike the Athenians,
he believed that words could harm action), his prestige was higher
than that of either Gladstone or Disraeli.

---

[1] *Notes towards the definition of culture*, pp. 83–6.
[2] *Ibid.* p. 87.
[3] See De Jouvenel, *The pure theory of politics*, Cambridge, 1963, pp. 169–75.
[4] Kennedy, *Salisbury, 1830–1903*, p. 355.

6

'DIFFICULTIES OF A STATESMAN'

Of Gladstone, Arthur James Balfour wrote in 1888 to Miss Margot Tennant: 'I am very glad you like the Old Man: for my part I *love* him, and *if* he be (as *I* think he is) the most unfair of Parliamentary speakers and the most unscrupulous of party managers, so I dare say would the most virtuous of mankind be, if, with his peculiar mental and oratorical endowments, they were subjected for 55 years to the blessed influences of free government.'[1] Balfour, Salisbury's nephew and successor as leader of the Conservative Party and Prime Minister, accepted with irony the liberal political order but was fully prepared to work and rule through it. What distinguished Conservatives from Liberals was their belief in rule: it was Salisbury who had once said that what Ireland needed was twenty years of firm government; it was Milner, in 1886, already moving, like Strafford, to the side of authority, who prayed that the House of Commons be shut up for ten years, so that 'poor politician-ridden Ireland' be transformed.[2] The Conservative Party, drawing now upon the business classes as well as the squirearchy, had many men of intellectual vigour, yet they had never been so much given to causes and declamation as the Liberals. (Their most notable declaimer after 1902, Joseph Chamberlain, had been bred in Radical Liberalism.)

Conservative objectives were more concrete than those of the Liberals. Conservatives were associated with power, anxious about defence; yet they tended to favour military service to create a nation in arms not so much for war as to brace the fibres of the nation. They were in sympathy with the transforming imperial energies at work in Africa and wished to make the most of British possessions in the world; they doubted if the critical and polemical Liberals would make much of them. Although there was a primitive force and realism in their political attitudes which often made the Liberals look anaemic or conscience-ridden, Conservatives were less articulate about what they came to stand for. They

[1] Quoted in Kenneth Young, *Arthur James Balfour*, London, 1963, p. 130.
[2] E. Crankshaw, *The forsaken idea*, London, 1952, p. 23.

had few intellectuals to set against the Liberal array; even imperial ideas had been mainly developed by Liberals (sometimes, admittedly, only *former* or *formal* Liberals)—Goldwin Smith, Dilke, Chamberlain, Rosebery.[1]

In *The New Machiavelli*, H. G. Wells's narrating politician-hero, Remington, looking for 'fine initiatives' that will reconstruct society, turns away from the Liberals, not to Labour, but to the Tories. The great landowners and financiers were just as progressive and open to imaginative appeals as their political opponents. They wanted a well-fed, well-exercised population and were just as likely to spend money on education and social services as the Liberals. Wells was impressed by their 'good temper' and saw them as potentially energetic and positive in a way that the Liberals were not. Conservatives promised efficiency, the rationalization of English political life. Moreover, they could, through the imperial theme, win genuine popular approval.

The faults of the Imperialist movement were obvious enough...The cant of Imperialism was easy to learn and use; it was speedily adopted by all sorts of base enterprises and turned to all sorts of base ends. But a big child is permitted big mischief, and my mind was now continually returning to the persuasion that after all in some development of the idea of Imperial patriotism might be found that wide, rough, politically acceptable expression of a constructive dream capable of sustaining a great educational and philosophical movement such as no formula of Liberalism supplied. The fact that it readily took vulgar forms only witnessed to its strong popular appeal. Mixed in with the noisiness and humbug of the movement there appeared a real regard for social efficiency, a real spirit of animation and enterprise.[2]

The Conservatives represented large and powerful interests while the Liberals suffered from 'multitudinousness' and at heart were opposed to social control. Nevertheless, the Tories did decisively lose the election of 1906 and, under Radical prodding, they also lost the good temper with which Wells had credited them. They became unduly alarmed. Balfour, for example, thought Campbell-Bannerman 'a mere cork, dancing on a torrent which he cannot control' and heard 'a faint echo of the same movement which has produced massacres in St Petersburg, riots in Vienna,

[1] R. B. McDowell, *British conservatism 1832–1914*, London, 1959, p. 103.
[2] *The New Machiavelli*.

and Socialist processions in Berlin'.[1] From then onwards as, in concert with Syndicalists, suffragettes and Ulstermen, they pounded away at the Liberal government, Conservatives were cast as the villains of the piece (in the historiography of the period, they seem to have remained such ever since).

The Tories might have lost the competition for political leadership yet they still considered the Liberals unfitted to govern at this point of time and were prepared to use all means to drive them out. The return to Parliament of fifty-three Labour members, most of them manual workers, and many Liberals with small means, seemed a clear portent. It was not just a question of men; it was a matter of policy too. In the world at large, it was the Tories who claimed to have the sense of power, who knew what should be done. Convinced, according to R. C. K. Ensor, that the greatness of England still depended on patrician rule, Balfour and Lansdowne deliberately exploited the Constitution, 'with no scruples regarding fair play', to hold up Liberal legislation.[2]

'Liberalism had its ideal, the era of universal peace, of mild democratic governments just keeping the peace and punishing breaches of contract, and of a great happy mass of humanity, of all races and colours, doing just as they pleased, their pleasures being presumed to be naturally virtuous and largely concerned with buying and selling.'[3] The Tories had a much more practical ideal in 'the conception of a united and developed Empire'. Moreover, it was sufficiently far off completion to provide 'the life-work' of two or three generations.

From the 1880s Liberalism was wearing out. Only the contention of Home Rule had given it the vestige of a cause. In default of practical outlets for their energies, Rosebery, Grey and Asquith had become imperialists but only to cut themselves off from many of the party. The party had not had the opportunity, perhaps not the nerve, to make a great deal of the radical Newcastle programme of 1891, and it is surprising that, in spite of its failure to propose to do anything very much about the condition of the people, its reluctance to interfere with the market, it retained as much working-class support as it did. Yet in 1906 Liberals might still claim that for twenty years events had run against them, that Ireland,

[1] Young, *Balfour*, p. 255.
[2] *England 1879–1914*, Oxford, 1944, p. 387.
[3] L. S. Amery, *My political life*, London, 1953, I, 255.

imperialism and the Boer War had all been distractions from the vital social themes that would now engage the attention of a unified party.

Moreover, it seemed that old themes still had some life. The Liberals still successfully defended—with much Tory support— the established position of Cobden, the big Free Trade loaf against the small one. Joseph Chamberlain's campaign for Tariff Reform was a gift to their journalists ('He will cement the Empire with the very life blood of the poor,' said the Radicals). The Non-conformists, long the driving force in the Liberal Party, and heavily represented in the Parliament of 1906, fought on long after the 1902 Education Act, perhaps against the light, to keep Church schools off the rates. And Morley and Lloyd George, representing old and new, were one in their opposition to the South African War. Morley still echoed the watchwords of Bright:

You may carry fire and sword into the midst of peace and industry; it will be wrong. A war of the strongest Government in the world with untold wealth and inexhaustible reserves against this little republic will bring you no glory; it will be wrong...It may add a new province to your empire; it will still be wrong. You may give buoyancy to the African Stock and Share market; it will still be wrong.

Indeed the moral fervour aroused by the Boer War was such as to divide the Liberals into Imperialists and Little Englanders. Only the coincidence of the possibility of Conservative Tariff Reform and Chinese 'slavery' on the Rand had served to reunite them.

But restraint, discrimination, moral elevation would not suffice. Unless the Liberals moved, as Lloyd George saw they must, into the sphere of social policy, got rid of their distrust of state power, their position, so solid-seeming in 1906, would melt. There had long been clear disagreement between Liberals and Socialists about the substance of politics. Liberals still mainly relied upon an unfolding social order, to try 'to elicit through rational persuasion the co-operation of individuals in the attainment of that degree of order of which they are capable'.[1] For Socialists the state 'was not a neutral organ seeking as best it could the well-being of the whole community, but a coercive power en-

[1] John H. Hallowell, *The moral foundation of democracy*, Chicago, 1954, p. 108.

forcing upon the working class the social discipline required by the owners of property in their search for profit'.[1]

For Liberals, Parliaments were, in theory, 'composed of representatives of the people, and thus by their very composition constitute a first selection and purification of social energies, a higher structure which moderates the violence of the interests that underlie it.'[2] For the fiercer Socialists, outside political society, who wished to transform the social order, Parliaments merely endorsed the rule of the privileged. William Morris had urged the workers not to vote, 'not to be accomplices of their own enslavement'; he had been without comprehension of Parliaments which merely patched up what ought to be destroyed. 'Morris,' said Tom Mann, 'was the man who enabled me to get a really healthy contempt for parliamentary institutions and scheming politicians.'[3]

There was some Socialism in the growing Labour Party: indeed the party had been founded under the stimulus of the Independent Labour Party and Socialist societies, but the Socialism was indigenous, did not concentrate upon class war. Moreover, the party was based on Trade Unionists who were not at all Socialist in outlook. Primarily they wanted a pressure group in Parliament to secure better conditions for Labour. To that end they would co-operate with any party.

Most of the twenty-nine Labour Party members returned in 1906 saw no barrier between their brand of Labourism and Liberalism. Indeed the Labour Party had acquired a foothold in Parliament through an electoral accommodation with the Liberals. The Liberal belief in reason and progress would automatically lead, thought Ramsay MacDonald, to Socialism. 'Socialism is a tendency, not a revealed dogma and therefore it is modified in its forms of expression from generation to generation.'[4] It had outlived the excitements of the revolutionary era and would absorb the best of Liberalism. MacDonald and his colleagues were hardly less the auxiliaries of the Liberal Party than were the twenty-four Lib-Labs who also augmented the great Liberal majority of 1906.

Between 1900 and 1910 was a period of rising political expectations and falling real wages. It was also a stridently articulate

[1] Harold Laski, *The rise of European liberalism*, London, 1936, p. 239.
[2] G. de Ruggiero, *The history of European liberalism*, Oxford, 1927, pp. 364–5.
[3] Dona Torr, *Tom Mann and his times*, London, 1956, p. 188.
[4] *The socialist movement*, London, 1911, p. 195.

period. Yet there was no real rejection by the working class of the two older parties which had for so long dominated the political scene. In Parliament, Labour were content with the Liberal legislative programme, school meals, medical inspection of school children, old age pensions, an eight-hour day for miners, labour exchanges and the Lloyd George Budget. By 1909, Keir Hardie had begun 'to feel almost, nowadays, that his occupation as a Socialist agitator had disappeared...Mr Lloyd George went to Limehouse and denounced the dukes and other mighty and respectable persons of that kind in a way which, up to quite recently, they had only heard on Socialist platforms.'[1] The respectable Labour Party was clearly not a threat to the Liberal Party.

England had, in fact, a true political society, selective, yet curiously capable of assimilating emerging political talent. Among the Socialists, only the most militant sects, like the Social Democratic Federation or its successor, the British Socialist Party, were resistant. Even the I.L.P. was assimilable. The Fabian Society, run largely by middle-class intellectuals, would conspire with whoever was in power. The Fabians kept off fundamentals. For them politics was without passion: it was a science in which 'everything can be done without anyone wishing to do it'.[2]

Within this political society, capture of the machinery of government was the prime objective and not the reflection of any common will. Will indeed struggled for expression. What policy and legislation emerged in such a process often seemed merely incidental to the contest for office. As a process it was wasteful of time, energy and ideas. It could only be afforded if there were a superfluity of political talent; the quality of politicians was crucial. No one has better stated the high demands of English politics than Joseph A. Schumpeter:

There may be many ways in which politicians of sufficiently good quality can be secured. Thus far however, experience seems to suggest that the only effective guarantee is in the existence of a social stratum, itself a product of a severely selective process, that takes to politics as a matter of course. If such a stratum be neither too exclusive nor too easily accessible for the outsider and if it be strong enough to

---

[1] As reported in *Woolwich Pioneer*, 27 August 1909. Quoted in S. Maccoby, *English radicalism, the end*, London, 1961, p. 47.
[2] C. F. G. Masterman, *The condition of England*, London, 1909, p. 150.

assimilate most of the elements it currently absorbs, it not only will present for the political career products of stocks that have successfully passed many tests in other fields—served, as it were, an apprenticeship in private affairs—but it will also increase their fitness by endowing them with traditions that embody experience, with a professional code and with a common fund of views.[1]

It was a political society capable of bitter and persisting divisions, and even short periods of 'knife and fork' hostility within the same party, but for most of the time the Government dined with the Opposition. Balfour could in all delicacy write to Charles Tennant, the Scottish millionaire, asking him to endow his son-in-law Asquith (potentially Balfour's most formidable opponent) sufficiently for political life and so free him from the necessity of earning his living at the Bar.[2] Asquith himself was staying at Hatfield House, the home of the Conservative Cecils, when Campbell-Bannerman was making the most important appointments to the Liberal Cabinet of December 1905. It was not until 1909 that the coherence of this political society was severely strained by sharp divergencies of attitude and, even in the early summer of 1911 at the height of the contest over the powers of the House of Lords, Asquith could appear in amity with Balfour at the same society ball.

Yet to those with no access to the élites, the Edwardian age seemed to be one of collusion. Hilaire Belloc and Cecil Chesterton agreed with Tom Mann that a united plutocracy commanded the age. Territorial rich and commercial rich were one: the landed aristocracy speculated commercially and the new rich bought landed estates. Blood, culture and money bound the two front benches together. England was still governed by a small friendly and interrelated clique:

On Thursday is the big Division which will wind up the Session I suppose: the Division which will give the Resolution in the Commons defying their brothers-in-law, stepfathers and aunts' lovers in the Lords. Thus Geoffrey Howard will defy Lord Carlisle while the more dutiful Morpeth will acquiesce in his father's power. Kerry will similarly support the privilege of Lansdowne but Fitzmaurice (oddly enough) will be of an adverse opinion. Alfred Lyttelton will think the powers of the Peers reasonable; not his sister's husband, Masterman,

[1] Joseph A. Schumpeter, *Capitalism, socialism and democracy*, London, 1943, pp. 290–1.
[2] Young, *Balfour*, pp. 169–70.

who will, however, be supported by his wife's first cousin, Gladstone; while the Prime Minister will not find his brother-in-law, Mr Tennant, fail him, nor need he doubt Mr McKenna, since he had married the daughter of the Tennants' chief friend...'[1]

Belloc admitted that there were still fervent adherents who looked on 'Mr Asquith and Mr Winston Churchill as the tribunes of a people rightly struggling to be free',[2] that there were some deeply committed by interest to one party or the other and that others would always back their fancy with the passion of sportsmen. He conceded, too, that the opinion upon which the party system operated was still honest and public-spirited. As in Namier's eighteenth-century 'structure of politics', there were honest backbenchers puzzled and frustrated by the collusive world at the top. Yet it was hard to resist its blandishments:

The Members of Parliament would disperse on Friday evenings to their country houses, and the stiff ritual of the week-end would follow its prescribed course. There would be baccarat and billiards, hock and seltzer and riding to hounds; the gloved hands which were clasped conventionally at Matins would pat the sleek quarters of the hunters as the party proceeded round the stables before luncheon...[3]

The tone of the House of Commons was not comparable with that of a good college or a good regiment.

Belloc had been even more disappointed than Wells's New Machiavelli with the election of 1906:

The accursed power which stands on Privilege
(And goes with Women, and Champagne and Bridge)
Broke—and Democracy resumed her reign:
(Which goes with Bridge, and Women and Champagne).

Belloc followed the old Radical habit of girding at, and tracing conspiracy within, establishments. He was temperamentally incapable of appreciating a political society in which there was a regulated competition for leadership. Like our own malcontents today, he preferred the ways of 'our prompt, centralized and lucid rivals abroad, notably the French and the Prussians'.[4]

[1] Robert Speaight, *The life of Hilaire Belloc*, p. 303. A letter from Belloc to Maurice Baring.
[2] Hilaire Belloc and Cecil Chesterton, *The party system*, London, 1911, p. 21.
[3] Speaight, *Hilaire Belloc*, pp. 226–7.
[4] Belloc and Chesterton, *The party system*, p. 167.

There were others more securely placed within political society who had doubts about the reality of the political contest. 'I feel more and more disgusted,' wrote Cecil Spring-Rice in 1903, 'I can't help believing that our Government (with the consent of the people) is becoming more and more the Government of interested people with the trail of finance over them all...I don't think the opposition are any better; the most able, Asquith and Rosebery, are in fact exactly the same.'[1]

C. F. G. Masterman's acute but perhaps too self-consciously 'literary' *The condition of England* described the vulgar ebullience of the times. At the top were 'the conquerors', in all their private opulence, with their motor cars, deer forests, banquets and long week-ends. Few had wit or grace or gave leadership to those below. Attached to them by interest or sympathy were the middle classes, Belloc's 'people in between', occupying a tasteless spreading suburbia, fearful of the workers only recently incorporated into the political nation. At the base were the drifting multitude, fun-loving and disliking the classes above them, but not much concerned to attack them. Masterman did not attribute insolence to the rulers; nor did he assail their integrity. What he criticized was 'the deflection of vigour and intellectual energy to irrelevant standards and pleasures'; the lack of will for positive things.

Parties, organized inside and outside Westminster, had long made Parliament an instrument of will, made a strong executive practicable. But where, now that Gladstone and Parnell were gone, was the will? Wells's Edwardian hero soon discovered that 'in politics a man counts not for what he is in moments of imaginative expansion, but for his common workaday selfish self; and [that] parties are held together not by a community of ultimate aims, but by the stabler bond of an accustomed life'. Only rarely could a politician 'lift his chin' and have a purpose. To speak and act appropriately a Conservative needed nerve, a clear consciousness that he served wider interests than his own. The Liberal, alternately critical and vaguely utopian, indulgent and easily sapped by luxury, needed work in hand.

What will there was in England seemed largely outside parliamentary politics, most obviously in the proconsuls, Cromer, Curzon and Milner, in Fisher at the Admiralty or Morant in the

[1] Quoted in William Scovell Adams, *Edwardian heritage*, London, 1949, p. 55.

Home Civil Service. These were all men who lifted their chins. In political society itself, Masterman saw 'a strange sterility of characters', and among the Tories who had ruled for so long 'nothing but a dialectic, a perpetual criticism of other men's schemes, clever, futile, barren as the east wind'. This might not be unfair to Balfour, whose hard will was refined almost to the point of nullity. It was certainly untrue of Joseph Chamberlain, the imperial visionary who sought by will to divert the very streams of world trade and at the same time restore the social fabric. Was any Conservative leading politician so lost in pragmatic caution as Asquith?

The reaction against words, unmeditated platform words unrelated to the seeming collusion in government and Parliament, was now in full flow. 'Whole pages could be filled', Sorel writes, 'with the bare outlines of the contradictory, comical and quack arguments which form the substance of the harangues of our great men; nothing embarrasses them, and they know how to combine in pompous, impetuous, and nebulous speeches, the most absolute irreconcilability with the most supple opportunism.'[1] In *Democracy and liberty* (1896), Lecky returned again and again to the same themes—the opportunities for and the dangers of political dishonesty. 'Ignorance in the elective body does not naturally produce ignorance in the representative body. It is much more likely to produce dishonesty. Intriguers and demagogues, playing successfully on the passions and credulity of the ignorant and of the poor, form one of the great characteristic evils and dangers of our time.'[2] The example of Gladstone, who had 'possessed every form of eloquence except conciseness...could rarely answer a question without making a speech', had been unfortunate. 'The dreary torrent of idle, diffusive, insincere talk that now drags its slow lengths through so many months at Westminster certainly does not contribute to raise the character of the House of Commons.'[3]

Eighteen years later, Graham Wallas found the speeches in the Commons, 'with their mixture of vague declamation, commonplace facts, and...tags', just as distressing. Nor had the coming of Labour improved matters. The Dissenting habit of praying extempore had had unfortunate results. 'One man obviously felt

---

[1] Georges Sorel, *Reflections on violence*, tr. T. E. Hulme, London, 1915, p. 129.
[2] W. E. H. Lecky, *Democracy and liberty*, I, 144.   [3] *Ibid.* p. 148.

something very strongly which had no relation to the typescript (prepared perhaps a month earlier) which he read with vibrating emphasis. Another, an experienced open-air agitator who spoke without notes, rambled on in that loose manner of trusting that every sentence will suggest another which constitutes the special disease of working-class rhetoric.'[1]

Instead of persuasion 'by pure logic in full session'—the assumption of the 'intellectualist' Whigs who passed the Municipal Reform Act of 1835—Wallas found 'a general atmosphere of intellectual slackness'. The House of Commons sat for organized discussion but no discussion took place. It was much more efficient as a Will-Organization than as a Thought-Organization. Even in Cabinet, Wallas suspected that there was often failure in oral argument. Cabinet Ministers no longer had 'one habit of speech and one social tradition'. 'The sincere and heart-searching letters...exchanged by the members of Peel's and Palmerston's Cabinets' had been 'admirable organs of thought',[2] but such communications were now too slow.

Those who wanted action derided not only the superfluous word but the whole political process:

I am going to ask you to begin our study of Democracy by considering it first as a big balloon, filled with gas or hot air, and sent up so that you shall be kept looking up at the sky whilst other people are picking your pockets. When the balloon comes down to earth every five years or so you are invited to get into the basket if you can throw out one of the people who are sitting tightly in it; but as you can find neither the time nor the money, and there are forty million of you and hardly room for six hundred in the basket, the balloon goes up again with much the same lot in it...[3]

Graham Wallas, unlike Ostrogorski,[4] who had excited and distressed himself needlessly by contrasting the facts of political behaviour with how 'free reason', as envisaged in the revolution of 1848, should have led men to behave, coolly examined politics as an area of 'non-rational inference'.[5] He censured Bryce for positing an ideal democracy in which 'every citizen is intelligent, patriotic and disinterested'. These qualities were in fact only

[1] *The great society*, p. 268.   [2] *Ibid.* p. 282.
[3] George Bernard Shaw, preface to *The Applecart*.
[4] M. I. Ostrogorski, *Democracy and the organization of political parties*, London, 1902.
[5] Graham Wallas, *Human nature in politics*, London, 1908, chapter III.

likely to be possessed by those civil servants and Fabian Socialists who pursued a science of politics or rather of administration, in a welter of partisan and scandalously ill-informed public opinion fed by a press which, since Harmsworth, had lost high seriousness, even common honesty. Did not 'the contents bills of two hundred newspapers denounce every day 'the "monopolists" and the "gold bugs", the "lies and shams" of the Bank Returns, and "the paid perjurers of Somerset House"'?[1]

Wallas was preoccupied with the practical art of statesmanship and, in the end, with political virtue. The politician would be subject like his audience to non-rational inferences: he, too, would find the symbols of political discourse dissolving before the complexities of fact and behaviour. Yet he had to continue to traffic in those symbols because he could only stir men, fix a scale of values, through the feelings. Because man was moved by passion and imagination to action, the politician had to contend with good passions against bad ones. He could not remain aloof.

There is first the danger that, becoming too proficient, developing too much conscious style, 'after a time the politician may cease even to desire to reason with his constituents, and may come to regard them as purely irrational creatures of feeling and opinion, and himself as the purely rational "overman" who controls them'.[2] Secondly, the politician may become too rigid, simply because he must speak 'in character'. Between the politician and his audience there is 'the party mask, larger and less mobile than his own face, like the mask which enabled actors to be seen and heard in the vast open-air theatres of Greece'.[3] Indeed, 'if an individual statesman's intellectual career is to exist for the mass of the present public at all, it must be based either on an obstinate adherence to unchanging opinions or on a development, slow, simple and consistent'.[4] There must be no stealing of the Whigs' clothing while they are bathing.

Responsibility denies the politician intellectual satisfactions. Faced with the contingent, changing world of politics he too must change and yet keep faith with commitments publicly undertaken. If he too swiftly and too publicly changes his opinions, he loses authority: if he publicly sustains opinions 'privately abandoned', he loses *character*. On everything that is not ripe for action, he will therefore equivocate.

[1] *Human nature in politics* p. 246.   [2] *Ibid.* pp. 173–4.   [3] *Ibid.* p. 91.   [4] *Ibid,* p. 95.

Like Schumpeter, Wallas stresses quality: 'The very existence of the Great Society requires that there should be found in each generation a certain number of men and women whose desire for the good of others is sufficiently reliable and continuous to ensure they will carry out the duty of originating leadership (mere dexterous self-advancement does not originate) either in administration or thought'.[1] He is not sceptical about the 'public spirit' of such political leaders. 'Whoever has known any such men will accept the statement, which they themselves constantly make, that no ambition, however lofty, would be sufficient to carry them through the unexciting toil, the constant disappointments, the ever-present uncertainty of result, which are involved in the intellectual organization of a modern community.'[2]

It was possible that the politics of the future might be purified through the triumph of enlightened will:

Some day the conception of a harmony of thought and passion may take the place, in the deepest regions of our moral consciousness, of our present dreary confusion and barren conflicts. If that day comes much in politics which is now impossible will become possible. The politician will be able not only to control and direct in himself the impulses of whose nature he is more fully aware, but to assume in his audience an understanding of his aim.[3]

On contemporary politics he is of the same mind as the conscience-stricken Arnold Toynbee. 'It is not that we care about public life, for what is public life but the miserable, arid waste of barren controversies and personal jealousies, and grievous loss of time? Who would live in public life if he could help it?'[4]

For the inconsequential ring of words on public platforms, ineffective and unreal debating in Parliament, Wallas would substitute a disciplined passion expressing itself in the 'grave simplicity of speech' of Japanese state papers,[5] in the unbought effort of mind which the Japanese sought in their generals. Wallas does not fully endorse Wells's Platonic rule 'of disillusioned and illuminated men behind the shams, and patriotisms, the spites and personalities of the ostensible world'[6]—Wallas's *illuminati* are not disillusioned—but he does seek the triumph of organized thought. In truth, this implies the end of politics as conflict.

[1] *The great society*, p. 152.   [2] *Ibid.*   [3] *Human nature in politics*, p. 198.
[4] Beatrice Webb, *My apprenticeship*, London, 1950, p. 158.
[5] *Human nature in politics*, p. 198.   [6] *Ibid.* p. 201.

Fabians generally sought a purified will in politics—a will which should reflect the possibilities within the social facts. Politics for them had long since moved away from oaths on the tennis court, from constitution-making, from drafts of social systems, to concrete choice and programme. Banner and manifesto had yielded to immediate preparation for action to be taken on the best knowledge available. This in turn meant reorganization of the means of action, the devising of long-rationalized processes within the bureaucracy. The politician is important as one who is to be persuaded to act.

Politics would be replaced by a science of administration—had not this been implicit in most of the nineteenth-century theories of social reorganization? It was not merely that words had long ago settled policy and that there were no more fundamentals to uncover. It was now assumed that practical policies, the removal of evils and anomalies, the doing of good things, did not begin in principles: they derived from social experience and social facts.

The demands on the politician therefore became more complex. In the past he had been assessed in character and style within a narrow political society; then, he had to raise heads of opinion and win public favour. Now he must develop an enlightened will. For this he must have access to a deepening knowledge of society. If he could acquire this last, listen intelligently to those who had ideas, Wallas and the Webbs would pardon the inexactitudes, equivocations and insincerities which the other demands necessitated.

In a sense this development was not the end but the consummation of liberalism in politics. For it was liberalism which had begun by subjecting the established religious, social and political order to the test of reason. Reason persistently applied to society produced social science. Before they act, politicians must now know this social science. 'We do not want clever school boys at the head of our great departments. We want grown men, "grown up" *in the particular business they have taken in hand*, doing their eight or nine hours' work for ten months in every year, whether in office or out of office; behaving towards their profession as the great civil engineer, lawyer, or medical man behaves.'[1] And as seekers and bearers of truth politicians would acquire a new authority.

Fabians aimed at influencing and refining will within the given

[1] Beatrice Webb, *Our partnership*, London, 1948, p. 133.

political society, a society to which, in the long run, their knowledgeable bureaucracy might prove inimical. But the immediate
threat to liberal politics and ethics came not from them but from
outside political society, from what Wallas called the Will-
Organization to be found 'in the fact of common industrial
employment'.[1] Syndicalism cultivated 'the roll of thunder', the
day that should swallow up all the days. The Syndicalist argued
that trade unionists, because they were bound to their fellow
workmen by 'a bond of things and deeds not of words',[2] were
uniquely capable of direct political action to achieve immediate
ends and of endowing their leaders with will. Those who acted
most passionately would fulfil themselves politically. Parliamentary government was too slow; it sought to reconcile by
compromise what could not be reconciled; it demoralized working-
class representatives. Industry could and should mobilize itself to
replace the existing state power by that of federated or autonomous
union-based industrial republics. In this way a new society would
emerge out of the shell of the old.

Direct action, the aggressive assertion of industrial strength
outside Parliament by boycotts, provoked lock-outs and strikes,
rejection of collective bargaining and all the civilities of liberalism,
became fashionable on the extreme left. The language of politics
became the language of industrial civil war. From 1910 the
Syndicalists were notably strong in the unions, strong in the
Celtic fringe, and had, in Tom Mann and Ben Tillett, the most
gifted agitators of the time. Yet it seems that the great industrial
unrest which began with the coal and textile strikes of 1910 and
culminated in the Triple Alliance of miners, railwaymen and
transport workers in 1913–14 was only partly due to these lucid
revolutionaries.

At some time towards the end of the first decade of this century,
the working class, who had lately drawn out a new kind of statesmanship from their old political rulers, turned away from their
rulers: they ceased to acquiesce. They turned away not only from
the Liberal politicians who had failed to satisfy their sectional
grievances; they also refused to recognize their own Labour Party
leaders who would have led them like a heathen sacrifice into the
collusion of parliamentary politics.

This political upsurge is certainly not explicable in terms of the

---

[1] *The great society*, p. 325.   [2] *Ibid.*

tardy response of wage rates to a rising cost of living. George Dangerfield saw it, almost mystically, as a demand for life: 'The workers did not want to be safe any more; they wanted to live, to take chances, to throw caution to the winds: they had been repressed too long. And so the deepest impulse in the great strike movement of 1910–1914 was an unconscious one, an enormous energy pressing up from the depths of the soul; and Parliament shuddered before it, and under its impact Liberal England died.'[1] Even Ramsay MacDonald, the leading advocate of parliamentary politics for Socialists, had to admit that 'the labour world responded to the call to strike in the same eager, spontaneous way as nature responds to the call of the springtime. One felt as though some magical allurement had seized upon the people.'[2]

Violence seemed imminent but there was in fact little of it. The government's intervention was confined to mediation. At this new task Asquith's ministers, with the possible exception of Lloyd George, did not acquit themselves very well. During one extremity, in the miners' strike of 1912, Asquith himself intervened —in all ignorance of the texture of the argument—only to find that he had made his government a party to negotiations that might lead to a general strike. He gave way in haste and induced Parliament to pass a Minimum Wage Bill. But the most significant thing was that he as a Liberal Prime Minister had to admit that further discussion was useless. 'We have exhausted all our powers of persuasion and argument and negotiation,' he told Parliament. So helpless were Liberal politicians in such contests between capital and labour that Asquith had to cut his losses and forbid ministers to mediate in future disputes.

The Syndicalist movement had its heroes in Mann and Tillett but the Parliamentary Labour Party threw up very few men of style or character. 'They are mostly men of laborious habits, teetotallers, of intellectual interests, with a belief in the reasonableness of mankind. The English working man is not a teetotaller, has little respect for intellectual interests and does not in the least degree trouble himself about the reasonableness of mankind.'[3]

Syndicalist will was powerful enough to disturb the government and 'the classes'. Yet it was utopian: it would have turned

[1] *The strange death of liberal England*, London, 1935, p. 226.
[2] *The social unrest*, London, 1913, p. 96, quoted in Dangerfield, *op. cit.* p. 227.
[3] Masterman, *The condition of England*, pp. 142–3.

the world upside down. It created tribunes and not statesmen. In practical politics it was necessary to look for creative intention among those who largely accepted the world as it was or as it could shortly be. The most powerful and practical idea—more powerful than and as practical as Fabianism—was imperialism. It 'made the weather' and had attraction for Liberals, Radicals and Fabians, for the whole of political society.

The imperial theme implied the mobilizing of all that was most vigorous in the British stock—what Wells called 'the good brown-faced stuff'—to lasting humane tasks: the civilizing or salvaging of primitive or archaic cultures in Africa and Asia. It meant organizing and moralizing on a process of expansion which had hitherto been haphazard or blind. It meant, too, that power that had been squandered would now be concentrated to assert Britain's place in the world and, particularly, among the powers of Europe.

If imperialism necessitated turning a blind eye upon the deeds of individualistic imperial entrepreneurs like Rhodes or Jameson, it also meant the creation of cadres of disciplined men for action under Cromer, Milner and Lugard. If in its conscious form from the 1890s, imperialism led (as the Boer War seemed to prove) to a recession in Liberalism, in the general siding with the puissant forces of history, those that enlarged, organized and improved, rather than with the freedom of small nations, it also meant *government*, the rationalization of British government overseas, some strenuous thinking about defence and even about the establishment of a true imperial executive at home. Above all imperialism kept men at work: 'When kings build, the carters have work to do.'[1] Imperialism gave social purpose to army, navy and bureaucracy.

Joseph Chamberlain took imperialism into the heart of popular politics. It was he who, in May 1903, came out openly for an organized world empire based upon reciprocal tariff preferences and taxes upon food. Britain's nineteenth-century prosperity had been built upon Cobdenite Free Trade, but she had not only become a fiscal eccentric by adhering to it, she was also steadily falling behind her rivals in trade and power. She could now only meet the economic and political challenge of Protectionist

---

[1] A line from Schiller quoted in Ortega y Gasset, *The revolt of the masses*, London, 1932, p. 155.

Germany and the U.S.A., the threats of closing foreign markets
and growing unemployment among skilled workers at home, by
going Protectionist herself, by building tariff barriers around her
economy and breaking them down in places for the benefit of the
Great Colonies. Upon Protection might be ultimately constructed
a federalized empire. Tariff Reform would once more make the
state a creative force in economic life, would develop natural and
mobilize human resources.

Tariff Reform was in fact a political decision; most of the
analytical economists were against Chamberlain and few colonial
politicians were enthusiastic. Chamberlain was prepared to go
against the grain: to divert the whole system of world trade to
make British power effective. 'We are going to talk about something else,' he said. From the revenues derived from Protection he
hoped to finance social reforms and improve the whole texture of
the life of the people. He asserted the community against individualism, control against chance, power against drift and disintegration. Britain would be prepared to compete in the world.
Two great middle-class agitators of the nineteenth century, Bright
and Cobden, had attacked the concept of empire, but Chamberlain's
was to be the empire not of the aristocracy but of the middle and
working classes. Like Bright, he was saying, 'Let us try the nation.'

Chamberlain is important because he was a proved creative
parliamentary politician. Although as a Liberal Unionist Cabinet
minister within a Conservative government he could not, after
1902, do much more than influence the Conservative leadership,
he was still an independent source of power in his own right as
the man who had designed Tory social reforms in the 1890s and
taken full responsibility during the Boer War. Of Chamberlain,
Milner wrote: 'In the long run he is swayed by big permanent
ideas, and they are not external to him, but, wherever he got them
from, *they have roots inside him* which alone can insure any vitality to
a policy or any greatness to its possessor.'[1] He was much more of a
democratic leader than Balfour ever was, much more of a political
educator: in Parliament his style was impeccable and on a public
platform he was still a master of exposition and argument. In his
last enterprise, from 1903 to 1905, the stylish Radical politician
was led by his heart and acquired the 'character' which his
opponents denied him.

[1] Edward Crankshaw, *The forsaken idea*, London, 1952, p. 135.

What faced Chamberlain was a task in persuasion—in his party, in political society and the nation. In party and political society he attracted zealots of the Tariff Reform League, the Tariff Commission and 'the Compatriots', who felt that 'at last there was a cause to fight for'. But he could only find his ground by leaving the Cabinet, going out of the centre of political society and, as a private individual, persuading the working classes that taxes on food would be to their benefit. But in a great debate lasting two years, he failed. The old polemic of Free Trade proved too strong.

No politician seemed to be able to measure the forces at work in Edwardian society. Democracy was still young but was already developing passions and appetites which leading politicians could not meet, prompt or anticipate.[1] Some were more at home than others: Winston Churchill in the battles of Sidney Street and Tonypandy and the perils of the Belfast Celtic football ground during the Ulster crisis of 1912; Lloyd George exercising his talents in industrial mediation; and Horatio Bottomley going from bankruptcy to bankruptcy with wit and effrontery unstemmed.

Lloyd George had the keenest awareness of what was possible. On the one hand, he sought a kind of political language which would divide people, give them adversaries—and objectives. In this he was feeling for a Radical 'hegemony', what today is sometimes called the 'natural' or 'sociological' majority. Failing the emergence of this hegemony, he was, with characteristic flexibility, quite prepared to bring about the kind of coalition that he proposed in 1910 to politicians on both side of the house, a coalition which would ignore party symbols and disputes and seek objectives agreed to be necessary. Lloyd George was uniquely capable of political action both as partisan and non-partisan. But his time was not yet.

Today, it may well seem that the man who came nearest to attaining considered objectives was Arthur James Balfour. Balfour was a rare combination of mind, sensibility and aristocratic presence in politics. He had entered Parliament rather doubtfully under the persuasions of his uncle, the marquis of Salisbury, never became involved in party organization and was never much of a platform man. He was forgetful of details; he would confuse, it

---

[1] Cf. J. A. Spender, *The public life*, II, 209: 'So we may pile up the tale of problems, defying reason, bewildering the human brain, making statesmanship an idle and helpless gesture before incontrollable forces of instinct and passion.'

was said, counties with provinces and squadrons with regiments.[1] Like his uncle he disliked professional politicians and, although he must have been very industrious in private, he achieved in public a remarkable detachment from matters of state. Politics interested him speculatively but he had no passion for them. H. G. Wells wondered whether, with all his parliamentary craft, Balfour cared about anything. 'Did anything really matter to him? And if it really mattered nothing, why did he trouble to serve the narrowness and passion of his side?'

Nothing could be more misleading than the impression of the desultory politician, the man who seldom read the newspapers. That he had courage had been proved long ago when he had accused Gladstone's government, in 1881, of negotiating 'in secret with treason' in their releasing Parnell and his associates under the 'Kilmainham Treaty'. That he had executive ability as well was shown by his four years as Chief Secretary in Ireland, where his resolute and effective government had earned him the name of 'Bloody Balfour'. That he had both an acute sense of power and political imagination is proved by his record as Prime Minister when, convinced that peace would not last and Britain was vulnerable, he personally pushed through lasting reforms in education (education for power) and defence (discovering in himself an unsuspected talent for military matters) and, through the *entente* with France and the alliance with Japan, brought the country out of isolation. The Liberal journalist, A. G. Gardiner, had to admit that 'in moments of great crisis and on the larger stage of things, he has been rapid, ruthless and able'.[2]

Like his uncle, Balfour was much concerned with Britain's place in the world. He developed his own geopolitics, sharing the prescience of both Cobden and Seeley about the rise of Russia and America to a dual dominance in the world. Yet, unlike Chamberlain, he did not believe that the world could be changed by a plan; he had precise and limited objectives and sought these first.

Who ruled was highly important. Democracy, he maintained, produced controls over government but contained no dynamic in itself. The problem of knowledgeable will troubled him as much as it troubled the Fabians. Significant movement in politics was always by the few. The perception, judgment and energy long

[1] Young, *Balfour*, p. 195, citing St John Brodrick.
[2] *Certain people of importance*, London, 1926, p. 86.

provided by his own class could not be guaranteed. There is in Balfour a consciousness of declining power; there had been one ice age and there might be another. Just as he doubted the capacity of 'untried races' to take over as the energies of Western races declined, so he doubted the ability of professional politicians from the new classes to rule effectively. This did not mean that he could not recognize political virtuosity wherever it turned up. Lloyd George (who, in turn, was to think Balfour merely 'the scent on a pocket handkerchief') always fascinated him.

Decadence, thought Balfour, arises 'when, through an ancient and still powerful state, there spreads a mood of deep discouragement, when the reaction to recurring ills grows feebler...'.[1] Yet he was not the kind to go on a mission: there was no mantle of Elijah on him. Against the times, 'genteelly devoid of passionate convictions',[2] he contended with rational statesmanship.

As a parliamentarian, he had no equal. Asquith thought him 'the most distinguished member of the greatest deliberative assembly in the world'. In the House, 'persistent, persuasive, indefatigable', he fought, with what Wells considered to be diabolical skill, to secure his essential programme and party unity. Balfour never doubted that anyone who mastered the House of Commons had the right to rule.

Balfour's conduct in Cabinet during the famous Protection crisis of May–September 1903 provides a clear picture of a master politician successfully working along a very narrow ledge.[3] On Protection Balfour had will but it did not take him so far as Chamberlain. He read with care the arguments and counter-arguments on Imperial Preference, or Tariff Reform as it became, and while devising no positive policy, came to the practical, undoctrinal conclusion that fiscal reform must be accepted in principle by his party. Yet he saw that food taxes were electorally impossible and that if the Free Trade–Protection controversy were opened up it would divide his party. He knew that four Free Trade members of his Cabinet, including the duke of Devonshire, would resign if Tariff Reform became policy. The precedents of 1846 and 1886 showed that a party which split would for a long

---

[1] Young, *Balfour*, p. 275.
[2] Harold Gorst, *The fourth party*, London, 1906, quoted in Young, *op. cit.* p. 64.
[3] The whole crisis has recently been re-examined in A.M. Gollin, *Balfour's burden*, London, 1965.

time be deprived of power to do the things that were necessary. And, unlike Chamberlain, he saw Protection as only one issue among many.

Faced with two factions in his Cabinet, Balfour skilfully got rid of both and achieved a personal mastery which would keep his party unified and in office long enough for him to proceed with the reorganization of the army and navy and to conclude the arrangements which would secure Britain some friends in the world. This was his prime aim: to hold on until he had concluded the work in hand for which he thought the Opposition Liberals under Campbell-Bannerman unsuited. There were times when only he and his kind could rule.

Balfour was quite willing to let Chamberlain go out from the Cabinet to conduct a platform crusade for Tariff Reform. For if he were successful Balfour could approve and take up Protection positively. If he lost, Balfour's position would not be damaged.[1] When Chamberlain failed, Balfour refused to be much more specific than he had been. Things went against him, and, after contending for two years against a seemingly irreversible current of unpopularity, the Conservatives went down, after a virtual hegemony of twenty years, to the biggest defeat they have suffered in this century.

L. S. Amery saw that what was demanded was a new language in politics to express the intensity of imperial feeling which bore Chamberlain up. Yet he admitted that many 'shrank back' from what was necessary: 'A complete remoulding, not only of British policy, but, harder still, of their intellectual outlook, and of their whole mental stock-in-trade of familiar and comforting phrases and formulas...'.[2]

Balfour, preferring party unity to action, would not be a shaper of ideas. 'He succeeded in his immediate object, but only at the cost of a paralysis of purpose and inspiration from which the Conservative Party has not shaken itself free to this day.'[3] Despite his liberality, lightness of touch, the serenity of his politics under harassment, his intellectual ability—F. E. Smith thought that he had 'the finest brain that has been applied to politics in our time'—Balfour was temperamentally incapable of finding 'a cause to fight for'. It may or may not be true that, as Neville Chamber-

---

[1] Gollin, *Balfour's burden*, pp. 125 ff.   [2] Amery, *My political life*, I, 236.
[3] *Ibid.* p. 259.

lain remarked, Balfour had 'a heart like a stone';[1] it certainly seems that he was at once a man of resolution and a man of doubts: because he was both, he sought limited *political* settlements. And, as Campbell-Bannerman commented, he was forced to live and die on tactics.

There is character, tenacity and courage in Balfour, but he ends in a severely limited style. After the eclipse and retirement of Joseph Chamberlain, Amery (and many others), seeking will and ideas in a truly compelling Conservative leadership 'which alone could transform the situation', thought of Milner. When contrasted with the finely tuned, cautious Balfour, Milner, with his formidable reputation gained as a creative public servant, a forcer of events, in Egypt and South Africa, had obvious merit as the man to bring things to a head. He had been strong enough to refuse both the Colonial Secretaryship and the Viceroyalty of India; his reputation was extremely high both in governing circles and with those journalists who specialized in what Beatrice Webb, in another context, called 'the melodrama of public affairs'.

Milner promised not 'politics' but that order, direction, statecraft which would make Britain impervious to changes in the hostile, uncertain world outside. With the imperial theme, he urged (like Chamberlain) effective social reforms. To these he added the civic discipline of military service. His energy and dedicated purpose had attracted younger men—the famous Kindergarten—to him in South Africa. He gave men work to do; he would develop the estate, not expiate sins.[2] He was also the man with the sense of the nation and, as has been well said, 'a leaderless host' awaited him.[3] He was the obvious guest of honour at patriotic meetings: the natural recipient of national testimonials, recognizing or vindicating not only his talents but also his moral power. For he denounced mere opportunism, condemned Cecil Rhodes because he sought 'to gain prematurely by violent and unscrupulous means what you could get honestly and without violence if you could only *wait* and work for it'.

Although he had been a Liberal, Milner was uncompromisingly hostile to the Liberal governments of Campbell-Bannerman and then Asquith (in spite of Asquith's Liberal Imperialist background). They lacked vision and 'workmanlike strenuousness'. Because of

---

[1] Gollin, *Balfour's burden*, p. 168.   [2] Cf. Crankshaw *Forsaken idea*, pp. 39–40.
[3] A. M. Gollin, *Proconsul in politics*, London, 1964, p. 117.

his imperial efficiency, his opposition to the conciliation of the Boers in South Africa, his fierce championing of the cause of Ulster (again to the point of action), Milner became anathema to radical Liberals. To his opponents in turn he attributed 'panoplied hatred, insensate ambition, invincible ignorance'. Because Milner had no guilt about power, Radical journalists thought him a pseudo-Bismarck, un-English. 'He is not placable,' wrote H. W. Massingham, 'he has no belief in any of our British prepossessions...'.[1]

Today he seems more like De Gaulle than Bismarck. He would certainly have subscribed to most of the maxims which De Gaulle claimed, in *The edge of the sword*, had schooled his public personality.[2] There is in Milner the same combination of *character* and *prestige*, the same willingness to wait for the groundswell which will carry him to power. There is in him, too, the same contempt for political life, the same promise of civilized autocracy. The idiom is different but within it there is the same uncompromising honesty, the same capacity to make himself heard above the din; '...in Milner's ideology', writes A. P. Thornton, 'there was a ringing appeal, an appeal that awoke echoes that even the iron clamour of the twentieth century never wholly obliterated'.[3]

Yet in default of war, external or civil, Milner could not come to power. He would not play the political game; he refused to accept a political system which left the determination of policy, first to the chance outcome of a muddy electoral battle between the major political parties, and subsequently to the hazards of political contention and collusion. Parliamentary government, he thought, was incompatible with an effective imperial executive. Of those who delighted in the traffic of politics, he was contemptuous. Churchill was 'the pot-boy of Downing Street'. As early as 1903 he wrote:

...the system is hopeless. Only one man in a hundred dares give effect or utterance to the statesmanship that is in him...Perhaps a great *Charlatan*—political scallywag, buffoon, liar...and in other respects popular favourite—may some day arise, who is nevertheless a *statesman* ...and who, having attained power by popular art, may use it for national ends. It is an off chance...[4]

---

[1] Quoted in Gollin, *Proconsul in politics*, p. 81.
[2] See, chapter 1, p. 5, n. 1.
[3] A. P. Thornton, *The imperial idea and its enemies*, London, 1959, p. 81.
[4] Quoted in Gollin, *Proconsul in politics*, p. 46.

In his fastidiousness, he insisted that he gave 'addresses', not political speeches; he thought that office imposed indignities and he would not do the hack work of opposition to attain it. To some extent this squeamishness merely disguised his own disability, what Amery called his *agoraphobia*, his fear of public places. He was quite incapable—as, of course, was Balfour in quite a different way—of bringing a movement into being, of starting a crusade, like the superbly equipped Chamberlain. And without either a crusade to gain popularity or connection, he could not gain office. No one would suspend the British Constitution for him.

Milner was the critic of Liberalism at many levels. Outside the political ring, he contended with the liberal imagination that, before the density and complexity of life denied the necessity of belief and preferred art to politics, was perturbed by 'character' and aesthetically repelled by political 'style'. 'I do not believe in Belief...,' E. M. Forster, whose mind and art were shaped in the Edwardian age, has declared. 'Faith, to my mind, is a stiffening process, a sort of mental starch, which ought to be applied as sparingly as possible.'[1] In *Howards End*, Helen and Margaret Schlegel would 'at times dismiss the whole British Empire with a puzzled, if reverent sigh'. There were whole islands of civilized people, guilty in their security, uneasy in their ascendancy, unwilling to acknowledge the stark power which sustained them.

Milner was also the enemy of the urbane, civilized office-holders, especially the Whiggish Asquith, who rarely extended themselves in action, who assumed that there was an automatic progression to an untroubled future, and would accept popular electoral verdicts as rough guides to what action was necessary. He was embittered too by the liberal order of politics which allowed good men to sink out of sight while it raised the operators. Milner was for policies, not for labels. 'I am not a Tariff Reformer because I am a Conservative. I am a Conservative because I am a Tariff Reformer.'

Yet another clash was with the 'Little Englandism' and conscience of the old Liberalism of John Morley. 'Twenty-five years ago', wrote A. G. Gardiner in 1914, 'the future of British politics seemed bound up with three friends, the most powerful triumvirate of our time. Citizen Chamberlain provided the driving power

---

[1] 'What I believe', in *Two cheers for democracy*, London, 1951, p. 77.

and the popular appeal, Citizen Dilke the encyclopaedic knowledge of detail and affairs, John Morley the moral motive and the
intellectual foundation.'¹ Morley is not much read today and even
in his prime he was regarded mainly as a master of the old watchwords, the idealizer of representative institutions as 'one great
taproot of our national increase'.² He had believed that the contention between parties in Parliament could be real and effective.
He had noted with approval how widening participation in
politics had 'helped both to fix our strongest and most constant
interests upon politics, and to ingrain the mental habits proper to
politics, far more deeply than any other, into our general constitution and inmost character'.³

He had no constructive idea. Beyond a passion for political
equality and liberty and the provision of a framework in which
individual energies could work their way, he hardly advanced. He
declined to examine the implications of 'social justice'. Right to
the end—and he lingered on as an office-holder until 1914, a
fitting symbol for a lost Liberal innocence—'as a public man he
was expected always to walk the high processional road'.⁴ Asquith
thought him the last survivor of an heroic age. He remained as a
kind of moral barometer. 'Tap him,' said Gardiner, 'and you shall
see whether we are set at "foul" or "fair".'

Yet Morley's politics was not merely the comfortable politics of
the political review and library—he was genuinely drawn to
political operating, to 'ulterior, political, practical, considerations
about ideas', as Matthew Arnold, with whom he had literary
affinities, once remarked.⁵ He gave politics priority over literature.

In his earliest work, *On compromise*, he had insisted (like Mill)
that truth should never take second place. He had urged the need
for real and sustained high convictions: intellectual symmetry and
integrity from both Conservatives and Liberals. He saw the
political arena neither as a mart for interests nor as an area of
non-rational inference, but as a strenuous mental gymnasium.

In action he was disappointing. He lacked character, the power
to instigate and hold on and finally the power to speak out. Neither
as Chief Secretary for Ireland nor in his later post as Secretary of

¹ *Prophets, priests and kings*, London, 1908, p. 58.
² John Morley, *On compromise*, London, 1874, p. 82.
³ *Ibid.* p. 83.
⁴ Spender, *The public life*, I, 105.
⁵ Cf. Warren Staebler, *The liberal mind of John Morley*, Princeton, 1943, pp. 211–14.

State for India (odd posts, as Spender remarks, for a Little Englander) did he show much political talent. Nothing perhaps shows his incapacity for action more clearly than his departure from politics in 1914. 'Morley, resolute for neutrality,' wrote Churchill, 'not indeed at all costs, but—as it seemed to me—at fatal costs in days, was absorbed by ideas of parley, of the fate of Liberalism, of the party situation. He had spent his life building up barriers against war, in Parliament, in the constituencies, and in the national mind.'[1] He resigned from the Cabinet because he disapproved of the way in which Britain had entered the war, but did not speak out to denounce the war or his colleagues. He was content with private virtue.

The Liberal governments from 1906, with their inner lining of Liberal Imperialists, could hardly be hostile to empire even when the Gladstonian Campbell-Bannerman was in charge. They were conscious of a civilizing, liberalizing mission for which the British were perhaps particularly suited; they were conscious of imperial sins to be expiated, of resistant nationalities to be conciliated; but they could not easily conceive of the empire as a system of power to ensure the survival of Great Britain in the politics of the world. Their approach was neither strenuous nor workmanlike. They were not moved to regenerate the nation through the execution of a single constructive idea; they disliked the regimentation and order which organization would entail.

Liberals favoured no central executive for a unified empire; they sought to create autonomous executives out of sight and out of mind rather than to wrestle with the absorption of intractable Irish and Boers into a single polity. In defence, it is true that they followed the Conservative lead and were competent. Britain was not ill prepared for war in 1914, even though the small efficient army was unloved by most Liberal politicians. The navy was largely built up through professional zeal from within and exhortation from outside.

In domestic affairs the Liberal governments used state power in the social field but organization was kept to a minimum. As the People's Party of 1906, as a *movement*, the Liberals were (whatever the party leaders might think) less concerned to improve the health of citizens in order to make the country fitter for success in the world than to ameliorate social ills. Doctrinally, Liberalism

[1] *Great contemporaries*, London, 1938, p. 104.

continued to stand, as the election of 1906 had proved, for Free Trade and the removal of obstructions to individual human development, for all the varieties of liberty.

Yet much of its impetus, as a movement, derived from its marked antagonism to the power of landed men as distinct (difficult though the distinction was in practice) from that of moneyed men. From 1906 Liberalism 'was directed against the whole amalgam of upper class society in Britain, rank, land, Church, services and varsity'[1]—against what it polemically thought of as privileged *hauteur* and parasitic splendour.

Behind the watchwords and this animus Liberalism was, as Wells observed, a 'huge hospitable caravanserai...a diversified crowd'. This diversification was reflected in its policy. The main stream of Liberalism, declared Lord Hugh Cecil in 1903 '...is Gladstonian in foreign, colonial and Irish questions; it is Nonconformist in ecclesiastical and educational questions; it is Radical in questions affecting property; it is Trade Unionist in questions affecting labour and capital'.[2] The Liberal leadership sought, without detaching itself from the comforts and civilities of political society, to use its parliamentary majority to legislate to meet the demands of the movement. Laws to right Tory wrongs in education and liquor licensing, to provide an eight-hour day for miners, to enable Trade Unions to use their funds for political purposes, to bring in old age pensions and national insurance, to disestablish the Welsh Church and give Ireland Home Rule, to satisfy the long-banked-up sectional grievances, were set in motion, sometimes checked by, and sometimes flowing round Tory obstructions, constitutional and non-constitutional.

The political conduct of Liberals did not always match their elevation of mind. Their electioneering in 1906, particularly on 'Chinese labour', had not been very scrupulous. The land taxes on unearned increments in the Budget of 1909 seemed a direct attack upon the political strength of the gentry. Lloyd George rejoiced in fomenting class antagonisms. The 'Peers versus the People' issue was artificially stimulated. The Marconi affair tainted the reputation of Lloyd George—even if he were acquitted of acting otherwise than in good faith and cleared of corruption,

---

[1] R. B. McCallum in 'The liberal outlook', *Law and opinion in England in the twentieth century*, ed. Morris Ginsberg, London, 1959, p. 70.

[2] Hamilton Fyfe, *The British Liberal Party*, London, 1928, p. 157.

a Radical tribune should surely not have had such a good eye for the financial main chance.

The Asquith government may, with one or two exceptions like Churchill and Lloyd George, have wanted a quiet life, but they were ineluctably set in motion by their own symbols, by the prescriptions in what Rosebery had called their 'fly-blown phylacteries'. The bare electoral victories were surely not sufficient authority for them to embark on the final emancipation of all Ireland. The fierce assertiveness of Ulster took them by surprise. So did the rough anger of the Tories. A government in power by the grace of the Irish Nationalist and Labour Parties, and visibly making concessions to both, might well be condemned for not assessing or even understanding the intensity of Tory and Orange feelings.

In their great faith in parliamentary majorities, the Liberals lost the sense of the nation. There was some doubt as to whether they could command the force of the nation. To their opponents it seemed as though the Liberal government believed that

those who have sufficient control of a political 'machine', or of two or more 'machines', to enable them, singly or in coalition, to maintain a majority in the House of Commons, are entitled to pass any legislation whatever, whether it affects some trifling interest or whether it breaks up the whole Constitution, whether it has been brought before the people or not, whether the opposition to it is weak and superficial or strong and passionately intense... [1]

Behind Asquith's composed front and lucid, contained speeches (lucid in expression, rather than in thought, Amery considered), the Tories sensed irresolution and lack of creative design and they refused to play the accommodating parliamentary game. They refused to let Parliament decide.

The great Tory conspiracy of 1912–14, perhaps as wild as anything that happened in the days of Harley and Bolingbroke, has now been largely forgotten, blotted out by the violence of the First World War. To the humiliating defeat of 1906 had been added the goad of the 1909 Budget: 'the Budget plus Lloyd George and the Limehouse speeches drove the Tory party off its mental balance'.[2] To these were now added Liberal dereliction of imperial

[1] Amery, *My political life*, I, 402.
[2] J. A. Spender, *Life, journalism and politics*, London, 1927, I, 231.

duty in Ireland and the betrayal of loyalists. The Tories had absorbed most of what was left of the old Whiggery but had acquired no elasticity from them. They decided that they were no longer squeezable. From the obstruction of legislation they moved to attack Parliament itself:

Everything they [the Tories] did in the next two years was aimed, not against Home Rule, but against the very existence of Parliament. Because Liberalism was already almost moribund, in spite of its appearance of health, their conscious aim was to destroy Liberalism: because the whole mood of that pre-war England was sudden, sombre and violent, their unconscious desire was to ruin an institution they were pledged to protect. An utterly constitutional party, they set out to wreck the Constitution; and they very nearly succeeded.[1]

In 1911, the Tories had rid themselves of Balfour, whose detachment and distaste for both the coarser and more theatrical kinds of politics had inhibited their response to Lloyd George and final resistance to the pruning of the powers of the House of Lords. His successor was Bonar Law, 'the man without unction'. In his uncompromising support of the Ulster minority, he was willing to reject parliamentary politics: he intended primarily to impress his own followers. 'He relied for effect on cold reasoning, hard facts and a bitter tongue. His idea of parliamentary debating was to be unsparing of his opponents. He judged the success of a speech by the degree to which it irritated the other side.'[2] He could draw astonishing parallels:

I remember this that King James had behind him the letter of the law just as completely as Mr Asquith has now. He made sure of it. He got the judges on his side by methods not dissimilar from those by which Mr Asquith has a majority in the House of Commons on his side. There is another point to which I would specially refer. In order to carry out his despotic intention the King had the largest army which had ever been seen in England. What happened? There was no civil war. Why? Because his own army refused to fight for him.

So contemptuous was Bonar Law of the government's courage, that George V instructed his Private Secretary, Lord Stamfordham, 'to urge Mr Bonar Law to be moderate in his own speeches and curb those of his supporters'.[3]

---

[1] Dangerfield, *Strange death of liberal England*, p. 91.
[2] Philip Snowden, *An autobiography*, London, 1934, I, 232.
[3] Harold Nicolson, *King George V*, London, 1952, p. 235.

The Conservatives were aided by Asquith's waiting upon events, by his hyper-parliamentary outlook—whatever happened at Westminster was sacrosanct. But if Asquith drifted, equivocated, the Roman presence revealing mind without imagination, the Tories, under Bonar Law complotting with Carson and Sir Henry Wilson, were made mad. In their anger and frustration they allowed an Irish faction to say where they were going. At Blenheim, in July 1912, Bonar Law had told a mass rally that he could imagine no lengths to which Ulster Unionists might go where his own party and the public at large would not follow them. This took defiance of parliamentary majorities to the point of rebellion. For the first time since 1688 a British government was uncertain of the allegiance of the armed forces. The opposition had gone to the brink of civil war. The screws, as Sir Henry Wilson had suggested, were really being put upon Asquith and his crowd.

Over the turmoil Asquith presided, as the bearer of the parliamentary tradition, in a cool and civilized manner. He concentrated on what could be immediately despatched, initiating very little but adjudicating among the policies of his colleagues, meeting with superb economy the arguments of the Opposition without perhaps seeing them whole or measuring their intensity. Because of the war we shall never know whether he had the sense of situation and good timing to prevent a civil war over Ireland. It seems unlikely that there would have been other than a solution by force. It is doubtful if Asquith would have worked hard enough to prevent one.

7

INNOVATIONS AND
RESTORATIONS:
LLOYD GEORGE AND BALDWIN

It is the career of Lloyd George which shows what was possible
for a leading politician in Britain in the early part of this century.
Not only did Lloyd George dominate Liberal social and industrial
policy before the war; he also turned from pacifist Radicalism to
become, as Minister for Munitions and Secretary of State for War,
the best known member of Asquith's war-time ministries. Then,
in a period in which the House of Commons lost authority and real
political discussion took place in the press, the newspaper editors
(not only Northcliffe) identified him as the man to prosecute the
war.

By the end of 1916 he had, with press and Tory aid, ousted
Asquith from the premiership and set out as organizer of victory.
H. W. Massingham of *The Nation* could not think of him as such:
rather, 'an attractive and ingeniously adherent FLY sat on the
mighty wheel and guided its whirl...Mr George did bad things
and good things and usually irrelevant things. But how could a
good military decision come from such a mind as Mr George's,
"slim", intuitive but ill-furnished and careless of detail?'[1] There
were some who would not give him credit for knowing what was
taking place on the other side of the hill. But, given that the war
had to be won outright, he was always visibly active and absorbed
in manipulating individuals and interests to that end. At the same
time he provided the popular leadership as no one else could. All
the while, Bonar Law, the Tory leader, 'held the stirrup iron' for
him.[2] Yet when the 1918 election endorsed the George–Law
combine, the two leaders were mutually obliged. The engine of
the coalition was the brute vote provided by Bonar Law's Tories.

---

[1] *The Nation*, 14 December 1918, quoted in S. Maccoby, *English radicalism, the end?*,
London, 1961, p. 285.
[2] Lord Beaverbrook, *The decline and fall of Lloyd George*, London, 1963, p. 175.

Yet Lloyd George's 'coupon', which had identified his followers
at the election, had divided the Liberal Party,[1] and his name had
everywhere swollen the Tory poll. From now onwards the
Tories were not certain of winning an election without him.

So, in the years of peacemaking, Lloyd George appeared
'visibly to all men the greatest man in the world'.[2] And all done
with little strain. For he thrived on politics, could master two or
three disparate crises at once. He met opposition with equanimity
and was strengthened rather than weakened by the hatred which
he aroused. He was the most accomplished demagogue of his day,
debouching at will from lay-preaching eloquence into fuliginous
diatribe or quick easy banter. In council or Cabinet he had
astonishing persuasiveness and an ability to charm or dominate
men of superior mental power. The mind held little detail, but he
had a good eye for emergent policy: he was, at the same time, said
Churchill, 'the greatest master of getting things done, of putting
things through that I ever knew'.[3]

A study of politics might indeed focus round this one man who
had all the endowments of both the platform and cameral politician. He began with specific causes but they did not obstruct his
development. The prospects of action dissolved his pacifism in
1914; in 1915, the manufacture of shells took precedence over his
scheme to nationalize the drink trade. 'One may marvel at, if one
can hardly admire, the lighthearted way in which Mr Lloyd George
picked up this vast new plan, as one might pick up a sovereign
from the pavement, and then dropped it again as quickly as if the
sovereign had turned out to be a hot potato.'[4] He was not diverted
from his causes by 'connection' or 'social allurement', but by
specific tasks in hand—making munitions, winning the war, making
the peace and, in the end, asserting British power in the world.
For these he disregarded personal or party ties, what Lord
D'Abernon called the 'conventional or contractual obligation of
comradeship'.[5]

Placation of 'the people', of rising opinion, had priority over

[1] It has been pointed out that, knowing that a Conservative-Unionist victory was
almost inevitable, Lloyd George tried, through 'the coupon', to save as many
Liberals as possible. A. J. P. Taylor, *English history 1914–1945*, Oxford, 1965,
p. 126   [2] See Sir Arthur Salter, *Personality in politics*, London, 1947, p. 52.
[3] *Thoughts and adventures*, New York, 1932, p. 60.
[4] Lord Beaverbrook, *Politicians and the war*, London, 1928, pp. 75–6.
[5] Quoted in *Slings and arrows*, ed. Philip Guedalla, London, 1929, p. xv.

the keeping of friends. His rapid 'slings and arrows', simple, emphatic exposition, unforced economical comedy, show acute sense of a popular audience, no longer as earnest as Gladstone's.[1] 'His critics have accused him of conscious cynicism in the composition of his politically idealistic public speeches, whereas his real fault was a desire to please his audience—his weakness was an extreme responsiveness to atmosphere and in place of an immovable candour a too adroit opportunism.'[2]

He spoke the language of the Radical editorial with Biblical overtones; his reading was meagre but always to hand. His 'picture language', unlike that of Ramsay MacDonald, sharpened rather than clouded the issue:

The Church is making tremendous efforts to regain its lost influence; that we admit. It builds new churches, and restores old ones; it founds extension societies and other societies; it multiplies its forces in the way of curates and lecturers; but it does not strike the right chords, and the heart of the Welsh people does not vibrate. It is nothing but a strenuous endeavour on the part of the organ-blower to play the organ. You can hear the whistling of the wind as it rushes through the pipes... you can see the sweating and perspiring of the man at the bellows; but not a chord of music can you hear. There is no one to press the pedals or to touch the finger board.

It is in his great speeches on the 1909 Budget in Limehouse, Newcastle and Caernarvon that his powers of exposition, his skill in exacerbation, are fully exhibited. The effects of the rating system, the nature of royalties and ground-rents, railway development and property rights, the meaning of urban increment, are all acted out with incredible skill. Against the landlord with 'the golden swamp', Lloyd George states the claims of those who want 'more air, more light, more room, more verdure'. Against Protectionist 'stomach taxes', he sets the land taxes of the Budget. The theme was an old one, his 'facts' were sometimes wrong or misleading, but he brought 'the land' back into politics—made an opening for his Land Campaign of 1912. It is an appeal to the simplest sense of right and wrong, to make men aware of the social consequences of ground landlordism, to divide them and set them moving. It is a declaration of intent, unclogged by detail.

---

[1] Thomas Jones, *Lloyd George*, London, 1951, p. 91.
[2] *Ibid.*

The five-shilling old age pension of 1909 becomes a lay preacher's felicitous image: 'It is rather hard that the old workman should have to find his way to the gates of the tomb, bleeding and footsore through the brambles and thorns of poverty. We cut a new path for him—an easier one, a pleasanter one, through fields of waving corn.' The redistribution of income is massively moralized: 'The great lesson of Christianity is this. You cannot redeem those who are below except by the sacrifice of those who are above...'

In 1911—not long before the Marconi scandal—he could see himself 'doing the work of the man of Nazareth'. The words were often facile but they carried. He made hardly any notes, talked as his mouth stood. Like Chamberlain, but in livelier idiom, he used language unusual in a Minister of the Crown and was at least as effective. He 'kept his audience howling with alternate rage and laughter; moment by moment, sentence by sentence, he assaulted the landlords, and outraged the gentry, and invited the dispossessed and cozened the dissatisfied: he shouted and implored and wheedled and mimicked'.[1]

The fine voice, the mobile face which could simulate any emotion, the sustained and homely metaphor, dissolved even English phlegm:

Have you ever been down a coalmine? I went down one the other day. We sank into a pit half a mile deep. We then walked underneath the mountain and we had about three-quarters of a mile with the rock and shale above us. The earth seemed to be straining—around us and above us—to crush us in. You could see the pit-props bent and twisted and sundered, until you saw their fibres split in resisting the pressure. Sometimes they give way, and then there is mutilation and death. Often a spark ignites, the whole pit is deluged in fire and the breath of life is scorched out of hundreds of breasts by the consuming flame. In the very next colliery to the one I descended, just a few years ago, three hundred people lost their lives in that way...

He continued:

And yet when the Prime Minister and I knock at the doors of these great landlords, and say to them: 'Here, you know these poor fellows who have been digging up royalties at the risk of their lives, some of them are old, they have survived the perils of their trade, they are broken, they can earn no more. Won't you give something towards

[1] Dangerfield, *Strange death of liberal England*, p. 22.

keeping them out of the workhouse?' —they scowl at us. We say: 'Only a ha'penny, just a copper.' They say: 'You thieves!' And they turn their dogs on to us, and you can hear their bark every morning.

He evoked love and hatred at all levels, even in the cottages where, according to Churchill, he was the best-known man in Britain. He might be a rascal, but to redeem him there was a kind of pantomime brio about him—very like that about Chester Nimmo, Joyce Cary's leading politician in *Prisoner of grace*:

There was perhaps some truth in the old joke that if Chester Nimmo, stark naked, were attacked by two desperadoes, armed to the teeth, there would be a short sharp struggle, and an immense cloud of dust, and then it would be found that the footpads had murdered each other and that Nimmo was wearing the full evening dress of an archbishop with gold watches in every pocket.

Beatrice Webb, too, saw the mobile face of an actor-conjurer and noted how one audience 'settled down to be amused and flattered. But his speech left a bad impression: it lacked sincerity. He told obvious little lies....'[1] Yet here surely, in person, was as near as could be got to Milner's 'political scallywag', the popular favourite who was 'nevertheless a statesman'.

His powers in conference and negotiation were, if anything, superior to his platform gifts. They derived largely from his capacity for concentrating upon the particular situation in order to change and adapt it. To Keynes there seemed to be little more to Lloyd George than this situational virtuosity.

Lloyd George is rooted in nothing; he is void and without content; he lives and feeds on his immediate surroundings; he is an instrument and a player at the same time which plays on the company and is played on by them too; he is a prism, as I have heard him described, which collects light and distorts it and is most brilliant if the light comes from many quarters at once; a vampire and a medium in one.[2]

These are Pateresque exaggerations, yet the testimony to his energy is universal. To Grey, his fertility and resource were wonderful; when the formidable Kitchener blocked his path, 'the torrent of Lloyd George's activity foamed against the obstruction' and swept it away.[3] For Salter, he had 'dynamic imagination':

---

[1] *Diaries 1912–1924*, London, 1952, p. 44.
[2] *Essays in biography*, London, 1933, p. 37.
[3] Grey of Fallodon, *Twenty-five years*, London, II, 242–3.

'No man in his great period approached him in his combination of creative force, courage and magnetism.'[1]

Force, imagination, adroitness, but no ideology. A vision, yet it was little more than the old Liberal individualism with a fairer start and a freer run—appealing to the small man, the shopkeeper, the farmer and the underdog. The imagery was of water, hills, valleys, sturdy peasantry and deserted villages. Lloyd George's initial model was the Joseph Chamberlain whom he had considered in 1884 to be the future leader of the people. To Chamberlain's industrial and agrarian Radicalism, attacks on 'the trade', and anti-Anglicanism, he had added Welshness. In the same way he had used the last surge of Nonconformity in English politics: the agitation against the 1902 Education Act which put the Anglican schools on the rates. His anti-imperialism faded: his post-war diplomacy showed how deeply he had absorbed the imperial theme. He believed in 'imperial righteousness'. For him, the Boers were, like the Welsh, an oppressed nation. Moreover, it was the Boer War that had effectively projected him, had given him the opportunity to challenge the Radical leader of the previous generation—'the gentleman from Birmingham, who had made no personal sacrifices for the war...the Mephistopheles of this play ...the marplot who stopped the piece'.

Nonconformity, Welshness and temperance were declining political assets but, as a minister in the Campbell-Bannerman and Asquith governments, he could still reaffirm his hostility to the men living in the big houses, exhibit his social origins, his home-brewed politics. 'Yonder smithy was my first parliament where night after night we discussed and decided all the abstruse questions relating to this world and the next....' Very early he had asserted that the Tories had not realized that 'the day of the cottage-bred man had at last dawned'.

Lloyd George was now quick to dramatize 'the social problem' and make it into practical politics. And like Joseph Chamberlain he would not be silenced by office. 'The quiet but certain revolution' must be taken over by the Liberals before Labour acquired momentum. No one knew better than he that Liberalism was worn out. In 1906, at Cardiff, he had 'one word for Liberals':

I can tell them what will make this I.L.P. movement a great and sweeping force in this country—a force that will sweep away Liberalism

---

[1] Salter, *Personality in politics*, p. 39.

amongst other things. If at the end of an average term of office it were
found that a Liberal Parliament had done nothing to cope seriously
with the social condition of the people, to remove the national de-
gradation of slums and widespread poverty and destitution in a land
glittering with wealth; that they had shrunk from attacking boldly
the main causes of this wretchedness, notably the drink and this
vicious land system; that they had not arrested the waste of our
national resources in armaments, nor provided an honourable sustenance for deserving old age...then would a real cry arise in this
land for a new party, and many of us here in this room would join in
that cry.

So he became through the People's Budget and National Insurance the nearest thing that England had to 'the revolution
man'.[1] It was the same prescience, the same sense of what was of
rising importance, that enabled him to make and take over the
Ministry of Munitions, to see, in 1915, that conscription, a small
War Cabinet, and the removal of Lord Kitchener from the War
Office were all necessary to the winning of the war.[2] His flair and
vigour were publicized by a press with more influence than it has
ever had since.

Yet throughout his career no one trusted him. His land taxation
scheme was sketchy, and of the passage of his National Insurance
measure Thomas Jones has written, 'His insecure acquaintance
with the minutiae of his own bill meant that he often skated over
a very thin sheet of knowledge, but it thickened as the debate
continued.'[3] But it was not merely that he did not work things
out. To some he appeared dishonest, a man who used figures as
adjectives. He acquired a reputation for double dealing. 'Are you
going to see Lloyd George alone?' James Craig, the Ulster leader
asked De Valera in 1921. 'Are you mad? Take a witness. Lloyd
George will give any account of the interview that comes into his
mind or that suits him.'[4] Did he dupe the Labour leaders in 1916
by promising extensive nationalization? Did he deliberately trick
and/or intimidate the Irish leaders in 1922?

Asquith distrusted him. So did McKenna. Haig thought him
not only an insufferable companion—'he talks and argues so', but

[1] G. E. Raine, *The real Lloyd George*, London, 1913, p. 103.
[2] Lord Beaverbrook, *Politicians and the war*, p. 193.
[3] Thomas Jones, *Lloyd George*, p. 37.
[4] Beaverbrook, *Decline and fall of Lloyd George*, p. 84.

also 'a thorough impostor'.[1] Beatrice Webb thought that he aroused none of 'the awe and instinctive deference' which Prime Ministers excited 'in all but the most sophisticated minds'. He had a 'low standard of intellect and conduct', was always trying to do a deal, always using people.[2]

Even Sir Henry Wilson found him tricky:

I had $1\frac{1}{2}$ hours this evening with Lloyd George and Bonar Law. I told them what I thought of reprisals by the 'Black and Tans', and how this must lead to chaos and ruin. Lloyd George danced about and was angry, but I never budged. I pointed out that these reprisals were carried out without anyone being responsible...It was the business of the Government to govern. If these men ought to be murdered, then the Government ought to murder them. Lloyd George danced at all this, said no Government could possibly take this responsibility.[3]

Paul Cambon, the French ambassador in London in 1917, in a confidential report on Lloyd George's handling of Austrian peace feelers, said: 'He is a Welshman, not an Englishman. In fact, he is the reverse of an Englishman: enthusiastic, bright, quick-witted, and unsettled. An Englishman never goes back on what he has once said; Lloyd George is apt to perform evolutions, his words have not the weight of a Balfour's or a Bonar Law's. On the other hand, he has some qualities of priceless value at the moment: among others that of not being obsessed by the fetish of Constitutionalism. Mr Asquith would never have consented to discuss a matter of this sort without telling his Cabinet, whereas Mr Lloyd George has solemnly promised not to mention it to any of his colleagues.'[4]

The 'infallible instinct of the public'[5] may, through the press, have identified him during a period of national extremity: but at large it was not clearly known then, nor for some time afterwards, just how he had attained power.

Whether Mr Lloyd George has been a willing instrument in their hands [of the Northcliffe Press and Tory Party] it is difficult for an outsider, like myself, to judge. But, like thousands of others, I have an uneasy feeling that he is not only fully aware of the dirty game that

---

[1] *The private papers of Douglas Haig, 1914–1919* ed. Robert Blake, London, 1952, p. 300.
[2] *Diaries 1912–1924*, pp. 111–12.
[3] Quoted by C. L. Mowat, *Britain between the wars*, London, 1955, p. 76.
[4] Thomas Jones, *Lloyd George*, p. 127.
[5] Beaverbrook, *Politicians and the war*, p. 275.

has been, and is still being played by Tory Press and Party, but he winked at it, seeing that amongst other things it aimed at making him Prime Minister...[1]

The alacrity of his co-operation with Bonar Law and the Tory Party machine in the election of 1918 did his reputation more harm.

In the post-war world Lloyd George had become a separate political interest, and the issue was whether he could use that interest to break the mould of British politics. 'He did not seem to care which way he travelled,' writes Beaverbrook, 'providing he was in the driver's seat.'[2] But in peacetime only the accepted leader of a party could be secure in that seat. And Lloyd George had no party, only a following. Could he then persuade his leading 'followers', aristocrats like Balfour intrigued by his resource and skill, political adventurers like Churchill and Birkenhead who thought that only he could bring in the votes, businessmen like the Geddeses whom Lloyd George had preferred to politicians in executive office, honest men like Austen Chamberlain bound by ties of loyalty to him—to form the nucleus of a new Centre Party?

Much of the habit background of British politics already seemed to be dissolving under his domination. Recognizing his true field of force and attraction as the platform and the newspapers, Lloyd George was appearing less and less in Parliament. The Cabinet was losing coherence as a true plural executive: while Curzon, the Foreign Secretary, was often ignored, Churchill, 'harsh, over-bearing, at times almost insulting',[3] at the War Office, and then the Colonial Office, often seemed out of control. And on the fringes of the Cabinet Office, there had appeared the 'Garden Suburb,' a personal intelligence centre for the Prime Minister, staffed with his own cronies, a standing affront to the knowledge and experience of the established civil service.

It was, of course, this capacity for creating his own sources of opinion and for refusing to be impressed by the views of accepted experts that made Lloyd George such an unusual *political* force. An administrative politician, like Lord Curzon, with his carefully garnered intelligence, his precious foreign affairs specialisms, his published works, was, in spite of greater knowledge, sometimes

---

[1] Tom Barnshaw quoted in Joseph Davies, *The Prime Minister's secretariat*, Newport, Mon. 1951, p. 31. What happened was, of course, not as simple as this impression. Asquith did contribute to his own fall. But the impression was widespread.

[2] Beaverbrook, *Decline and fall of Lloyd George*, p. 140.   [3] *Ibid.* p. 30.

better judgment, merely an instrument for Lloyd George, useful but rigid.[1]

With the policies of the old parties in ruins, a new party seemed feasible. It was for a short while possible for him to pick and choose policies at Versailles, in the Middle East and Ireland, and even in the world of industry. The future, as he had forecast, was briefly molten. Lloyd George himself was a master in raising new heads of opinion. He had at his disposal an enormous party fund got from the indiscriminate sale of honours. He had assumed as Prime Minister the personal power to ask for a dissolution of Parliament when the time was ripe to project himself on the nation. Finally, there was his strength in the constituencies, where his reputation as a card, rascal or hero obscured all others.

But the design seemed less and less realizable from 1920 onwards, for coalitions, as L. S. Amery has remarked, coalesce more closely at the top than lower down. He retained the support of most of his Tory ministers to the end but the Tory chairmen and agents in the constituencies, led by Sir George Younger, the chairman of the Party, were hostile. They distrusted Lloyd George's Irish, labour and foreign policies, fearing, quite correctly, that he intended to break the Tory Party as he had broken the Liberals.

The problem was this. Could Lloyd George find a suitable issue for going to the people before the backbench Tories brought him down? With the retirement of Bonar Law from the Cabinet and leadership of the Tory Party in the spring of 1921, his chances receded. For the man who had held him up could now pass judgment on him. At any time Bonar Law could come out of retirement to defend true Conservatism. And Beaverbrook has shown how the man who had once said, 'We must never let the little man go,' became convinced that Lloyd George was no longer suited to high office.

The occasion for another plebiscitary election to give Lloyd George a lease of virtually presidential power eluded him. The best opportunity was in January 1922 after the successful conclusion of the Irish treaty, but neither Younger nor Austen Chamberlain, the new leader, would agree. Lloyd George had lost his flair. 'The great war leader who was capable of ordering armies and navies to advance into battle was incapable of ordering a dissolution of

[1] See F. S. Northedge, 'The ideal civil servant?', *The Listener*, 31 December 1959.

Parliament.'[1] He thought of joining up with the Asquith Liberals again, even speculated on giving up politics and becoming editor of *The Times*. 'He had', says Beaverbrook, 'no future.'

There followed the Philhellenic policy (Lloyd George hated the Turks because, like the English gentry, they had been those 'in possession') which led to Chanak in September 1922, the unrealistic appeal to France and Italy and the British Dominions to unite in resisting the resurgent Turks under Mustapha Kemal, the vain attempts to forestall the inevitable Tory revolt, the fateful meeting of the Tory Parliamentary Party at the Carlton Club on 19 October, the withdrawal of the Tories from the Coalition and the eclipse of Lloyd George at the November election.

Beaverbrook sees the protagonists as Lloyd George and Bonar Law. And it is true that Bonar Law's letter to *The Times* of 7 October, insisting that this was not the time for foreign adventures, and his reluctant appearance at the Carlton Club to pull the Tories out of the Coalition were decisive. But the destruction of Lloyd George was the penultimate act of Bonar Law's career; for Baldwin, the chief dissentient in the Coalition Cabinet, it was the moment of self-discovery. When at the Carlton Club meeting he said of Lloyd George that 'a dynamic force is a very terrible thing; it may crush you, but it is not necessarily right', he was announcing with vehemence that for him at least success dissolved no moral distinctions.

There is no explanation of Lloyd George except in terms of political virtuosity—of managerial and oratorical power unequalled among his contemporaries. In a period of peace he might well have constructed a really formidable party. As it was, personality made a mark against the grain, *against* the structure of politics. Had there been no European war—the war was initially a distraction to him, as Irish Home Rule was to Joseph Chamberlain—he might well have continued as the main focus for Radicalism in Britain.

It is difficult to interpret him in terms of pressures—Welshness, Agrarianism, Nonconformity, Radicalism, the Newspapers—in the end he controlled all these diffuse forces. There was no reverie and no set purpose either. What he did was to make politics out of his own gifts and to realize himself through events—the Boer War, the Education Act, the People's Budget, the Munitions

---

[1] Beaverbrook, *Decline and fall*, p. 141.

crisis. And within the canons of Churchillian historiography it also may be true that 'when the English history of the first quarter of this century is written, it will be seen that the greater part of our fortunes, in peace and in war, was shaped by this one man'.

Yet he lowered the tone of politics; he would perhaps have been as successful in the deplorable politics of Louisiana as in England. So absorbed was he with getting things done that he might not have noticed the difference. He bewildered, if he did not demoralize, the electorate. Popular journalism aided his rise, wartime journalism made him the necessary man: he was the journalists' politician, enlivening and dramatizing not only domestic but also foreign policy. 'His mind leapt with that of Fleet Street; he dealt with public affairs', said Spender, 'as if he were editing a popular newspaper with its "splash" for every day, its headlines, its pictures.'[1]

Shortly after the fall of the Coalition, Lord Beaverbrook declared that 'Mr Lloyd George, the greatest living force in British politics, has been rendered half-impotent by the disloyalty of his followers in the House of Commons'.[2] The disloyalty presumably lay in the insistence of the Tories, after having made electoral capital out of the name of Lloyd George at the Coupon Election, that they should once more be led by leaders whom they recognized, that the party should come into its own again. Like most of the Liberals, the Tories rejected magnetism. They rejected, too, the tensions which Lloyd George had created in foreign and domestic affairs, his wilfulness, his ultimate irresponsibility. In doing so they may well have inaugurated what C. L. Mowat calls 'the rule of the pygmies'.[3] But in a longer perspective it was perhaps the rule of 'the first class brains' (if we can agree that what Lloyd George, Birkenhead and Churchill had in common was 'brains') which was anomalous.

The 'pygmies' (MacDonald, Baldwin, Neville Chamberlain, Halifax) did not, it is true, reconstruct English politics. Rather they restored its familiar outlines. It is an odd view of English history which sees only either betrayal or incapacity to recognize will and imagination (and 'brains') in this resistance to the bending of an ancient and successful mode of politics in the flame

---

[1] Spender, *The public life*, I, 120–1.
[2] Beaverbrook, *Politicians and the press*, London, 1926, p. 86.
[3] *Britain between the wars*, p. 142.

of either a single genius or two or three geniuses. It would be more appropriate to see character re-asserting itself when the times made stylish swashbuckling dangerous. As it happened, things were never quite the same after Lloyd George. He had worn too large a hole for himself. The aggrandizement of the office of Prime Minister, the subordination of Cabinet and Foreign Secretary—these have been the more easily accepted because of Lloyd George.

There is no final verdict, and the words addressed in 1923, by that heavyweight scholar—and angry Liberal—J. M. Robertson, to the broken Liberal Party are not the last:

To judge of the fitness of any man who claims to lead them they have to take note of his past, his record, his capacity to handle real difficulties, his value in counsel, his hold on principles, as well as his conduct towards those who have worked with him. All these items constitute his public character which is what they are concerned with. To put it all aside on a plea that it will 'pay' to take him is to make politics contemptible, to reduce Liberalism to the plane of the Byzantine Circus.[1]

Lloyd George's electioneering skill, declarations of intent and political 'magic' were no substitutes for political reliability.

'I am glad that idol—the honest but stupid man—is discredited. It takes big intelligence to be honest in politics,' wrote Beatrice Webb in her diaries, 'there is no meaning in an honesty that does not know its mind from one day to another...Honesty *is* security for other people's warranted expectations—that is the test of honest behaviour between man and man.'[2] She was writing about Stanley Baldwin. This is a very early attack but the indictment is one that has stuck: that Baldwin, a Prime Minister concerned primarily with being rather than doing, was neither intelligent nor resolute enough for his times.

A revaluation of Baldwin means a re-assessment of Britain in the inter-war years, years of disappointment and decline, of the failure to cope with unemployment at home and the Rhine frontier abroad, to realize the aspirations of the League, to comprehend the brutalities of continental politics. It was a period when the two most potent politicians in Britain were rejected by the nation. Today, many are convinced that the hard-backed men, Churchill, Lloyd George, Birkenhead, even Beaverbrook, should

---

[1] *Mr Lloyd George and liberalism*, p. 116. [2] *Diaries 1912–1924*, p. 251.

have been in power. Instead, so runs the accepted story, the invertebrate Baldwin presided over an age in which resolution decayed, the facts of power were not faced, and hideous strength grew unchecked.

When war came, Baldwin fell into obloquy from which his reputation is only now slowly recovering. The Press Lords whom he fought and defeated have retained more virtue. And Churchill, who so seldom put a foot right even when he was right, has become the prescient man; Lloyd George, the lost national leader. Compared with Baldwin, Neville Chamberlain at least was a man of action; if he failed it was through excess of zeal, not indolence.

And yet, in 1937, Baldwin retired in all honour. He had been three times Prime Minister and in power, actually or in effect, for half the inter-war period. 'Upon four occasions of first-class importance', says Sir Samuel Hoare, he had proved himself the indispensable man, 'a feat unique in the history of British Prime Ministers.'[1] He had rid the country of Lloyd George; he had settled the General Strike; he had smoothed the way in 1931 for stable government; and had managed the Abdication. In and out of office he had faltered; in 1931 he almost lost the Tory leadership, and in 1935 he barely withstood the fierce attack on the Hoare–Laval Plan, but on each occasion he had been resilient enough to recover.

A catalogue of legislation would tell us very little about Baldwin's achievement. 'Baldwin cared greatly for the *tone* of government, but for particular measures of policy only as they were needed to set and keep up that tone.'[2] It was what he stood for personally that mattered. This was the recognition which he received from other leading politicians. Asquith wrote: 'In regard to yourself, let me say that I have never found, and could never desire, a more straightforward and scrupulously honourable opponent, or one who more completely satisfied my ideal of an English gentleman.'[3] Of the speech on the Macquisten Bill in 1925 on the Trade Union political levy, Haldane said that it 'had lifted public affairs to a higher level and recalled to me things that happened fifty years ago'.[4] For Baldwin's 'great utterance' on

---

[1] Lord Templewood, *Nine troubled years*, London, 1954, p. 32.
[2] Lord Eustace Percy, *Some memories*, London, 1958, p. 127.
[3] G. M. Young, *Stanley Baldwin*, London, 1952, p. 53.   [4] *Ibid.* p. 94.

India in 1929, the dying Balfour expressed his 'intense admiration' of the way in which he had treated 'the greatest of political themes'.[1]

From where did Baldwin get his moral certitude, his barely fallible appeal to the people, to party and to Parliament? The crucial act of his career was his part in the destruction of the Lloyd George Coalition in 1922. Milner had gone, Bonar Law had resigned: control was passing to a triumvirate of political stylists, Lloyd George, Birkenhead and Churchill. Austen Chamberlain, the embodiment of private and public honour, remained as the representative of orthodoxy and manners.

We see Baldwin as an obscure, dissentient minister brooding on adventurism and political degeneracy. Churchill he appreciated but distrusted; Birkenhead he despised. It was the influence of Lloyd George that Baldwin feared, 'the morally disintegrating effect of Lloyd George on all whom he had to deal with'.[2] What made Baldwin wonder 'if English politics would ever be clean again'? It was not merely the traffic in honours, or the odour of Tammany detected by indignant Conservatives, or the intangible 'disreputability' of the régime; the dangers lay in the febrile political excitations, what Lord Eustace Percy called 'all the stridencies and the varied policy-mongering of the years since the Armistice'.[3] Lloyd George, without respect for either political institutions or usages, was an alarming and unpredictable force. His Cabinet were 'trusties' to be moved by the master of the offices to whatever tasks seemed appropriate. Even the civil service, the repository of integrity and experience, was unsafe. He had created his own staff and intermediaries to bend the bureaucracy more easily. It seemed quite possible that he might create a new pattern of power in the Constitution, that by liaison with the Press Lords he might insulate himself and his aides from parliamentary and public pressures. What most alarmed Baldwin was that Lloyd George had broken the Liberal Party and now he and his bravos seemed on the point of destroying the Tories too. Baldwin might be a latitudinarian Tory but he was also, paradoxically, a passionate one, convinced that his party sustained national values that should not be lost.

Yet Baldwin's fellow Coalition ministers stood by Lloyd George

---

[1] G. M. Young, *Stanley Baldwin*, p. 148.   [2] Amery, *My political life*, II, 226.
[3] *op. cit.* pp. 127–8.

and were prepared to fight an election to perpetuate his régime. They had lost faith in alternations of government: Tory and Liberal would now stand together to fight Bolshevism. Everything depended on the support of the Conservative Party machine and the backbenchers and the availability of Bonar Law as an alternative Prime Minister. At the 1922 Carlton Club meeting, the Conservative Party rallied to Baldwin's passionate denunciation of Lloyd George, and the 'Fusion' movement was defeated. The Conservatives would fight the imminent election as an independent party. This was a revolt against personal government. Baldwin did not do it alone. Without Bonar Law he would not have done it at all. But it was he who sensed the rising discontent in the party; he spoke first: 'it was Baldwin's rather than [Bonar Law's] speech that settled the issue of the day'.[1]

From now onwards, Baldwin was privileged to moralize on the intercourse of English politics. The Constitution had not been made by *first-class brains*. It had flourished through the wealth of character available in Parliament. It would live through the reputation of its politicians. His personal contribution was to be the trustworthy man, the politician of character. As such, he may be regarded as the major architect of English politics in the inter-war period.

Baldwin thought that the national interest was endangered by footloose, careerist politicians striking styles to catch fleeting moods. Secondly, he was, like Ernest Bevin, suspicious not only of stylists but also of intellectuals in politics: '"Intelligentsia"', he said, 'bears the same relationship to "intelligence" that "gent" does to "gentleman".' 'What he was afraid of was a government of so-called intellectuals, who pushed over on the working man theories, not of British extraction, but theories that had never worked anywhere by men who had never managed anything so much as a whelk stall, men who would never get into Parliament except on the backs of the Trade Unions.'[2]

Englishmen should not fill their bellies 'with the east wind of German Socialism and Russian Communism and French Syndicalism'. Baldwin was, despite ancestral Celtic links, as G. M. Young has said, an Englishman 'by election'.[3] After his coming to

---

[1] Templewood, *Nine troubled years*, p. 31.
[2] *The Times*, 22 February 1935. Quoted in A. W. Baldwin, *My father, the true story*, London, 1955, p. 163.   [3] *Stanley Baldwin*, London, 1952, p. 56.

power in 1923, 'presently there shaped itself in his mind', wrote L. S. Amery, 'the idea of what a Prime Minister ought to be. It was, to begin with, to be as unlike Lloyd George as possible—plain instead of brilliant; steady instead of restless; soberly truthful instead of romantic and imaginative; English and not Welsh.'[1]

It was Baldwin's self-imposed task to restore to politics something of the *gravitas* that it had had before those whom C. E. Montague called 'the virtuosi of political blatancy' had got to work. 'The bitterness of the country was of the devil; no one in the higher political world seemed to realize it or give it a thought.' Hence Baldwin's conciliatory approach to Labour from 1924 to 1929. MacDonald came more than half-way to meet him and R. Bassett has rightly insisted that the 'almost general acceptance of the methods of parliamentary democracy, and the much wider appreciation of what they in practice involve, owe much to the two outstanding statesmen of the inter-war years'.[2]

Protection was dished at the 1923 Election and after that Baldwin was a Prime Minister without commitment to anything very much except the English way of doing things. His greatest moment came during the Macquisten Bill debate of 1925. The immediate issue was whether or not the system by which the Trade Unionists paid their political levy to the Labour Party should be one in which those who wished to do so should deliberately commit themselves by 'contracting in'; or whether the existing system dating from 1913 which required those who were unwilling to subscribe to the funds of a political party to 'contract out' should continue. Baldwin refused to use his majority to destroy Labour's acquired position. To dissipate the lowering conflict, he evoked from his own recollections of the Baldwin family business a picture of an organic industrial community; temporarily he created a world of harmony for both sides of the House. He went on:

We find ourselves, after these two years in power, in possession of perhaps the greatest majority our party has ever had, and with the general assent of the country. Now how did we get there? It was not by promising to bring this Bill in; it was because, rightly or wrongly, we succeeded in creating an impression throughout the country that we stood for stable Government and for peace in the country between

---

[1] *My political life*, II, 506–7.
[2] *Nineteen thirty one*, London, 1958, p. 19.

all classes of the community...That being so, what should our course be at the beginning of a new Parliament?...I want my Party today to make a gesture to the country...and say to them: 'We have our majority: we believe in the justice of this Bill which has been brought in today, but we are going to withdraw our hand, and we are not going to push our political advantage home at a moment like this.'

His magnanimity unified party and Cabinet and won over the Opposition. David Kirkwood compared him to Lincoln and one Labour member said to him, 'It was true, Prime Minister, every word was true. But those times have gone.'

'At last,' cry the Diehards after the fateful Carlton Club meeting... 'We have found a hero.' 'No hero at all', they say, as later they sit gloomily silent while he ascends the pulpit and talks to them of peace and goodwill when they are hot on the trail of blood—'no hero at all, but little better than a psalm-singing Puritan.'[1]

Twenty-five years later, *The Financial Times* was to say that he was the first revivalist produced by the Tory Party. And, they greatly hoped, the last.[2]

What Baldwin cultivated in the country, in Parliament and in the Cabinet was the sense of the nation; for years he did it more convincingly than anyone else, much more than Churchill. His personality now seems to suffuse the 1920s as Gladstone's had been impressed on the 1870s and 1880s. He deferred to popular feeling but was not dominated by it. He merely did not consider that you could carry a country further than it would go. Yet he often thought 'it was only by the mercy of God that Englishmen, when gaining experience by running their heads into a stone wall, only stunned themselves and did not kill themselves outright'.[3] It is this tactile sense of the people which explains his so-called indolence over rearmament in the 1930s. Effective action could not be taken on any major matter until the mind of the country was made up.

The country liked a contemplative as Prime Minister, one who set his face against action as such—action could be as purposeless as 'the electric trams in Hell'. But some saw his rule as a soporific. Lloyd George was always a threat ('Baldwin knifed me and I shall

[1] Gardiner, *Certain people of importance*, p. 1.
[2] *Financial Times*, 10 November 1952, quoted in Baldwin, *My father, the true story*, p. 168.   [3] *Ibid.* p. 292.

knife him') but a threat which diminished. Churchill, for whom Baldwin was 'an astute and relentless politician', quarrelled violently with him over the future of India and was prepared at all times to make a *pronunciamento*. Yet Churchill held little real threat. His insistence on making his own political divinations had deprived him of support in high politics and he was popularly assessed as a careerist—a man without a steady public purpose. Nearly everything he had touched had turned out badly and, after 1929, Churchill seemed, like Lloyd George, to have a future only as a journalist. By 1935, he was ruefully to admit, Baldwin 'had gathered to himself a greater volume of confidence and goodwill than any other man I recollect in my long public career'.[1]

The Press Lords, Beaverbrook and Rothermere, were more persistent assailants. Baldwin disliked the popular press, its brisk daily excitations, its irresponsibility. 'You are bombarded today', he told the Junior Imperial League in March 1935, 'by a series of utterly disconnected impressions; unless you can put yourself outside the events of the day, you will lose your perspective, and find yourself unable to maintain that careful, steady, balanced judgment which is essential in politics.' A man had to stand still within ancestral grooves to make any sense of the world. It was from Beaverbrook and Rothermere that the main challenge to Baldwin's hold over the nation and party came, particularly after 1929, when the Conservative Party became restive under his quietism and began to look for a programme. Today, the pretensions of the Press magnates have been largely forgotten, but in the First World War Northcliffe had, through his newspapers, engineered changes of policy and even of the personnel of government. After the war, Rothermere and Beaverbrook had tried once more, as 'trustees of public opinion', to mould governmental policy, even to make governments. Had not the *Daily Express*, Beaverbrook insisted, supported the victorious Lloyd George in 1918, the victorious Bonar Law in 1922, opposed the premature Baldwin dissolution in 1923, backed the successful Baldwin in 1924?[2]

From the mid 1920s both the great newspaper proprietors pushed a policy of Empire Free Trade by special crusading campaigns, by running independent Conservative candidates against official ones. From 1929 they made a dead set at Baldwin

---

[1] Baldwin, *My father, the true story*, p. 166.
[2] Beaverbrook, *Politicians and the press*, p. 55.

either to persuade him or to bring him down. At Caxton Hall in
June 1930, Baldwin accused the Press Lords of moving out of
their province of journalism 'to dictate, to domineer, to black-
mail', comparing their challenge to that of the T.U.C. in 1926:

We are told that unless we make peace with these noblemen, candidates
are to be run all over the country. The Lloyd George candidates at the
last election smelt; these will stink...Here is a letter from Lord
Rothermere which I have permission to read ... 'I cannot make it too
abundantly clear that, under no circumstances whatsoever, will
I support Mr Baldwin unless I know exactly what his policy is going to
be, unless I have complete guarantees that such policy will be carried
out if his Party achieves office and unless I am acquainted with the
names of at least eight, or ten, of his most prominent colleagues in the
next Ministry'...Now those are the terms that your leader would have
to accept, and when sent for by the King he would have to say: 'Sire,
these names are not necessarily my choice, but they have the support
of Lord Rothermere.' A more preposterous and insolent demand was
never made on the leader of any political party. I repudiate it with
contempt, and will resist that attempt at domination to the end.

His audience of Conservative M.P.s and prospective candidates
acknowledged his victory. He seemed to have won the battle that
Asquith had lost. Yet in February 1931 the Chief Agent of his own
party, under pressure from malcontents, asked him to reconsider
his position as leader in the interests of the party. He was not only
challenged on Protection but also on his support for Labour's
liberal attitude to Indian self-government. The press continued to
attack him. But he still had words 'to put the matter to the touch'
in the Commons and on the platform. At the St George's, Westminster, by-election, where the initial Conservative candidate had
withdrawn because of lack of faith in Baldwin, and where the
Press Lords were sponsoring an Independent candidate, he went
down to support Duff Cooper and delivered the final blow to the
hostile newspapers:

What are their methods? Their methods are direct falsehood and mis-
representation, half-truths, the alteration of the speaker's meaning by
publishing a sentence apart from the context...These words appeared
in *The Daily Mail* of yesterday week: 'These expressions come ill from
Mr Baldwin, since his father left an immense fortune which, so far as
may be learned from his own speeches, has almost disappeared. It is
difficult to see how the leader of a party who has lost his own fortune

can hope to restore that of anyone else, or of his country'... The first part of that statement is a lie, and the second part of that statement by its implication is untrue. The paragraph itself could only have been written by a cad. I have consulted a very high legal authority, and I am advised that an action for libel would lie. I shall not move in the matter, and for this reason: I should get an apology and heavy damages. The first is of no value, and the second I would not touch with a barge-pole. What the proprietorship of these papers is aiming at is power, and power without responsibility, the prerogative of the harlot throughout the ages.

If words delivered at the right time are deeds, Baldwin exhibited again his capacity for political action. Yet, if from now onwards he seemed to be unassailable, he was in the long run to fall into the hands of all his detractors, so that, as his son has remarked, 'what in Baldwin was once wise is now at best shrewd, and at worst cunning..., what was patient and statesmanlike is now indolent..., what was honest is now shifty or, more pityingly, self-deceptive'.[1]

What brought about this transvaluation? Primarily lack of prescience. He failed to recognize the unappeasable appetite of Nazi Germany. The accusation extends to lack of insight into the needs of his time and to inertia as a national leader. Charge after charge in concatenation insists that Baldwin followed and did not lead public opinion; that he took little interest in foreign affairs; that it was a dereliction of duty to assume, as he did, that the people themselves must resolve to play a great part in the world.

He has been charged with specific errors and omissions: in assessing the growth of German air-power; in failing to challenge the Nazis when they broke the Treaty of Versailles to enter the Rhineland; in failing, after winning an election in 1935 on a mandate to support the League of Nations, to make a real stand against Mussolini's invasion of Abyssinia and merely going through the motion of imposing sanctions; in not executing the policy of rearmament rapidly enough and in not creating a really effective Ministry of Defence; and, gravest of all, in neglecting to make his country aware of its predicament or, more crudely, in hiding the truth in a matter of national security in order to win a general election. And in each case the ingenuousness which was his virtue has served to reveal his backsliding all the more clearly.

[1] Baldwin, *My father, the true story*, p. 14.

Many of these charges are the products of hindsight; all become part of the polemics of Munich. Of Baldwin's lack of interest in foreign affairs it may be said that this has sometimes been claimed as a merit in other Prime Ministers. It also surely means that if Baldwin was wrong, so too were his Foreign Secretaries.[1] Some of the keenest intelligences of the time saw that it might be disastrous if Britain were involved in conflict in the East and in Europe at the same time. John Strachey, no admirer of the National government, considered that cautious inaction was the appropriate policy for Britain in the 1930s and saw Baldwin as 'the one man of to-day who in the perspective of history, will be found to have attained the stature of a statesman of the heyday of British capitalism'.[2] Baldwin knew that the limits of profitable action in Britain were 'becoming narrower and narrower'[3] and that, at all costs, she must keep out of war.

The currents of opinion in his own party, in the opposition parties and in the country all ran strongly against a dangerous foreign policy. Everywhere there was a growing recognition of the inequity of the Versailles Treaty, of the necessity of admitting Germany to parity with the other European nations. It is often forgotten, too, that British governments had all taken their commitment to the League seriously, particularly to Article 8 of the Covenant, which obliged them to reduce 'national armaments to the lowest point consistent with national safety and the enforcement by common action of international obligations'. There had been a widespread reception both at large and by those who had studied the origins of the First World War of the moral pointed in Grey's *Twenty-five years*: that 'great armaments lead inevitably to war'. It was now a doctrine, accepted as a fact, that all cries for increased defence expenditure were promoted by armament manufacturers and warmongers.

Weak though it was, the Labour Party was the alternative government. Until 1935 it was led by Lansbury, who had said, 'I would close every recruiting station, disband the Army and dismiss the Air Force. I would abolish the whole dreadful equipment of war and say to the world "Do your worst".' The words were addressed to the voters of East Fulham in October 1933.

[1] D. C. Somervell, *Stanley Baldwin*, London, 1953, p. 36.
[2] *The coming struggle for power*, London, 1932, p. 276.
[3] *Ibid.* p. 282.

The by-election there had seemed[1] a famous pacifist victory; the Labour candidate, denouncing all rearmament, had converted a Conservative majority of over 14,000 into a minority of nearly 5,000. Lansbury's successor, Attlee, had said, as late as July 1935, that his party was sick to death of all this talk of armament. A year before, on the increased Air Ministry estimates, Attlee had stated that his party 'had absolutely abandoned any idea of nationalist loyalty'.

Point by point Baldwin can be defended. When he said on 28 November 1934 that the German air force had not achieved parity with the British, it seems that he was right and Churchill was wrong.[2] The failure to act in 1936 when Germany, in defiance of Versailles, occupied the Rhineland, may well have been crucial. But Britain was not prepared to fight 'to keep Germany out of her own backyard' at the time, even if, as Churchill maintains, such a military operation was practicable. Nor was France. Invoking the principle of collective security to aid Abyssinia meant fighting Italy without French help—single-handed action in fact. And single-handed action in the Mediterranean against another imperial power in such a familiar setting would soon have taken on the colour of an old-style imperialist war.

Baldwin was sensitive to opposition and public opinion in a way that Churchill was not. He knew that the government might not carry the 1935 election if 'great armaments' were in the programme. Yet, even if he promised 'no huge forces', the election was in fact fought and won on rearmament. And there is no real reason to believe that if substantial rearmament had been embarked on earlier, the second German war would not have occurred. There is no assurance that if Churchill had been in power things would have been much better. And even if Germany had been checked would that check have been other than momentary? As for the failure to appoint a really powerful Minister of Defence— was this so very lax in face of Service opposition and four major reports? Twenty years later, there was, in peacetime, still no effective Minister of Defence.

But what of the 'appalling frankness' speech on 12 November 1936? Churchill had accused the government of not making up

---

[1] It is likely that housing and unemployment were more important issues. See Taylor, *English history 1914–1945*, p. 367.
[2] *Ibid.* p. 387.

their minds on air strength. 'So they go on,' he had said, 'in strange paradox, decided only to be undecided, resolved to be irresolute, adamant for drift, solid for fluidity, all-powerful to be impotent. So we go on preparing more months and years—precious, perhaps vital, to the greatness of Britain—for the locusts to eat.'

Baldwin replied:

I would remind the House that not once but on many occasions in speeches and in various places, when I have been speaking and advocating as far as I am able the democratic principle, I have stated that a democracy is always two years behind the dictator. I believe that to be true. It has been true in this case. I put before the whole House my own views with an appalling frankness. From 1933, I and my friends were all very worried about what was happening in Europe. You will remember at that time that the Disarmament Conference was sitting in Geneva. You will remember that at that time there was probably a stronger pacifist feeling running through the country than in any period since the War. I am speaking of 1933 and 1934. You will remember the election at Fulham in the autumn of 1933, when a seat which the National Government held was lost by about 7,000 votes on no issue but the pacifist... My position as the leader of a great party was not altogether a comfortable one. I asked myself what chance was there—when that feeling given expression to in Fulham was common throughout the country—what chance was there within the next year or two of that feeling being so changed that the country would give a mandate for rearmament. Supposing I had gone to the country and said that Germany was rearming and that we must rearm, does anyone think that this pacific democracy would have rallied to that cry at that moment? I cannot think of anything that would have made the loss of the election from my point of view more certain.

According to Churchill this statement 'carried naked truth about his motives into indecency. That a Prime Minister should avow that he had not done his duty in regard to national safety because he was afraid of losing the election was an incident without parallel in our Parliamentary history.'[1] G. M. Young says too that 'an opponent—even a friend—might say that Baldwin had confessed to concealing the truth in order to win an election'.[2] Indeed the passage has already passed into the textbooks as an example of failure in political leadership.

[1] *The Second World War*, London, 1948, I, 169.
[2] *Stanley Baldwin*, p. 230.

He knew [writes C. S. Emden] that the people were ignorant of the facts; and if he had had the courage and inspiration of a genuine political leader, he would have disclosed the whole situation to them and called on them to support him in the policy which he realized was the right one and the urgent one for the country's safety.[1]

These are interpretations which the words as they stand can just bear: this is the penalty of 'appalling frankness'. But in fact the situation was hypothetical. Baldwin was not—this is clear from the context—referring to the 1935 election but to one that might have taken place a little time after East Fulham. What he meant was that if, at that time (1933 or 1934), rearmament had become the central election issue, the National government would certainly have lost the election. Baldwin was, in fact, impressing on the House the truth that a democracy must be taught by events, must learn from experience. This was something he knew from his own premature appeal to the people on Protection in 1923. The point was underlined when he went on to say that 'the country itself learned by certain events that took place during the winter of 1934/35 what the perils might be to it. All I did was to take a moment perhaps less unfortunate than another might have been, and we won the Election with a large majority; but frankly I could conceive that we should at that time, by advocating certain courses, have been a great deal less successful. We got from the country—with a large majority—a mandate for doing a thing that no one, 12 months before, would have believed possible.'

Baldwin was not prepared, as Churchill was, to rearm without popular authorization and considered that such authorization was not obtainable in 1933 or 1934. This was his open acknowledgment of the 'two years' lag of democracies to dictatorships. It is not true that Baldwin failed to warn the country of the Nazi menace merely because he wished to retain power. With remarkable ingenuousness, he was merely reflecting in public on dangers safely passed.

'Supposing I had gone to the country and said...' The failure was a failure of language: it was an unnecessary foray into the hypothetical and did untold harm. It discredited Baldwin. Yet the very discrediting showed that the political tradition, seemingly so mild, had its own rigours, and that speech could still be momentous. Baldwin was the kind of politician the English liked and

---

[1] *The people and the constitution*, Oxford, 1956, p. 233.

trusted. His lack of prescience might have been forgiven him. For Hitler was outside the British political experience—a prodigy even in Europe.[1] Even Baldwin's faltering judgments in his last administration might not have counted too much against him. What really unravelled his reputation all the way back and cast doubt on the 'character' that had contended so effectively with the first-class brains and the political stylists of the 1920s, what to-day still obscures his achievement in restoring the familiar outlines of English politics in the post-war period, is those few careless words in an unnecessary public rumination—words which in fact proved his prudence but which seemed and were made to prove the honest politician dishonest, capable of sacrificing the interests of his country to the electoral prospects of his party.[2] Yet, paradoxically, only the most transparent of politicians could have exposed himself to such a danger in such a way.

---

[1] Perhaps the best comment on the *incredibility* of Hitler is that of Lord Eustace Percy: 'It is the weakness of Mr Darcy that he can only despise a cad and laugh at an adventurer, that he has no eye for the exceptional and no sense of the uncanny.' *Some memories*, p. 187.

[2] 'The confusion resulting from these efforts to press a false charge against Baldwin instead of presenting a reasoned case against him' is very ably sifted by R. Bassett, 'Telling the truth to the people: the myth of the Baldwin "Confession"', *The Cambridge Journal*, November 1948, pp. 84–95.

8

LABOUR'S LOST LEADERS

'We were', wrote J. R. Clynes of the early Socialists, 'out with a spiritual appeal, as well as to win material concessions. We urged that men did not live by bread alone. We wanted more than wages. We demanded a share for all in freedom and beauty, and a system of life that should be organized and not left to the accidents of birth and environment.'[1] Henry Snell, too, has recorded how

men who had grown old in years had their youthful enthusiasms renewed under the glow and warmth of a new spiritual fellowship. They were born again: they joyfully walked many miles to listen to a favourite speaker; they sang Labour hymns; and they gave to the new social faith an intensity of devotion which lifted it far above the older political organizations of the day.[2]

In the Labour churches of Lancashire and Yorkshire the texts were from Carlyle, Ruskin, Morris, Whitman and Bellamy: the preachers were Ben Tillett, Tom Mann (who might have taken Anglican orders), Robert Blatchford and Philip Wicksteed. Keir Hardie grew up in a freethinking household but it was through the Good Templars and the Evangelical Union that he came to political journalism and labour organization. Philip Snowden, after Hardie probably the most effective Socialist platform propagandist in the Edwardian period, had the appeal of a 'Come to Jesus' revivalist.

Men came out of a long silence to witness to their regeneration, their new sense of communion. Thus, wrote Snowden, 'men who had never before attempted public speaking were given courage and the gift of effective oratory by the new passion for social justice which consumed them'.[3] In London, William Morris was not, in tone, so very remote from the secular preachers of the West Riding: 'Forsooth, brothers, fellowship is heaven, and lack

---

[1] J. R. Clynes, *Memoirs*, London, 1937, I, 103.
[2] Lord Snell, *Men, movements and myself*, London, 1936, p. 147.
[3] P. Snowden, *An autobiography*, London, 1934, I, 71.

of fellowship is hell: fellowship is life, and lack of fellowship is death: and the deeds that ye do upon the earth, it is for fellowship's sake that ye do them...' Then there was the life-affirming, essentially undenominational journalism of Robert Blatchford and his colleagues on *The Clarion*, often excessively laced with literary 'gusto', yet persuasive enough to create the open-air fraternities of the Fellowship, the Glee and Cycling Clubs. Even the Fabian Society, the source of so much 'wizened rationalism' in the drawing-rooms, which looked upon these ardours merely as part of the necessary business of 'stoking up', had stemmed originally from the Owenite New Life movement, which had sought among other things 'the cultivation of a perfect character in each and all'.[1]

At his best the Labour leader embodied what A. D. Lindsay was later to call 'the wisdom of the plain man':

The democratic leader turns up. He is recognized by his fellows and carries them with him. He has the power of calling out the best in ordinary people. Because he shares the life and experience of ordinary men and women he knows, almost unconsciously, 'where the shoe pinches' and 'what people are prepared to do'...Knowledge of the common life and its possibilities; understanding of the things which produce in it bitterness and thwart men's activities are the wisdom most wanted for politics. The state will be wisely directed if the final control is in the hands of 'ordinary' men...[2]

Hyndman, Burns and Henry Hyde Champion seem, in contrast, to draw on postures in the European insurrectionary tradition. Their Social Democratic Federation was for 'Bullet, Bomb or Ballot Box'; there were vague hopes of an 1889 Revolution to celebrate the French centenary, and Champion prepared men to fight for a Commune of London. It was Champion who declared that 'if the propertied class had one throat I should cut it'. John Burns may or may not have said, 'We must have bread and they must have lead,' yet there was a striving for violence in his early postures. Even Clynes, in a fleeting romantic mood, was capable of seeing future parliamentary Labour leaders 'emerging from the smoke of the muskets that the troops fired over the heads of insurgent mobs'.[3]

---

[1] E. R. Pease, *History of the Fabian Society*, London, 1916, p. 32.
[2] *The modern democratic state*, London, 1943, p. 279.
[3] Clynes, *Memoirs*, 1, 54.

Yet the political models remained mainly native. Like Tom Mann, the young Snell looked to Bradlaugh.

I had an unclouded belief in his sincerity and capacity, and in his absolute devotion to the truth... Taking him all in all—as man, orator, as leader of unpopular causes, and as an incorruptible public figure, he was the most imposing human being that I have ever known and I do not expect to look upon his like again. His energy upon the platform was cyclonic... There was nothing quite like it during that generation.[1]

Hyndman pilfered Marx to write *England for All*, but he also, said Eleanor Marx,[2] set Englishmen against foreigners, and detested Engels. Shaw saw Hyndman as one of the

freethinking English gentlemen-republicans of the last half of the nineteenth century: with Dilke, Burton Auberon Herbert, Wilfred Scawen Blunt, Laurence Oliphant: great globe-trotters, writers, *frondeurs*, brilliant and accomplished cosmopolitans so far as their various abilities permitted, all more interested in the world than in themselves, and in themselves than in official decorations; consequently unpurchasable...[3]

Hyndman appreciated Disraeli and, in some ways, remained a Tory to the end. Snowden thought that the gentlemanly John Redmond fitted more nearly to 'one's idea of a leader and orator than any other man of his time in the House of Commons',[4] and considered Henry Chaplin ponderous but 'ever courteous to his opponent' and 'the ideal type of an English country squire, both in appearance and manners... '[5] In the same way Snell found Lord Henry Bentinck, a Tory of the old school who opposed him at a South Nottingham election, 'as fine a gentleman as ever lived...' On some, the deepest impress was still that of Gladstone. 'The influence of Gladstone among trade unionists was unprecedented and apparently unassailable: what he wanted they too wanted; what he hated they despised. He was the creator, inspirer and chief bulwark of... Liberal–Labourism... '[6]

It might be considered that a party of movement would be more likely than a party of order to produce politicians of architectonic power, that its enthusiasm and purpose would keep the leaders up as symbols of, and makers of, change in a way that the older

---

[1] Snell, *Men, movements and myself*, p. 31.
[2] C. Tsuzuki, *H. M. Hyndman and British socialism*, Oxford, 1961, p. 61.
[3] Quoted in Henry Pelling, *Origins of the Labour Party 1880–1900*, London, 1954, p. 21.
[4] Snowden, *Autobiography*, 1, 133.   [5] *Ibid.* p. 309.   [6] Snell *op. cit.* p. 139.

parties could not. And yet no party has been more disappointed in its leading politicians than Labour, and this in spite of the initial cloth-cap fidelity of Keir Hardie. From the beginning Labour has feared the lost leader, the man of charm, eloquence and promise who attains the political élite and is corrupted. 'Some amongst us have turned traitor. Some have been bought with position, others have betrayed their trust for money.'[1]

'The day of the cottage-bred man has at last dawned,' declared Lloyd George. And it would in fact be the men from the one-roomed and two-roomed cottages of Newarthill, Ickornshaw and Lossiemouth who would provide the fund of style and character for the Labour movement. These were the strenuous autodidacts who lived laborious days on oatmeal and hot water, on Ruskin and Henry George, rose from obscurity to marvel at their own fortunes.

An engine-driver rose to the rank of Colonial Secretary, a starveling clerk became Great Britain's Premier, a foundry-hand was changed to Foreign Secretary, the son of a Keighley weaver was created Chancellor of the Exchequer, one miner became Secretary for War and another Secretary of State for Scotland, while I, the mill boy, reached the position of Lord Privy Seal, so that I might lead the House of Commons, and, later, became Home Secretary.[2]

These were achievements of individual energy. Yet, 'the finest individuals are nothing till mastered by a cause'.[3] To cause and man the main danger was parliamentary 'collusion', particularly in the years before the First World War, when Labour had a strategic position in Parliament and entered the calculations of the older parties. It was because Keir Hardie was considered resistant to political bargaining, 'because of his rare courage in loneliness, and his incorruptible will',[4] that he was revered. Hardie, wrote A. G. Gardiner,

glowers at life from beneath his mournful eyebrows...He is the only man who could have created the Labour Party...But he is almost the only man in the party who is not fitted to lead it. It is plain common-sense men like Mr Shackleton and Mr Henderson, and astute politicians like Mr Ramsay MacDonald, who have made it a political instrument.[5]

[1] Clynes, *Memoirs*, I, 17.
[2] *Ibid.*
[3] R. H. Tawney, *The attack and other papers*, London, 1953, pp. 57–8.
[4] Snell, *op. cit.* p. 149.
[5] *Prophets, priests and kings*, pp. 214 and 218–19.

When Hardie resigned the chair of the Parliamentary Labour Party in 1907 in order to speak out, it was not to Parliament but to the people. 'His opportunist and even sentimental socialism,' wrote G. D. H. Cole, 'exactly suited the mood of the more advanced group of workers....'[1] Yet as a parliamentarian he was a failure; he would not be assimilated.

Snowden, too, in the early days—although he would become a great parliamentary performer—made no friends in the Commons and developed a hard uncompromising style, concentrating rigorously on drink and national finance. But the parliamentary sketch-writers probably made too much of Socialist intransigence; both Hardie and Snowden were well aware that the pre-1914 Parliamentary Labour Party operated as little more than a pressure group on the Liberals. MacDonald differed mainly in his being more at home in Parliament ('a born parliamentarian', said Balfour) and in his open admission of affinities with the Liberals and open advocacy of co-operation with them.

Less compromising, for example, was Robert Smillie, a designer of the industrial Triple Alliance, who made forceful politics out of the discontents of the miners. He found difficulty in getting into Parliament and was never in danger of diluting his simple socialist faith. How he resisted the social embrace is told in his autobiography *My life for Labour*. During the miners' strike of 1912 when he was vice-chairman of the Miners Federation, Margot Asquith sought him out to urge him to use his influence for industrial peace. She wrote: 'But keep your blood warm. Don't let it get cold. Use your great power for an honourable settlement. Destruction is a sad exchange for construction. Help my husband. He is a self-made man like yourself...You have great power. See that you use it for good.'[2] Smillie refused to meet her; he was incorruptible.

The cherished were those who rose from obscurity and remained faithful: those who were obtuse, would not compromise, and sulked in their own honesty. 'New Models,' as Tawney was to write, 'are not made by being all things to all men.'[3] Parliamentary experience was suspect because it drew men into the gentleman class. The silk hat and frock coat which Thomas Burt the Liberal—

---

[1] *DNB*.
[2] R. Smillie, *My life, for Labour*, London, 1924, pp. 223-4.
[3] Tawney, *op. cit.* p. 62.

Labour miner M.P. wore for over forty years were symbols of capitulation to the class structure. For those who wished to retain grassroots support, social recalcitrance became an acceptable style. Among these was Victor Grayson, the engineering apprentice, diverted from the Unitarian ministry by revivalist street-corner Socialism, who won the Colne Valley by-election in 1907 after some remarkable mob oratory. In Parliament he would not join the Parliamentary Labour Party or give attention to parliamentary business; refused to speak on the same platform as Keir Hardie; with rank-and-file support, defied the council of the Independent Labour Party. In the end he was beaten but Blatchford's biographer writes that years later you had only to mention his name in the North to see old faces light up.[1] Tom Mann, the itinerant agitator, was another who remained incorruptible, but he had passed from Parliamentarianism to Syndicalism and was to find his place finally in the Communist Party.

'How can followers be Ironsides,' asked Tawney, after the débâcle of 1931, 'if leaders are flunkies.'[2] But distaste for the symbols and gratifications of social ascent was not all. What distinguished the Labour Party fundamentalists in the British political tradition was their reluctance to acknowledge the prerogative necessarily vested in parliamentary leaders. The political leader was thought of as a delegate. Blatchford opposed 'the idea that the Parliaments or committees are elected to "rule", or "govern" or "command" the people'.[3] He had little room for the organization and leadership which the Independent Labour Party and the Trade Unions were seeking to provide. The people 'want champions, and they want servants. They want men to fight their battles in Parliament. But they don't want Parliamentary "leaders".' Professional leaders were false, even Gladstone, 'a splendid fellow—but splendid fellows made splendid blunders unless they were watched'.[4]

Fred Jowett wanted leaders to carry out agreed policies and remain all the time in closest contact with the rank and file. 'I believe', he said, 'that the Party which sets itself to establish the authority of elected representatives of the people against the successive Juntas of which Cabinets are composed will do a great

[1] Laurence Thompson, *Robert Blatchford*, London, 1951, p. 202.
[2] Tawney, *op. cit.* p. 67.
[3] Thompson, *Blatchford*, p. 135.   [4] *Ibid.* p. 54.

service to the country and increase the respect of the public for
Parliamentary government.'[1] The ascendancy of leaders was not
for him. Nor for Emanuel Shinwell when, in 1920, he declared
that the Parliamentary Party was the property of the Labour
movement. Nor for Mrs P. Popplewell, a delegate from Nottingham Central to the Scarborough Conference of 1960, who declared,
'There will be those who say we are seeking to tie our Parliamentary members hand and foot. Yes, that is exactly what we do
want.'[2] What this implied was repudiation of government by discussion or mediation at the top, the process by which 'the ideas
of the majority are widened to include some of the ideas of the
minority which have established their truth in the give and take of
debate'.[3] England has always been generous to politicians,
trusting them to interpret and act in situations to which they alone
can give attention.

On the platform, at the street corners, in the Labour churches,
in the bright hopeful journalism, the gap between words and
action necessarily widened. Whether sentimental or militant, the
early leaders had circulated words which meant revolution. Tom
Mann knew that when he abandoned parliamentarianism for direct
action. The truth was that Labour had to be corrupted if the
civilities of the Constitution were to be maintained. The Socialism
of William Morris, Robert Smillie, or James Maxton has never
been compatible with parliamentarianism. With the possible
exception of Lansbury, all Labour's leaders since Hardie have
known that. 'Stoking up' and leadership were two different
things.

Labour's propagandists continued to see the smoke of battle.
After 1931, Tawney saw two things:

The first is that, if a Labour Government, when it gets the opportunity,
proceeds to act on it, it will encounter at once determined resistance. The
second is that it will not overcome that resistance, unless it has explained its aims with complete openness and candour. It cannot avoid
the struggle, except by compromising its principles; it must, therefore,
prepare for it. In order to prepare for it, it must create in advance
a temper and mentality of a kind to carry it through, not one crisis,
but a series of crises, to which the Zinovieff letter and the Press cam-

---

[1] Fenner Brockway, *Socialism over sixty years*, London, 1946, p. 104.
[2] *The Times*, 5 October 1960.
[3] Ernest Barker, *Reflections on government*, Oxford, 1942, p. 67.

paign of 1931 will prove, it is to be expected, to have been mere skirmishes of outposts. Onions can be eaten leaf by leaf, but you cannot skin a live tiger paw by paw; vivisection is its trade, and it does the skinning first.[1]

Inter-war Labour governments were not like that. They wished to prove that they were 'fit to govern'; they wanted, in all humility, to assimilate to the political tradition. Of the Labour Party on the eve of office in 1923, Snowden later wrote that it was 'composed in the majority of new and undisciplined members who would expect the Labour government to do all sorts of impossible things'.[2] There were those who urged a demonstration and the introduction of 'bold socialist measures, knowing, of course, that we should be defeated upon them. Then we could go to the country with this illustration of what we would do if we had a socialist majority.'[3] These courses were rejected by the Big Five, MacDonald, Clynes, Snowden, Henderson and Thomas. MacDonald and his Cabinets worked the system as they knew it. In the second ministry they held their ground 'while the masses were grumbling, business-men despairing, intellectuals ranting'.[4] Schumpeter thought that it was probably 'one of the best performances in the history of democratic politics'.

Moreover, since Labour politicians were, compared with Liberals and Conservatives, inexperienced in office, they had to be sedulous. 'All the time', wrote Clynes, 'I found the permanent officials extraordinarily helpful and kind. They were always beside me, advising, coaching and checking...'[5] Ministers became absorbed in administration, became concerned more with understanding than controlling or directing: they could not keep their minds open. They were not fully involved in the work of the plural executive; could not make a collective impact on policy. Too often 'they threw themselves into the role of *The Obsequious Apprentice or Prudence Rewarded*, as though bent on proving that, so far from being different from other governments, His Majesty's Labour Government could rival the most respectable of them in cautious conventionality'.[6]

Consider John Burns, never a member of the Labour Party, but

[1] Tawney, *op. cit.* pp. 62–3.
[2] Snowden, *Autobiography*, II, 595.   [3] *Ibid.*
[4] Schumpeter, *Capitalism, socialism and democracy*, p. 368.
[5] Clynes, *Memoirs*, II, 45.
[6] Tawney, *op. cit.* p. 53.

the first of Labour's lost leaders, a biographical homily. Here is the stylist, one of Joyce Cary's spellbinders 'who, in preaching, creating, move the crowd; those who take their part among all artists in renewing life and the passion of life to peoples always growing bored or stale in their own achievement'.[1] There is the squat robustness, the handsome head, the astonishing fluency and the voice which, said Tom Mann, downwind, could reach 20,000 people. In the thick of the great agitations, the smashing of Pall Mall windows and of Bloody Sunday in 1887, in the great Dock strike, he vindicated his class by heroic energy conspicuously displayed, was unmistakably identified as the 'Man with the Red Flag' or the 'Man in the White Straw Hat'. He had read his Marx but also his Carlyle and Ruskin. He had taken as one model Voltaire's *Charles XII*.

For Burns and the Scottish aristocrat, Cunninghame Graham, who marched breast forward to be arrested, Bloody Sunday was a triumph. Burns was a Chestertonian figure in the Chestertonian scene described by J. W. Mackail:

No one who saw it will ever forget the strange and indeed terrible sight of that grey winter day, the vast sombre-coloured crowd, the brief but fierce struggle at the corner of the Strand, and the river of steel and scarlet that moved slowly through the dusky swaying masses, when two squadrons of the Life Guards were summoned up from Whitehall.[2]

Yet it was in the Dock strike of 1889 that Burns achieved unrivalled authority, both as orator and organizer. It was one of the few industrial struggles that have ended in a mood of moral elevation. The glow was on him and his words on Tower Hill were felicitous:

'This, lads, is the Lucknow of Labour, and I myself looking to the horizon, can see a silver gleam—not of bayonets to be imbued with a brother's blood, but the gleam of the full round orb of the docker's tanner.'

Mothers brought their children to him, the blessed man, the English Garibaldi, that he might lay his hands upon them. Understandably it was prophesied that he would be 'the salt of the

[1] *A fearful joy*, preface to Carfax edition, 1952.
[2] *The life of William Morris*, London, 1901, II, 191, quoted by William Kent, *John Burns*, London, 1950, p. 29.

Labour's lost leaders 187

Labour Party'—despite the provincial bias of the movement against his London base. He seemed to be one of Blatchford's self-denying 'champions'. For Burns had protested, 'I have not the slightest desire for office. It is for me to give hostages to disinterestedness...Office! I am prouder of my present office—Judge Advocate of the poor—than I should be of the premiership itself.'[1]

Yet pride, individualism, jealousy of the other working-class leaders, took him away from Labour. He lacked persistent class consciousness, became 'tired of working class boots, working class trains, working class houses, and working class margarine'. He continued to think of himself as the righter of wrongs, the Lion's Mouth of the Venetian Republic, the Tribune of Battersea and much more, but he was never mastered by a cause and the Labour movement grew up without him, indeed despite him. Hardie reproached him: 'With your magnificent voice, your rich imagination and attractive personality, you could rouse and lead your fellows as no other man in public life could, and had you followed this course you might at this moment have been the greatest political force in England.' He had 'neither relation nor fellowship' with the movement.[2]

Ambitious, isolated, but of symbolic value, he allowed himself to be captured by the Liberal administration of 1906—'the crowning act and the reward', said the Battersea branch of the Social Democratic Federation, 'of a whole series of betrayals of the class to which he once belonged...'.[3] He developed 'into the most reactionary President of the Local Government Board in our history',[4] one who told his own Battersea constituency that poor relief could be 'illusory and extravagant', might 'sterilize men's self-reliance and destroy their capacity to make strong men and citizens'.

'John Burns did a great deal for the workers and the workers did much for John.' To his audience he was, like Lloyd George, an entertainer as well as a hero, although of a more athletic kind. He embodied a sporting and Puritan ethic (no gambling, no drinking) which was widely admired. In 1893 Beatrice Webb had

[1] Kent, *op. cit.* p. 53.   [2] *Ibid.* p. 125.
[3] *Ibid.* p. 158.
[4] Joseph Burgess, author of *The rise and progress of a Right Honorable*, London, 1911, quoted in Kent, *op. cit.* p. 173.

seen him as 'a born ruler of barbarians, impressing his followers with will and determination, not guiding them by reason'. She thought it 'pitiful to see this splendid man a prey to egotism of the most sordid kind...'.[1]

Burns remained magniloquent but he relinquished the style of an agitator without regret. By 1907, Beatrice Webb's former 'untrained enthusiast' had become 'a non-responsible being'. 'He talks incessantly and never listens to anyone except the officials to whom he *must* listen in order to accomplish the routine work of his office.'[2] He was by no means versatile, writes his biographer, 'his one acquirement was talking';[3] he ended as a raconteur of the National Liberal Club. But in fact he liked work in hand and his own evolution from agitator to administrator, which he had foreseen, was not unhappy.[4] From his first entry into Parliament he had believed in co-operating with the Liberals to achieve practical social reforms.

It is possible that the vanity of a politician may keep him out of office, preserve his integrity. Of Burns, Bruce Glasier said in 1903 that 'his vanity has quite eaten his moral energy up'.[5] He continued: 'He will wake up some of these days and discover he is a man of the past.' If Burns did discover this, there is little evidence during his thirty years' retirement from national politics (he resigned from the Liberal government at the outbreak of war in 1914) that it disturbed him.

In Burns, the Labour Party lost a potential leader but there was also a sense in which he brought credit upon his constituents by rising to a place within the political élite. The renegings of Thomas, Snowden and MacDonald were different: they threw a whole party into disarray. For the Labour leading politician was a man who spoke for the movement, held its disparate elements, Socialist and Trade Unionist, together. He was given no authority to treat with the enemy even though, from the very beginning, he had had to come to terms with Liberal ministries, to count on Liberal and even Conservative forbearance. What 1931 revealed was that instructions and solemn engagements mattered less than the exigencies of the political situation, that leaders, loved and

[1] *Our partnership*, pp. 39-40.
[2] *Ibid.* p. 393.   [3] Kent, *op. cit.* p. 360.
[4] Obituary notice in *The Times*, 25 January 1943.
[5] Quoted in Philip P. Poirier, *The advent of the Labour Party*, London, 1958, p. 218.

trusted by the rank and file and accorded necessary ascendancy, might have wider loyalties than those of the party.

MacDonald's 'treachery' was the most important but both Thomas and Snowden had considerable status in the party. In spite of his obvious enjoyment of cigars, champagne in silver tankards, his odd addiction (in a Labour leader) to horse-racing and Stock Exchange speculation, Thomas had very deep roots among the working class. They too enjoyed his social rise. As G. K. Chesterton had once written: 'Working men are not at all like Mr Keir Hardie. If it comes to likeness, working men are rather more like the Duke of Devonshire.' Moreover, despite the cultivated 'h-dropping', the unabashed vulgarity, Thomas was a remarkably able negotiator to whom the railwaymen owed their relatively high wages between the wars.

Long before 1931, Thomas's fidelity to the Labour movement was suspect. He had backed the Labour Council of Action in their defiance of the Coalition government's Russian policy but he had never wanted Labour to be more than an estate of the realm with a strong bargaining voice. After the railway strike of 1919 he had said, 'We did not want to defeat the Government.' He opposed direct industrial action, insisting that unionism must not override citizenship. For years extremists attacked him for the part he had played as leader of the railwaymen on Black Friday, 1921, when the Triple Alliance of miners, railwaymen and transport workers collapsed.

Thomas was an alert and able minister in the first Labour government and *The Times* thought that he had done more than any other man to prove that 'Labour is fit to govern'.[1] He became a symbol of reconciliation between labour and capital, a Mond–Turner man. He was confessedly no Socialist: 'I don't read any of those bloody books.'[2] Yet up to his failure in the second Labour government to contend with unemployment, Thomas was thought of as a possible Labour Prime Minister. After that there was a rapid decline in nerve and ability until the perhaps undeservedly cruel humiliation and dishonour of 1936.

The parliamentary journalists had chosen to see in Snowden an implacable Socialist, but far more characteristic was his Yorkshire Englishry, his uprightness and his devotion to the craft of

[1] *DNB.*
[2] Hugh Dalton, *Call back yesterday*, London, 1953, p. 193.

Gladstonian finance, the 'primitive liberalism' which had, says Dalton, replaced his Socialism. His self-reliance, strength of personal judgment, meant that he could not easily subordinate himself to a cause. Yet by established institutions he was completely captured. He was a gifted expositor of received public finance, who became absorbed and fascinated by Treasury expertise (Schumpeter calls his performance as Chancellor of the Exchequer in 1924 'excellent'); could appreciate even Joynson-Hicks (not at all a popular Conservative politician) simply because of his grasp and urbanity as Financial Secretary to the Treasury.[1] He made ephemeral heroic politics out of the defence of British interests at the Hague Conference on War Debts in 1929.

He remained very much a parliamentarian and hostile to instruction or domination by outside bodies. Like Gaitskell at Scarborough in 1960 he maintained that the parliamentary party was not responsible to the party rank and file but to its constituents in the country. He became contemptuous of the party's annual assembly. 'Of the hundreds of resolutions I have seen passed by Labour Conferences outlining a drastic programme of reform, I can hardly call to mind one which has had any practical effect. Conferences will talk, let them talk.'[2] He deplored the emotional indecorum in Parliament of both Grayson and Lansbury and for the parliamentary oratory of the Clydesiders he had nothing but harsh contempt: 'We recognized their speeches as having done duty on many previous occasions. The other parties in the House were very tolerant of these speeches, and were more entertained than indignant at the thundering denunciation of the capitalist system, which was something new to them.'[3]

Snowden was an uncharitable, complacent man, yet it must be difficult for even an unsympathetic reader of his autobiography, from the early conversion to Socialism to the indictment of his associates in the 1931 Labour government, to be unimpressed by his strength of character.[4] In the negotiations of August 1931 Hoare contrasted MacDonald's 'Ossian-like complexities' with

[1] Snowden, *Autobiography*, II, 590.
[2] *Ibid.* I, 87–8.
[3] *Ibid.* II, 577.
[4] In 1931, P. J. Grigg was 'full of admiration for Snowden—something "really great about him". He had put through the Tories and the Liberals the identical Budget which he had proposed to the Labour Cabinet.' Thomas Jones, *A diary with letters*, Oxford, 1954, p. 11.

Philip Snowden's hard and immovable determination to balance the budget at any cost. His doctrinaire, radical mind was inspired by an unquestioning belief in the infallibility of a balanced budget, whilst his whole nature rebelled against the political evasions and complacent generalities of many of his ministerial colleagues. From start to finish in our talks he was never deflected from the course that he had set himself, nor, I believe, was he ever blind to the destination to which it was undoubtedly leading him, much as he disliked it. My first memory, therefore, of these inter-party discussions is of the alert, dogmatic and explosive Chancellor of the Exchequer...[1]

MacDonald was the master and victim of a style. The impress may be superficial, yet he seems the most Gladstonian of modern British politicians. Gladstone and MacDonald both felt the attractions of the inherited social order and were assimilated to it. Both were romantic figures; their achievements counted for less than what they were; the centre of both has proved impenetrable. Each served the Crown rather than party. In each, there is the same irresolution and cloudy language, the same accepted ascendancy over his colleagues and capacity for evoking love from afar. They had contrasting fates and reputations. MacDonald is perhaps what happens to Gladstone in the twentieth century.

MacDonald had a presence, a voice, assiduity and a schooling in the humanities which he claimed tightened up every bolt in his intellectual being; a tendency to take flight into lyrical uplift— not always happily: 'With the approach of the sun to the earth in spring, the breeze warms and the wayside bursts out into colours. Life is the companion of the hours of Spring. So is socialism the companion of democracy.' Prose like this, flowing abundantly, beautifully delivered, might well make him 'a match for all those underbred and under-trained workmen who surround him on the platform and face him in the audience'.[2] But what was it that established his ascendancy in the parliamentary party?

It was not doctrine, for he did not 'want anything done in particular'. The answer, in part, was simply political talent tenaciously and professionally exercised: in particular, the astuteness by which, after relinquishing the party chairmanship because he opposed the First World War politically, he had yet managed to stay close to Arthur Henderson and keep the Trade Unionist

[1] Templewood, *Nine troubled years*, p. 19.
[2] Webb, *Diaries 1912–1924*, p. 17.

and Socialist segments in the party together. There was, too, his industry as secretary of the Labour Representation Committee from 1900 to 1906, when with hardly any staff he had built up the electoral organization of the party.

It was these achievements, added to great personal distinction, which enabled him, after he had become 'the most unpopular and distrusted man in Britain', narrowly but conclusively to secure the leadership of the Labour Party over Clynes in 1922. Moreover, he became, says Pelling, leader in a sense that none of his predecessors had been.[1] From 1922, he was chairman *and* leader of the Parliamentary Party—a positive leader and not just a voice for the party. Clynes, Henderson and Lansbury could not rival him. When Prime Minister he used his full discretion in selecting his administration, going with assurance beyond the party for men of ministerial timber.

In Cabinet, his primacy was acknowledged. His sedulous ministers were absorbed in their tasks and he was able to keep a great deal to himself. He was surprisingly slow to see the dangers of the Campbell prosecution (when the government was accused of tampering with the judicial process) to the life of his administration and also to assess the implications of the publication of the Zinoviev letter during the ensuing election campaign. Yet in his initial year of office he generally showed much soundness of judgment, especially in foreign affairs.

To many it seemed that in his first administration MacDonald was conceding too much to the left, but the Independent Labour Party who had helped to make him chairman were already moving away from him. They continued to do so during the Baldwin period, joining the miners in condemning the parliamentary leader's lukewarmness for the General Strike, and objecting to the conciliatory Mond–Turner talks between industry and labour. MacDonald had always discountenanced direct industrial action. The I.L.P. were intent on maintaining their separate identity within the Labour Party and in keeping their parliamentary representatives under strict control. In 1927 they refused to nominate MacDonald for the Treasurership of the Labour Party, but within the Parliamentary Party his authority steadily grew: he was annually re-elected as leader.

Because MacDonald was a secretive man who found conflict

---

[1] Henry Pelling, *A short history of the Labour party*, London, 1961, p. 52.

between what had raised him and what he had to do, between what he felt as fact and what he had to say, it has been only too easy to discover in past evasions and half-expressed wishes evidence that the great 'betrayal' of 1931 was premeditated, as though from the beginning there had been no honesty in Mac-Donald. Both the Webbs saw 1931 as the consummation of a long-maturing plot. Snowden, too, considered that, for a long time before the crisis arose, MacDonald 'had been turning to the idea of a new party orientation and government by what he called a Council of State'.[1] There was ground, he thought, for suspecting 'that Mr MacDonald had deliberately planned the scheme of a National Government'.[2]

To support this there is little more evidence than a few extracts from MacDonald's early writings in which he had visualized a patriot Prime Minister as the chosen national leader, unattached to party, responsible to the king and nation, and also his first speech in the House of Commons as Prime Minister in 1929, in which he speculated how far it was possible 'without in any way abandoning any of our party positions, without in any way surrendering any item of our party principles, to consider ourselves more as a Council of State and less as arrayed regiments facing each other in battle...'. To these scraps there may be added Snowden's impression that in 1929 MacDonald had sought a bargain with Baldwin to keep Labour in office and, further, that when his government resigned in 1931 'he neither shewed nor expressed any grief at this regrettable development. On the contrary, he set about the formation of the National Government with an enthusiasm which shewed that the adventure was highly agreeable to him.'[3]

Against MacDonald, too, was his personal acceptability in the houses of the great, the vanity which made him so vulnerable to sustained 'social allurement'. There were also his observed amicable relationships with Baldwin, their mutual sense of the country, their willingness to accommodate each other. So there grew the stories that he had long dined secretly with the Opposition, that more and more he had found the ideas, vocabulary and manners of his Labour colleagues unpleasing, and frequently disparaged them, that all the while he had been preparing for a crash which would enable him to escape from them.

[1] *Autobiography*, II, 954.   [2] *Ibid.*   [3] *Ibid.* p. 953.

Just as Sir Robert Peel was finally restored to the Tories, so, Schumpeter hoped, would Ramsay MacDonald eventually be redeemed within the Labour Party.[1] Yet he is still a man without a character and only the rags of a style. Had there been only a temporary recourse to a National government 'of persons' to carry out a highly unpopular policy for which no single party was willing to be entirely responsible, perhaps his redemption would have been possible. For there is nothing inherently wicked in coalitions. The Labour Cabinet had after all agreed to considerable economies and might even have accepted the specific cuts in unemployment benefits had it not been for the T.U.C.—their objections were crucial. What established '1931' as 'the greatest betrayal in the history of the party', to be instanced by the Labour movement on its most solemn occasions, was the 1931 general election, fought in a highly emotional atmosphere and perpetuating a reconstruction of government declared at the outset to be temporary only.

It was highly unfortunate for MacDonald, as Salter remarks, that his public life continued after his break with the Labour Party, in the full prominence of the premiership. 'It was MacDonald's cruel destiny, unusual in a country with Parliamentary government, to outlive himself, neither in retirement, nor in the intermittent activity of opposition, but in the office of Prime Minister.'[2] Without party, without even the kind of 'following' that Lloyd George had had, MacDonald lived on, a kind of uplifted Antaeus, a Prime Minister who was also a political ruin. From 1931 onwards, he was in the stocks, as 'Tory prisoner', 'royal favourite', or 'court politician' for every Socialist pamphleteer.

The hostile judgments have stuck. Snowden took the trouble to tell us[3] that when MacDonald was appointed Secretary of the Labour Representation Committee in 1900 it was only after two other people had turned the post down.[4] Even before 1914 he

---

[1] Schumpeter, p. 368.   [2] Sir Arthur Salter, *Personality in politics*, p. 65.

[3] *Autobiography*, I, 92.

[4] Dalton maintains that on three occasions MacDonald benefited from being the victim of mistaken identity: when those who voted for him in 1900 thought that he was James MacDonald, Secretary of the London Trades Council; when the Clydesiders who gave him a narrow victory over Clynes in the contest for the Labour leadership in 1922 thought that he was a Socialist of the left; when King George V, appointing him to head the National Government in 1931, thought that he was a party leader 'whom a majority of his followers would still follow'. Dalton, *Call back yesterday*, p. 188.

suffered 'from a failing, which has grown upon him with advancing years, of being unable to make a speech which was not open to any interpretation a person chose to place upon it'.[1] After the 1931 election he found the Prime Minister 'as usual discursive and incoherent'. For the aged Blatchford, writing about the same time, MacDonald was 'a windy spasm' who 'wiped his boots on Keir Hardie's whiskers'. Lansbury thought MacDonald's whole mind 'one web of tortuous Conservatism'. And Churchill called him 'the boneless wonder'. One would hardly expect Leonard Woolf to say anything very good about him but one wonders at the resentment which prompts:

I have never known a vainer and a more treacherous man than Ramsay ...When Ramsay talked about himself he seemed to ooze vanity. One of Ramsay's most marked characteristics was tortuousness of mind...Finally there was a curious streak of treachery in Ramsay. Some people in the Labour Party who knew him much better than I did, and therefore suffered much more from him, used to say that his instinct to double-cross and stab his friends in the back was derived from the traditional habit of the Highland Scot to pursue secret feuds.[2]

How much light do these or similar comments in Beatrice Webb's *Diaries* ('egotist', 'snob', 'poseur') throw upon the man whose desertion was, says Miss Jennie Lee, 'spiritual death to thousands of Labour people who had worshipped him'?[3] Perhaps Mrs Webb was fairer to the public man on another day:

The leader of the Labour Party was in his best form. He is an attractive creature; he has a certain beauty in colouring, figure and face, a delightful voice and an easy unpretentious manner, youthful enjoyment of his prestige as a Prime Minister...

MacDonald might be distinguished in neither intellect nor character, yet she had to admit that

he has great gifts as a political leader, he has personal charm, he has vitality, he is assiduous, self-controlled and skilful. In all these respects he is unique in the inner circle of the Labour Party made up, as it is, of fanatics, faddists, refined and self-effacing intellectuals and the dull mediocrities of the Trade Union Movement.[4]

---

[1] Snowden, *Autobiography*, 1, 218. [2] 'Some portraits', *Encounter*, May 1964.
[3] *Tomorrow is a new day*, London, 1939, p. 143.
[4] *Diaries 1924—1932*, London, 1956, pp. 111–12.

Michael Foot, who, in *Guilty Men*, helped to keep the story of the Baldwin–MacDonald plot circulating, has now, in a more recent book, deliberately to raise his voice to insist that Mac-Donald was not the empty rhetorician usually presented. 'He was a skilled Parliamentarian and a towering platform and conference orator; he stood head and shoulders above all rivals, the clear master of his Party.'[1] Sir Samuel Hoare, an observer of MacDonald under stress in 1931, gets close to the centre of the matter when he sees MacDonald as a tired man who could no longer resolve his intellectual difficulties.

Being both proud and sensitive, he could never bring himself to the complete acceptance either of his colleagues or even of his own programme. With the Fabians, he was for Independent Labour, with Independent Labour, for the Fabians.

There was an 'eclecticism' which showed through more and more as he got older.

The result was that he never seemed to be a hundred per cent for or against any one course of action. The pale cast of his complicated thought was apt to tone down the colour of his generous sentiments, and to obscure both the intentions and the words with which he expressed them.[2]

He was without that saving obtuseness which might have stemmed his steadily growing scepticism about his Labour colleagues and Labour policies. He lacked the character to make a public turn-about; he lost his ground in the country and his audience too. Hence the incoherence of his public words. Oddly enough, there was the same conflict, but much more effectively resolved, in Baldwin, the same apperception of a common good.

The rejection of MacDonald was the rejection of a single ascendancy over the party. From now onward the disparagement of MacDonald's personal conduct and qualities (not necessarily of 'MacDonaldism') was a criterion of Labourism. 'Better a pedestrian speaker who meant what he said than a spellbinder who bemused himself with his own words.'[3] It was not to be as simple as that. The immediate successor, it is true, was Henderson, and he was no orator. He was a negotiator, 'a fine combination', wrote Clynes, 'of secretary, treasurer, advocate, organizer and

---

[1] *Aneurin Bevan*, London, 1962, 1, 99.   [2] Templewood, *op cit.* pp. 27–8.
[3] Roy Jenkins, *Mr Attlee*, London, 1948, pp. 102–3.

dependable agent'.[1] He had always had difficulty in getting him-self elected—he was of course defeated in the election of 1931—and had never therefore been much of a parliamentarian. Moreover, he was thoroughly subordinated not only to the cause but to the party machine.

Certain words invariably came from his mouth with capital letters. They were words of collectivity. Rarely did he speak in the first person singular; but when he said 'Party', 'Party Conference' or 'Socialist Movement', something big loomed up. 'This Great Movement'—does any phrase bring him back more vividly? He conveyed the sense, most actual to his mind, and constant in it, of a mighty confraternity, whose solid centre would swing on, no matter what snarlings or scufflings might be happening on the wings.[2]

Henderson had solidity, was an estimable, deeply religious man who could betray neither his party nor the unemployed directly hit by the economy cuts of 1931, yet did not differ markedly from MacDonald in outlook. His roots were in late nineteenth-century liberal politics; he had been an admirer of Gladstone and Morley and began his life in national politics as an agent to a Radical M.P. He did not find MacDonald's crime of helping to form a National Government a heinous one.

I am not so sure that there was very much shame in it, because as I have said before, if this situation is all that we have been told, if, in its magnitude, if, in its possible consequences, in its urgency it was such as has been described, I have no hesitation in saying that I would have preferred that the idea of National Government had been seriously considered and approached in the proper way...[3]

Lansbury, who took over the leadership, was hardly 'pedestrian'. He had run *Lansbury's Weekly* against the I.L.P.'s *New Leader* before 1914. His models had been Gladstone, Cobden and Bright but the man who had 'affected his mind' was Hyndman. He had swung over from the Liberals (like Henderson he had been an election agent for a Liberal M.P.) because he had wished 'to preach Socialism' and had created a devoted personal connection in very much the same way as Keir Hardie.

[1] *The British Labour party*, ed. Herbert Tracey, London, 1948, III, 187.
[2] M. A. Hamilton, *Arthur Henderson*, London, 1938, p. 266.
[3] TUC Annual Conference Report, 1931, p. 400, quoted by Ralph Miliband, *Parliamentary socialism*, London, 1961, p. 184.

Lansbury was a fierce and persistent moralist who found the whole structure of society insupportable. He was deeply religious and deeply English and had a large and urgent desire to reconstruct society. He identified Christianity with Socialism. Snowden thought he had more vigour than any man that he had known except Lloyd George and Tom Mann. Lansbury had championed Mann when he had gone to gaol in 1912 for his 'Don't Shoot' pamphlet to the troops. As editor of the *Daily Herald* he had been a vehement critic of the régime, of the game of Ins and Outs in the 'House of Pretence', of the Marconi scandal. Because Parliament had seemed to be failing as an instrument of change, he had been associated with Syndicalist direct action.

After the First World War, Lansbury had thought, like Smillie, that it was legitimate to use industrial force against a government so iniquitous as the Lloyd George Coalition. He had a melodramatic view of politics. He warned George V of the fate of Charles I when it was rumoured that the king was advising Baldwin to hold on to power without majority support in Parliament after the election of 1923.

Lansbury had been an uncritical admirer of Lenin as one who had acted clearly and unequivocally.

Cabinet Ministers in other countries would have talked of their troubles, of their difficulties, would have surrounded themselves with a group of officials to prevent the possibility of any mistake in their answering of questions: but Lenin takes the field alone, and this because he is not a diplomat—that is, he does not use language of a double meaning but wants you to understand what he means. He hates compromise... Those who would be his friends must be as purehearted as he: he has no room for any of us who are half and half, and he wants us to be one thing or the other.[1]

In Parliament, Lansbury reverted to the beleaguered virtue of Keir Hardie, practised simple evangelism on the floor. The *Red Flag* was sung in the division lobbies. But the parliamentary game was played: he never gave up. He coached both Cripps and Attlee. Naïve and sentimental, he nevertheless had courage; he was one of those who 'provided, in the unassuming but undeniable honesty of their characters, evidence that a Socialist could easily be a better man than the "get-rich-quick" business-

---

[1] Raymond Postgate, *The life of George Lansbury*, London, 1951, pp. 205–6.

man whom Liberal politics held up as a model'.[1] He always seemed, even if Bevin said he was not, free from guile.

Yet he too was to be a lost leader. For in his deep, emotional pacifism he lost contact with the realities facing his party, broke indeed with the declared policy of supporting collective action against aggression. 'One day the party seems all important, the next day quite unimportant because its interests seem to conflict with truth.'[2] In the end he stood, unaware and vulnerable, in the Dome at Brighton at the 1935 Annual Conference of the party, opposing the defence policy of the National Council of Labour, declaring 'that God intended us to live peaceably and quietly with one another, that if some people do not allow us to do so, I am ready to stand as the early Christians did, and say: "This is our faith, this is where we stand, and, if necessary, this is where we will die."'

Ernest Bevin's rejoinder was an attack upon the egotism of one who, like MacDonald, had allowed his personality to 'protrude as compared with this great Movement', upon Lansbury's presumption in remaining leader while repudiating the policy of the party. Where MacDonald was secretive, Lansbury, like Baldwin, was 'appallingly frank'. But the conscience of a leader, if unsubordinated to the movement, might well create a dangerous prerogative power. To the Conference Bevin said, 'I hope you will carry no resolution of an emergency character telling a man with a conscience like Lansbury what he ought to do. If he finds that he ought to take a certain course, then his conscience should direct him as to the course he should take. It is placing the Executive and the Movement in an absolutely wrong position to be taking your conscience round from body to body to be told what you ought to do with it.' Bevin carried the Conference overwhelmingly against the leader of the party; Lansbury resigned.

Bevin was to prove the decisive man in the 1930s. After 1931, the Trade Union movement which for so long had been preoccupied with industrial matters came back into the centre to guide and control the Parliamentary Party. For Bevin, master of the biggest union in the country, controlling personally one-tenth of the votes at the Annual Labour Conference, the sights were set. It was now a matter of defending the interests of British Labour in a struggle which extended into continental Europe beset by

[1] *Ibid.* p. 97.   [2] *Ibid.* p. 284.

Fascism; of beginning the slow ascent to real power again through a majority at some future General Election (he disparaged the minority Labour governments) and, in the meantime, of sustaining the pressure of a united Trade Union movement on the government. For although Bevin had once said that 'there is nobody in the world who submits to anything but force', and had been hostile to parliamentarians, he now acquiesced in parliamentary methods. From now onwards the National Joint Council, on which the General Council of the Trades Union Congress had dominating representation, determined the line of Labour policy.

The egotism or discretion of Labour leaders was to be bridled. In 1933 the Annual Conference of the Labour Party accepted a National Executive Committee report which, among other things, recommended that the National Joint Council should advise the Parliamentary Labour Party about taking office in the future; that in conducting his government, the Prime Minister should be subjected to majority decisions of the Cabinet and should only dissolve Parliament on the decision of the Cabinet. Policy would be according to the resolutions of the Annual Conference as embodied in the General Election manifesto.

But outside both Parliament and the unions there was still ground for heroes to stand on. Mosley, whom Beatrice Webb had seen to be, with his charm, good looks, delightful voice and the gift of oratory, a possible successor to MacDonald, was, it is true, already lost to Labour. After resigning from the MacDonald government he had anticipated future new departures with a plan to be achieved by a super-Cabinet, national planning and the virtual supersession of Parliament. He built an Action Group within the party to which he attracted John Strachey, Aneurin Bevan, W. J. Brown and others and, in 1930, nearly carried the Labour Annual Conference against its leaders. He then formed his own New Party, which unsuccessfully contested seats in the 1931 election. After that he took his own brand of romantic authoritarianism to the streets.

Yet there was a stronger swell than Fascism. The vocabulary of politics was moving in Socialism's favour. The National government, although achieving much more domestically than it is usually given credit for, lacked words, could neither persuade nor convert. It was the kind of provisional government which endures. The monopolists of moral fervour were on the left and all the more so since the left was so far from power. Mass unemployment, the Distressed Areas, Hunger Marches, the rise of Fascism in Europe, the fate of Republican Spain, the heroism of Soviet Russia, tearing a new world out of the old, gave a new excitement to politics, seemed to dwarf English men and measures. It was an excitement which Labour backbenchers and Trade Unionists seemed not to share. Miss Jennie Lee, in MacDonald's time, had been totally unprepared for 'the solid rows of decent, well-intentioned, unpretentious Labour backbenchers. In the long run it was they who did the most deadly damage. Again and again an effort was made to rouse them from their inertia. On every occasion they reacted like a load of damp cement.'[1] Moreover, she liked 'the cash plus voting power ascendancy of a trade union junta headed by Sir Walter Citrine and Mr Ernest Bevin'[2] no better than the supremacy of MacDonald.

Politics on the left was now open to new initiatives of the sects opposed to MacDonaldism. The Independent Labour Party had long evangelistically sought Socialism here and now. It was a kind of cave of burning eloquence within the party. But it had insisted on its distinctiveness, on the control of its rank and file over the conduct of its representatives in Parliament, and at last had withdrawn its affiliation to the Labour Party in 1932. It was now in decline. Its characteristic leader was Maxton, like Bruce Glasier primarily an agitator, happiest on the public platform or romantically contemplating Lenin, politically hardly more than a flourish.

More important as a rostrum was the Socialist League, a group which claimed to have learned the lesson of 1931, that the inevitability of gradualness in realizing Socialism in Britain could no longer be taken for granted. The argument was that the ruling class would not, when next Labour was returned to power, accept its authority to govern. Parliamentary majorities were therefore no longer enough and a future Labour government should be prepared for action from the moment of taking office.[3] The Socialist League thought in terms of 'civil wars' and struggles for power. What Tawney invoked was not the long English tradition of trimming, of coming to terms with the adversary, but the zealotry of the Puritan Rebellion and even the dedication of the Russian revolutionaries of 1917.

[1] *Tomorrow is a new day*, pp. 144–5. [2] *Ibid.* p. 183.
[3] See Miliband, *op. cit.* pp. 196 f.

Labour was far from power (indeed neither of the shortlived ministries between the wars had truly enjoyed it) and this, together with growing political class consciousness, led to a great seething of amateur politics outside the party. The ground was Marxist. Not much more could be made out of English Radicalism but Marxism was a universal creed and had peculiar excitations in an age of foreign violence. It clarified and divided and, pure or corrupted, could raise head after head of opinion. To the Marxists nothing was safe: every institution was perverted, even the League of Nations. Capitalism caused wars: the League was merely the 'International Burglars Union'. 'At no time,' declared Sir Charles Trevelyan, supporting a resolution proposing a General Strike in the event of war, at the Labour Party Annual Conference in 1933, 'has there been such a black outlook for the world. The great instrument for keeping the peace, the League of Nations, some day will be the machinery for international safety, but it will be when hearts are different and Governments are different... The rulers must know that if war comes, they will fight with a divided nation. They can make their bourgeois war themselves but they will make it without the workers.'[1] The National government itself was seen as a forerunner of Fascism. Had it not flouted the system of party government and, with the agreement to differ on tariff policy, the convention of collective responsibility? Was there not a tendency to reduce the power of parliamentary scrutiny of government, to restrict opportunities of free speech and assembly?

A much favoured concept was of a distressed capitalism unable any longer to tolerate the demands of Socialism or reformism and therefore seeking to protect itself by creating or adopting a mass movement from discontented elements. The diehards, the experienced politicians of the right (the terms 'left' and 'right' acquired wide circulation at this time), were considered more dangerous than Mosley. 'No doubt,' wrote Harold Laski, 'if the problem came to an issue in this country, we should wear our fascism with a difference.'[2] For many the National government in Britain already seemed 'sometimes like a grey shadow of what was in power on the Continent'.[3] Attlee detected the phrases of Mussolini and Hitler on the lips of Ramsay MacDonald. And

[1] Eric Estorick, *Stafford Cripps*, London, 1949, p. 131.
[2] Introduction to W. A. Rudlin, *The growth of fascism in Great Britain*, London, 1935, p. 8.   [3] Postgate, *George Lansbury*, p. 281.

because MacDonald constantly made a distinction between party and national interests and assumed that there was some ideal course to be followed for the good of the country, from which party policies were merely factious deflections, MacDonaldism was 'essentially Fascist'.[1] For H. N. Brailsford, Fascism had already happened:

The forms of democracy were preserved but something also of the authoritative procedure of Fascism was attained and without the trouble of dressing in coloured shirts. What had been done for the defence of the realm was done for the defence of capitalism and no one was startled or shocked. The English alone possess the art of making the boldest constitutional changes without raising their voices by a fraction of a tone.[2]

Political heroism was widely diffused on the left. It was achieved mainly by assailing the National government and embarrassing the official Labour leadership. Among the heroes one could include Cole, Tawney and Laski (all on the executive of the Socialist League), men who were borne up by the eddying circles of opinion which they created. The left rank and file has always been readier than the right to accept the authority of those whose knowledge of politics is entirely 'of the book'. Laski, in a flood of books, pamphlets, speeches and lectures which were speeches, observed no limitations to his talents, and now it may fairly be said that he was at least as much a politician as a scholar. When the constituency party members elected members to the Labour National Executive Committee in 1937 it was not surprising that both he and Cripps were elected. He made politics out of a few 'vulgar' Marxist ideas repetitiously asserted. Although he claimed, through acquaintance with the great, to be close to the grain of politics, he was simple and chiliastic in his prescriptions. He was skilled at plucking from his very wide reading such historical parallels or antitheses as seemed appropriate to the occasion; yet his rhetoric was over-exercised and, in time, he wore his knowledge to the bone.

But although Laski virtually became a politician, he still kept one foot firmly planted in the academic world. He could not attract a following in quite the same way as Sir Stafford Cripps. Cripps was an unlikely hero, a late recruit to Labour politics, a

[1] *The Labour Party in perspective*, London, 1937, p. 60.
[2] *Property or peace*, London, 1934, p. 60.

dedicated Churchman and a Chancery lawyer. But he had deliberately come into politics and, having survived the electoral
disaster of 1931, rapidly became a front-bencher. He was the
financial backer and the leading light of the Socialist League and,
as early as 1933, was seen as a future Prime Minister. Some
claimed that he was the ablest leader since Mosley (Ernest Bevin
said that there was not much to choose between them).

Here was one of Tawney's energumens, 'at once dynamic and
antiseptic'. His politics were simple and inflexible. The divisions
within the Labour movement meant nothing to him—they had
happened before he became active. As a lawyer he had a capacity
for being right at the centre of the live issues of the day: the
jurists' inquiry into the Reichstag fire; the question of British
retaliatory action over the Moscow trials of British engineers
accused of sabotage; the inquiry into the Gresford Pit disaster.

His attack on the gradualism of the Labour leadership was
based on a simple hypothesis. It was that a future Labour government would certainly have its programme blocked by the House
of Lords and would quickly be replaced by a minority Conservative government, unwilling to go to the country and ruling by
armed force. In these circumstances 'it would probably be better
and more conducive to the general peace and welfare of the country
for the Socialist Government to make itself temporarily into a
dictatorship until matters could again be put to the test at the
polls'.[1] He did not confine himself to propaganda. At the 1933
Conference of the Labour Party he demanded the specification of
the means to secure the rapid and complete conversion of the
capitalist system to Socialism.

In 1935, Cripps resigned from the Labour Party Executive so
that he might freely express his own views. Like Joseph Chamberlain before him and Bevan after him, he needed his own untrammelled field of persuasion. From now onwards there was no
Labour politician who could more easily fill a public hall. His
preoccupations now were War and Fascism. Again, his prescriptions were startlingly clear. At Brighton, just before the destruction of Lansbury, he declared that only a Socialist government
could be trusted to pursue the correct policies. 'Had we a workers'
Government, as they have in Russia, the whole situation would

[1] *Can socialism come by constitutional means?*, London, n.d., p. 5. Quoted in Miliband,
op. cit. p. 200.

be completely different. Then, with a Socialist Government, there would be no risk of imperialist and capitalist aims being pursued, as today it is certain they are being, and will be, pursued.' A year later, at Stockport, he declared that he 'did not believe that it would be a bad thing for the British working-class if Germany defeated us. It would be a disaster to the profit-makers and capitalists, but not necessarily for the working-class.'[1]

By 1937 he was in open conflict with party leadership and, supported by Bevan, Strauss and Brockway in the 'United Front of the Working Class to fight Fascism and War', was co-operating with the I.L.P. and the Communist Party. As Sidney Webb noted, the alliance was hardly worth it in terms of numbers and, if anything, it only served to stiffen the government. 'He may be right', Webb went on, 'in giving up his position inside the Labour Party and taking on the role of a preacher or prophet, in the wilderness, if he is convinced of the ultimate rightness of his gospel. But I am a pedestrian accustomed all my life to be in a minority and looking for nothing but being outvoted...'[2]

When the Labour Party National Executive declared membership of the Socialist League to be incompatible with that of the Labour Party and shortly afterwards threatened to excommunicate any member of the party who appeared on United Front platforms with I.L.P. and Communist heretics, Cripps and his associates appealed to the Annual Conference. There they were defeated; yet, on the day after, the rank-and-file delegates from the constituencies elected Cripps, Laski and D. N. Pritt to the National Executive.

From now onwards Cripps abandoned his class-conflict policy, even his Socialist purity. To win the next election, he now advocated an alliance of all Opposition groups against the National government. In 1939, in a memorandum to the secretary of the Labour Party, he advocated Labour leadership of a Popular Front movement which would invite 'the co-operation of every genuine anti-Government Party or group of individuals' to protect the democratic rights of the British people from internal and external attack and 'to secure a positive policy of peace by collective action with France, Russia, the United States of America...'. The

[1] For a selection of Cripps's odder statements see Hugh Dalton, *The fateful years*, London, 1957, pp. 149–51.
[2] Estorick, *Stafford Cripps*, p. 156.

Labour leaders were hostile and when Cripps sought to distribute the memorandum throughout the Labour Party organization he was expelled—as were Bevan, Strauss and Trevelyan shortly afterwards—from the party.

Today, it seems strange that a man of such political innocence should rise again and again with renewed strength. To Dalton he appeared 'a dangerous political lunatic':[1] to his aunt, Beatrice Webb, 'oddly immature in intellect and unbalanced in judgment, ...ignorant and reckless in his statements and proposals'.[2] Yet it is clear that he was supported by a steady surge of political idealism from below. His words were notable only in their irresponsible, unpolitical lucidity, but the established parties seemed to have no memorable words at all. He was always credited with honesty of purpose. In Cripps, the audience sensed the Christian conscience at work in politics and the kind of rectitude which ensured action.

In the end Bevin and the General Council of the T.U.C. beat Cripps in the contest for the mind of the Annual Conference. Bevin's judgments were simple and lasting. A British General Strike to prevent war would be useless because Trade Unionism had been destroyed in Italy and Germany and did not exist in Russia. Labour was pledged to collective action in support of the League and that might mean war. War would have to be faced and the British Government must be trusted to wage it. The movement had made up its mind to oppose a dictatorship of right or left and things must go forward. Moreover, the empire was redeemable in a changing world and imperial interests need not inhibit action. Rearmament must be accepted as a necessity to fulfil obligations and defend the country. By 1937, the Labour Party were approving, after sustained prompting by Bevin and Dalton, the Defence Estimates. The Socialist League had been dissolved.

Bevin's vocabulary and syntax were clumsy but thought and emotion were strongly welded. In humiliating Lansbury at Brighton, says Mrs M. A. Hamilton, 'he compelled a naturally sentimental body to see an issue in larger than personal terms'.[3] He was sceptical about intellect in politics. Ramsay MacDonald, Mosley, Maxton, Cripps, Bevan and Laski were all febrile, in-

---

[1] Dalton, *The fateful years*, p. 42.
[2] *Diaries 1924–1932*, p. 304.
[3] Quoted in Alan Bullock, *The life and times of Ernest Bevin*, London 1960, 1, 569.

constant creatures. For them, politics was a perpetual seminar with inconclusive and drifting discussion and bright sallies—a sphere for egotism or sentiment. Intellect ran so frequently to sentiment. Intellectuals were forever dividing, forever cultivating their discontents. 'When we have tried to associate with the intellectuals, our experience is that they do not stay the course very long...It is the necessity to work out our own salvation which is the driving force; whether the intellectuals are with us or not, we must carry on.'[1]

Bevin had the passion, responsibility and strength to make a working-class revolution, yet he chose to reach an honourable settlement with the political order. He recognized the strength of the forces which British society could still raise against even a united Labour movement; for a disunited movement, forever probing its own premises, forever hypothesizing circumstances, seizing oratorical initiatives, he saw no hope at all. This was a time for organization and loyalty, for measuring what could be done here and now. His own ideas were deeply examined but now was the time for considered action. His feet never left the ground; when he spoke one seemed to hear 'the very embodiment of all natural and unlettered men'.[2]

Of the intellectuals, the one who was to come nearest to making a lasting style out of his sensibility was Aneurin Bevan. The rank and file of the Labour Party found Bevan exciting because what concerned him was the bold initiative. Details bored him and Michael Foot[3] sees him deliberately seeking to wean Labour away from Fabian gradualism. He was not temperamentally suited to 'strong and slow boring of hard boards'.[4] Some of this may be attributed to his Dissenting (Baptist and Methodist) family background: his basic political education was acquired in the Sunday school and the public library and these gave him, as they have given others, a dramatic view of life and some apocalyptic political perspectives.

His intellectual diet, H. G. Wells, Jack London, Noah Ablett (the Welsh Syndicalist), Thorstein Veblen and Marx, was coarse but sustaining. His authors left a mark on him; and like many

[1] *Ibid.* p. 532.
[2] Francis Williams, *Ernest Bevin*, London, 1952, p. 178.
[3] *Aneurin Bevan*, 1.
[4] 'Politics as a vocation', in *From Max Weber*, ed. by H. H. Gerth and C. Wright Mills, London, 1947, p. 128.

self-taught men he could always mobilize his learning. Although he would seek to play the part of John Bright or Charles James Fox (George Otto Trevelyan's biography was a later favourite), for much of his early life he was Ernest Everhard,[1] the muscular and omniscient hero of Jack London's *The Iron Heel*, the scourge of the drawing rooms (Beaverbrook's included), the foe of the Oligarchs.

He outgrew his early I.W.W. Syndicalism, but what attracted him to the Marxism which succeeded was not the tactics, which he thought irrelevant, but 'the largeness of its conception, its profound philosophy and its sure grasp of history...'.[2] It was this love of the thunderous which sometimes took him out of the grain of the English political tradition; would send him, for example, on those long Audenesque tramps through the Welsh hills preaching Marxism at the head of his followers from the Tredegar Workers' Freedom Group.[3]

Foreign ideologies went down well in alienated South Wales but they could blunt understanding, lead to such excesses as: 'Political toleration is a by-product of the complacency of the ruling class. When that complacency is disturbed there never was a more bloody-minded set of thugs than the British ruling class.'[4] These exciting simplicities could result in misjudgments of the kind which made him urge resistance to continental Fascism and at the same time refuse, like Sir Stafford Cripps, 'to trust Chamberlain with a revolver'. He could be naïve enough to think that the only thing that kept Britain from going Fascist was the power of organized Labour; like John Strachey and others he saw the jack-boot in most unlikely places. This internationalization of national issues and tensions had unfortunate effects on the right as well, but particularly on the left. It made politics more interesting but ignored the *genius loci*. When the war broke out he and Jennie Lee played Spanish marching tunes. When the war was on, Bevan was immoderately angered by Churchill's assertion that the country was fighting 'in defence of the values of traditional England'.[5]

His Syndicalism faded but it left him a residual truth: that power in society is all important. To be Fox or Bright was not enough: he must move to the centre of power while keeping open to the left. It is this which explains so much that seems inconsistent in

---

[1] Foot, *op. cit.* p. 59.   [2] *Ibid.* p. 38.
[3] *Ibid.* p. 169.   [4] *Ibid.* pp. 170–1.   [5] *Ibid.* p. 347.

his behaviour. In 1930 he endorsed Mosley's emergency plan but would not go along with the New Party—and Mosley then seemed to be the rising power on the left. He sympathized with the fundamentalism of the I.L.P. members but would not join them. He was a member of the dissident Socialist League until its dissolution; from 1937 he was at the heart of the Unity Campaign which Foot calls 'the most ambitious bid made by the British Left throughout the whole period of the 'thirties to break the stultifying rigidity of Party alignments'.[1] He co-operated with and openly admired Sir Stafford Cripps. Yet Bevan never burned his boats. He was always ultimately willing, and this was to be true of the years after 1950 too, to come back into the party. The sects could never obtain power; and he wanted power.

This explains, too, his ambivalent attitude towards Parliament. Parliament was the place where property must come to terms with power. Bevan had no doubt that the transformation of Britain into a social democracy could be achieved by parliamentary means. And yet he could, at the same time, appeal to the streets against Parliament and seek to bring into it some of the outside turmoil.

He insisted that politics should be principles in contention. What the political leader had to do was to identify himself with policies, strike attitudes if necessary but, above all, personalize politics. No one claimed so much for open politics, openly audited, as he. Yet Bevan was imperfectly liberal in that he seems to have lacked either a saving irony or the capacity to reconstruct within himself the mental processes, the ideas, of others. He could be ungenerous to opponents and allies.

During the war, untrammelled by office, he kept the debate open, attacked Churchillian strategy, urged the Second Front— the thousand-bomber raids belonged, he said, to the realm of rhetoric. He denounced the quality of British generalship and class prejudice in the army. In 1942, he declared Churchill's continuance in office to be 'a major national disaster'. Above all, he wanted the House of Commons to master Churchill.

But his chief targets were never the leading politicians. He could indeed appreciate the virtuosity of Baldwin ('medicine man talk') and Churchill, although he would say that 'the *hero's* need of the people outlasts *their* need of him. *They* obey the pressures of

[1] *Ibid.* p. 243.

contemporary conditions whilst *he* strives to perpetuate the situation where he stood supreme. . . .'[1] What he really detested was the bureaucracy of the modern party system which breaks the contact between the politician and his audience. As strongly as A. D. Lindsay he believed in 'the wisdom of the plain man', that it was from 'the unencumbered minds of ordinary people that vigorous ideas will emerge'.

He had Lloyd George's intemperance of language—it probably cost him more—but in other ways he differed from his compatriot. For Lloyd George cared little for theory, for what Foot calls 'the interplay between political principles and the point of action';[2] he became the master of men and situations, of what is to be done now. Bevan was not a good judge of men, of situations or of tactics. He failed to do justice to men like Attlee, Dalton and Morrison. Political passion was expended too often without responsibility, without discrimination. As F. R. Leavis has said of Swift, he was 'distinguished by the intensity of his feelings, not by insight into them'.

The early leading Labour politician was typically one who could, through his facility with words, his moral authority, dominate a restricted homogeneous circle. He was more likely to begin in the I.L.P. side of the movement than in the Trade Unions. He had schooled himself as a public speaker, but he was to the manner born. He discovered his own kindling power. As his circle widened he became a platform orator, perhaps a pamphleteer or journalist, an exponent of the crowd, of the social crisis. He promised choice, freedom, to men alienated. He cannot be explained functionally; he was not merely one who in the latest language 'emits stimuli and is responded to integratively'. Rather he was, as Michels insists, a man of high attainments, higher than those of politicians in other parties, intrinsically disinterested, with a wider range of knowledge, stronger convictions and a higher opinion of his own worth than had his audience.

At first he embodied aspiration, cleansing political passion, and as long as he did he made and mirrored the mind of his audience. But the failure of the older political parties, the war, and persistent social tension rapidly pulled him to the centre, away from instigation and resolution, to the gravity and responsibility of attentive

[1] Foot, *op. cit.* p. 468.   [2] *Ibid.* p. 117.

government. 'When they got to Parliament their national reputations grew, and when, in 1923, they became Ministers...—MacDonald, Prime Minister and Foreign Secretary, and Snowden, Chancellor of the Exchequer, neither having had any previous experience of office—their national and international reputations swelled still further with a loud blast of sudden fame. But, with both of them, it all began with public meetings.'[1] At the same time the Labour leader was making a social rise; in attaining the political class, he was making his own revolution.

It was unusual for the Labour orator to be well grounded in theory; his words had come from a generous and humane native literature, from Carlyle, Ruskin, and Morris; his ideas from Henry George rather than from Marxism (which, when it was an influence, was only one among others and exotic at that).

It is in Parliament that his political education begins. The Commons, he discovers, is not a sounding-board for oratory; indeed, in time, he becomes embarrassed for those who, like Grayson and later the Clydesiders, used it as such. Innovation is difficult but he rapidly becomes aware that it is possible to co-operate with those in occupation for limited objectives and that this means application and detailed knowledge. Ends recede: 'parliamentary labours [are] undertaken at first with reluctance but subsequently with increasing satisfaction and increasing professional zeal...'[2] And as the Labour parliamentarian acquires skill, so he gains a parliamentary rating which he values.

The leading politician becomes responsible and as such vulnerable to younger men who want dramatic initiatives. Outside, there are bursts of irritability but the movement has begun to accept parliamentary knowledge as indispensable, to regard the installed leader as one in whom they have an investment. They do not wish to withdraw support and create a crisis of confidence. They cannot in fact deny him the discretion which parliamentarians must have. This means much more than rank-and-file forbearance. It means acquiescence in leadership. These are the conditions in which MacDonald acquired his ascendancy. It meant a continual adjustment to group after group, to circle after circle. The cost of this to Labour politicians has always been heavy. Snell did not rise so high, but he says: 'The politician, especially if he has any capacity

---

[1] Dalton, *Call back yesterday*, p. 186.
[2] Michels, *Political parties*, pp. 82–3.

for research, exposition, organization or administration, requires powers of endurance and great reserves of strength which he can draw on at all times, and in almost unlimited measure, and in my case these powers were seriously damaged before my real work in life began.'[1]

MacDonald was the leader who acted out in full the whole transition from agitation to administration. And the original ties between leader and followers which he sought to maintain during his political and social ascent, in increasingly strained and empty rhetoric, were, in the end, completely unravelled. He lost his audience; at the close he did not know whom he was addressing. The crumbling of MacDonald is still the crucial event in Labour history. For what men and women had come to hope for was a man who would seem to control events like the great Victorian master politician. In stature, mien and rhetoric he seemed in the line; not a functional, not a fabricated or used leader, but a creative statesman.

Since MacDonald, the Labour Party has not sought or installed a Great Man as leader, in spite of the tensions of the 1930s and wartime visions of a New Order of Society. The model of the highly esteemed Attlee is now accepted: a man outside the factions, somewhat left of centre, widely acceptable and capable of being built up, but not to heroic stature. This does not mean weak leadership; every Labour leader will, after all, be a potential wielder of the full prerogative of the Crown. Even when some distance from office, Gaitskell showed appetite for conflict and command. And the journalists say that Mr Wilson's favourite politician is Mr Gladstone. The Labour leader is now sustained not by an audience but by a following drawn on one side from the politicking middle and lower middle classes and on the other from the professional Trade Unionists. His ability and character have been assessed and approved by men who are increasingly recognizable as professional politicians. For society he need no longer turn to Snowden's duchesses. There is now a well-established 'Left Wing Society' which nurtures and advances those who wish to be political.[2] The leader can still fall but if he does it is no longer likely that he will seek either refuge or reception on the other side.

[1] Snell, *Men, movements and myself*, p. 45.
[2] See W. L. Guttmann, *The British political élite*, London, 1963, pp. 251–3.

There is of course a notion widely entertained, and particularly on the left, that in the kind of government and politics we are likely to have in the future there is only a limited use for politicians of character and style. All that is necessary is a single political eminence, presentable and persuasive, to preside over executives, acting on the right information assembled by experts. In such inerrancy there would be no betrayals.

9

THE PRESUMPTIVE VIRTUE
OF CONSERVATIVES

In a notable essay Professor Samuel P. Huntington insists that
Conservatism—a universal Conservatism which he epitomizes
from the resistance offered to liberal movements in European and
American history over the last four centuries—has no autonomous
set of ideas and no *Wunschbild*.[1] Conservatism is basically *situational*, i.e. it 'arises out of a distinct but recurring type of historical
situation in which a fundamental challenge is directed at established
institutions...'. Conservatism only puts on its armour when
Apollyon is in sight. It is made articulate, perhaps briefly passionate (as in Burke), by events, but it has no substantive ideal.
Into existing institutions and human relationships the Conservative breathes life and value. Yet to the truths of emergent reason
he is sceptical, discriminating, sometimes obtusely resistant. This
does not mean that Conservatism is without intellectual content.
On the contrary, writes Huntington, 'Conservatism is the intellectual rationale of the permanent institutional prerequisites of
human existence...It is the rational defense of being against
mind, of order against chaos.'

English Conservatives rarely analyse their beliefs in depth; they
affirm the Conservative rationale when necessary but are often
incurious about why they are what they are. Yet those Conservatives who are articulate have produced a literature rich in both
insight and persuasive power. 'There is no text book of Conservatism,' it is claimed, 'except the history of Britain,' and it is true that
this literature is at core a commentary upon history, an extraction
of perennial values from insular habits and practices. English
history is seen neither as the flowering of institutions nor as a
chapter in the history of liberty, but in terms of human character
contending with and yielding to the processes of change. Conservatives are concerned with what Coleridge called 'the genius of
G. Britain...that blended result of Laws, Language, Customs,

[1] 'Conservatism as an ideology', *American Political Science Review*, LI, June 1957.

long enjoyment of personal and political Independence, illustrious Forefathers and whatever else constitutes a Grand national character and makes a Nation more than an aggregate of Individuals'.[1] It is a concern with men, and a criticism as well as an appreciation. No one was more severe than Coleridge on the limitations of the younger Pitt as a statesman.

The Tory is not on the side of history. History is an enchafèd flood which may sweep away a known and loved world. There are times when history must be held up, dammed so that reason may come to terms with human establishments and human prejudices. Indeed, one of the reasons why English Conservatives have been the dominant political party since 1867—in power for almost two-thirds of the time—is that they are allied with establishments, prejudices, estates of the realm. These allies are faithful and stubborn—particularly the Tory working man. Moreover, because Conservatives have been in power so often, they are much more occupied with what is to be done now than with theory. And, having had so much authority, Conservatives expect to have it again. 'If a guiding principle must be looked for, it is simply the assumption, unquestioned at any level of the party, that the Conservative Party ought to govern and will govern, even though there be no other principle to guide its course when in power...'[2] Conservatives believe that there are times when they alone can rule. It was this that made them so arrogant in the years before 1914.

Yet if English Conservatives have something only just short of passion for asserting their intrinsic authority, they protest that they have no passion at all in actually exercising power, in governing. Government is a matter for the reason and judgment of responsible men, not for passion. Conservatives usually contrast their modest use of reason and judgment in concrete circumstances with all that unreasoning commitment to orders of harmony and justice devised in the heads of the politically innocent. 'A politician', says T. E. Utley rather melodramatically, 'is a man whose business it is to manipulate as justly and humanely as he can the most powerful instrument of torture and destruction which human ingenuity has invented, the sovereign State. He is

---

[1] *Observations on Egypt*, quoted by John Colmer in *Coleridge, critic of society*, Oxford, 1959, pp. 84–5.

[2] 'The adaptable party', in *The Political Quarterly*, July–September 1961.

not paid to exhort, like a moralist, or to imagine, like a poet, but to govern; and government is the application of force and the threat of it to human beings.'[1] Conservatives do not believe that 'to govern is to turn a private dream into a public and compulsory manner of living';[2] they reject the accepted stereotype of the modern politician, 'the activist dreamer'.

'The door of the Cabinet has a quality the most opposite to the ivory gate of Virgil; it suffers no dreams to pass through it.'[3] But the rejection of redeeming or transforming politics does not mean that Conservatives will not use state power to achieve security among men, and to remedy abuses in society. Toryism has sunk its deepest shafts into English history during periods when England was *governed*, notably in Tudor times. 'We are not', R. A. Butler has said, 'frightened at the use of the State. A good Tory has never been in history afraid of the use of the State.'[4] But Conservatives have no 'High State Theory';[5] Conservatives do not identify liberty with obedience to law. Society is 'the product of a system of real relationships *between* individuals, classes, groups and interests'.[6] It is this tactile sense of politics that characterizes Conservatism. Power is held in by a consciousness of the diversity of human aims and passions in society. Conservatives may have a will to power, or rather a desire for office, but are mistrustful of untrammelled will in government. Cripps's 'country gentleman's Fascism' was an illusion.

Conservative politicians must be guarded in what they disclose about their fundamental beliefs. Convincing statements may be made about these but not easily in public. There may well be time and place for asserting the rights of property, small and large. There are occasions when open declaration of the hard primacy of the national interest in foreign affairs will rouse more than two cheers. In asserting 'principles' like these which may be said to be particularly theirs, Tories need not, indeed, be so embarrassed as they often appear to be. They know that the vocabulary of politics

[1] *Essays in conservatism*, Conservative Political Centre, 1949, p. 1.
[2] Michael Oakeshott, *Rationalism in politics*, London, 1962, p. 186.
[3] S. T. Coleridge, quoted in Keith Feiling, *Sketches in nineteenth-century biography*, London, 1930, p. 104.
[4] [434] H.C. Debates, p. 1247, 10 March 1947, quoted in S. H. Beer, *Modern British politics*, London, 1965, pp. 270–1.
[5] R. J. White, *The conservative tradition*, London, 1950, p. 5.
[6] *Ibid.* p. 8.

long ago took a leftward turn: what they seem to forget is that this vocabulary is tired and worn out.

Yet there are two things in which Tories must believe, which are difficult to affirm: first, rule through a political class taking its cue from a relatively small political nation; second, the moral necessity of inequality. Such Tory sociology as is articulated insists that 'there are different classes each with its own customs, its own loyalties, and its own obligations',[1] that society consists not of conflicting classes but mutually supporting sub-cultures, and that 'a class can be a source of comfort, reassurance, and orientation to those who belong to it'.[2]

Burkean assertions like these will pass in club, in common room or *Times* editorial (perhaps no more), as 'inside' beliefs, as rationalizations of 'private politics', but the tone of voice, as Timothy Raison has reminded us,[3] is not at all that of current academic sociology, which had its roots in social reform, was developed and is still developed by 'outsiders', and has therefore always tended to swing away to the left both in themes chosen for investigation and in findings. Because Conservatives have little footing in academic sociology in Britain, because they have neglected to bring their critical faculty to bear so effectively in this sphere as, say, on economic organization, the social services, or foreign policy, the contest seems to have gone to their opponents by default.

The Conservative knows that 'equality' is a dangerous nostrum to be applied to a rich and living education system; that the welfare state may weaken 'the national character', that effective law and order may be better secured by recourse to practical wisdom than to the findings of 'tender-minded' critics of police and penal systems.[4] He knows that a nation should not in the name of 'modernization', or other cant, rashly cast aside institutions and usages sustaining political manners and social disciplines which, if once lost, may never be re-created.

It is not just that what the Conservative *knows* cannot be squared with fashionable sociology; there is also the difficulty of fitting his beliefs—often his perturbation—into the kind of

---

[1] Lord Coleraine, 'Conservatism today', *The Times*, 2 October, 1956.
[2] T. Raison, *Why conservative?*, London, 1964, p. 24.
[3] 'Towards a Tory sociology', *Crossbow*, October–December 1963.
[4] *Ibid.*

enlightened political rhetoric that is expected of him. Indeed, so difficult of public communication are his convictions that the Conservative may sometimes be tempted to abandon them and utter the truths of his opponent. But it is not his business to do this. As Lord Coleraine has written: 'There are no doubt many things to be said for the classless society, but they are not normally said by Conservatives.'[1]

The Conservative does not officiously affirm, although he believes it to be true, that a *privileged* ruling class is indispensable if power is to be responsibly exercised. No one has better expressed this than A. K. White:

Power as a trust and personal and class privilege hang together. To take them apart may be desirable but it will produce something other than responsible government. For real responsibility cannot be exercised until the individual is privileged, that is, until he fills a place in the community which no one else can fill or fill as well. In other words, to be privileged is to be free, free absolutely or in a moral sense, free, that is to say, not merely to use his power on behalf of the community but also free to act, if one cares to, against the public interest. No other person or body of persons has the right to dictate to the responsible agent what his conduct should be. The final decision is entirely his, is his prerogative as a free moral being.[2]

Nor does the Conservative openly expound what he thinks about equality: (with Kant) that 'inequality is a rich source of much that is evil but also of everything that is good', that every historical society, as distinguished from Utopia, must have its ruling values and that those who do not adapt themselves to those values are less equal than those who do.[3] This is an unspoken truth, as is the Conservative's conviction that the state's business is not to enforce justice and charity but order and equity.[4]

Too much public candour, then, may be dangerous. What the Conservative must be is first critical and then practical—his criticism is directed to the 'truths' openly expounded by his radical opponents and since, as Plamenatz has said, the vocabulary of politics now favours not the established but the radicals, this is the

[1] *The Times*, 2 October 1956.
[2] *The character of British democracy*, Glasgow, 1945, p. 15.
[3] Ralf Dahrendorf, 'On the origin of social inequality', in *Philosophy, politics and society, second series*, ed. P. Laslett and W. G. Runciman, Oxford, 1962, pp. 105 f.
[4] Garry Wills, 'The convenient state' in *What is conservatism?*, ed. Frank S. Meyer, New York, 1964, pp. 167–8.

main part of the Conservative's political discourse. Then there is the criticism which illuminates the political tradition from within. These insights are explorations and affirmations within the system. They are not typically the insights of politicians. Few recent Conservative politicians have had imagination; few have been committed by ideas, developed style. Two come to mind: Disraeli and Joseph Chamberlain, each with a single branching idea which lasted: the one of an aristocracy serving the common interest of one nation; the other of strength and justice in the imperial theme. Each was inspirational; each founded a Conservative school of politics. Each, as might be expected, elaborated (like Bolingbroke) his ideas out of office. Chamberlain indeed found that his were incompatible with office.

The Conservative must also be practical—capable of taking and executing decisions. 'People vote Conservative because they expect integrity and competence in administration and stability in their daily lives.'[1] Conservatives stand on their record. It is only because of *reliable performance* that a party which has so long persisted in giving authority to an inner circle within a class can continue to expect to have the business of government confided to it by a mass electorate. Conservatives themselves often seem amazed that a party without vision, without a *Wunschbild*, which at heart contends with popular demands for the provision of this and that, sustains momentum and can win elections. We were all made aware of Labour's worrying in the 1950s about whether or not there would ever be a Labour government again. But there is an even more deep-rooted unease at the heart of Conservatism. 'The Conservative politician of these days,' wrote Lord Coleraine when the Tories were in power in the early 1950s, 'is apt to suppose that it is only by a kind of miracle that a Conservative government can be returned, and he is constantly seeking auguries in the public opinion polls.'[2] Conservatives are worried by the thought of some transcending wave of opinion, some hegemonic political force which will sweep them, as the party of Wellington was swept, onto the rocks of a permanent second, or even third, position in the political system. Since 1964 the fit has come and gone again.

Performance means keeping up to date. Tories must always keep their ears to the ground to hear what is burrowing and shaking

[1] Coleraine, *The Times*, 2 October 1956.   [2] *Ibid.*

there. They need generous endowment with 'the sense of real politics, of people feeling their way; of moles digging frantically about to dodge some unknown noise overhead; of worms all driving down simultaneously because of some change in the weather, or rising gaily up again because some scientific character has spread the right poison mixture.'[1] Conservatives will listen to all insistent voices. Comprehension of the situation is a primary activity—one thinks of Salisbury, Balfour, Baldwin. But Conservative leaders are also capable of seizing situations, of pursuing intimations to the point of innovation. Peel, Disraeli, Neville Chamberlain and Macmillan were all Tory men with Whig measures.

It is not the business of Conservatives to promise either a new order of justice or comprehensive management of human affairs. Yet, while reluctant to raise hopes and trusting the people never to demand too much, they must have programmes to win popular support. People must be able to predict how they will behave in power; there must therefore be 'principles of action'. This means sober reflection in order to develop specific and consistent policies. Only when long out of office—as Jacobites—are Conservatives likely to take to drama. (Even the Jacobites tended to be sturdy, truculent men idealizing an order disrupted, not really believing it could be recalled.) In recent times the Conservatives have never been far from power. Order has been shaken and events have disturbed them but they are seldom tempted to take up extravagant ideas; witness, despite the aspersions of the Left Book Club, their immunity to Fascist infection in the 1930s.

In fact, as S. H. Beer has pointed out, the Tories were doing some serious and constructive thinking in the 1930s.[2] It was then that they accepted the managed economy and through 'the great policy' of Neville Chamberlain created a new framework in which business would operate. The thinking was from within. The policy meant a change in direction but did not appear to Conservatives as either a capitulation to Socialism or to interests. Rather, it seemed, with its emphasis upon Protection and rationalization, a legitimate revival of Elizabethan mercantilism—the belated discovery of economic coherence. It was what had to be done *now* after hard appraisal of the situation. For, as Beer says: 'A party may have its own political culture inherited from different historical moments

---

1 Joyce Cary, *To be a pilgrim.*
2 *Modern British politics*, London, 1965, chapter x.

—and quite possibly, in the case of an old party, internally in-consistent—which from the resources of a distant past provides principles of action in a new situation.'[1]

Given these political attitudes Conservatives, one might think, would produce attentive and cautious rulers for quiet times. Labour and Liberal politicians can speak the lucid truth, with the gap between promise and performance widening all the time. The Conservative politician labours at modest tasks. He is typically the man of character rising not so much from obscurity as from English inertia, out of the silences and brief interchanges of the English club. For the Tories are, as Ford Madox Ford's man of integrity in *Some Do Not* insisted, primarily men together.

In electing to be peculiarly English in habits and in as much of his temperament as he could control...Tietjens had quite advisedly and of set purpose adopted a habit of behaviour that he considered the best in the world for the normal life. If every day and all day long you chatter at a high pitch and with the logic and lucidity of the Frenchman; if you shout in self-assertion, with your hat on your stomach, bowing from a stiff spine, and by implication threaten all day long to shoot your interlocutor, like the Prussian; if you are as lachrymally emotional as the Italian, or as drily and epigrammatically imbecile over inessentials as the American, you will have a noisy, troublesome and thoughtless society without any of the surface calm that should distinguish the atmosphere of men when they are together.

This insulation has its drawbacks. The times may not be quiet: the tasks may be too severe, demand more energy than the Tory can command. Yet it was out of this close, but not necessarily inbred, society that the statesmanship of which Tories were capable was distilled.

Tories give their leader much independent power. How much he should exercise is left to him; he is trusted to do what is necessary—like a civil servant drawing on the residual authority of the Crown. Because he has this prerogative power his character is of the greatest importance. Tories therefore spend an inordinate amount of time judging the qualities of their leader. 'Conservatism finds the pledges of responsibility on the part of men entrusted with authority, in the personal character and public repute of the individual politician.'[2] Yet the leader is not raised to power by popular acclaim—but selected by the knowledgeable. Conservatives

[1] *Ibid.* p. 300.   [2] R. J. White, *op. cit.* p. 60.

believe in the rule of the right man, providentially endowed, but rationally chosen. This does not mean that criticism is subsequently suspended. 'Virtue and wisdom may be the objects of their choice,' declared Burke, 'but their choice confers neither the one nor the other on those upon whom they confer their ordaining hands.' There is a countervailing critical power which may check and depose, and it is in this, the constitutional faculty within the party, that the Tory intellect is grounded. Tories are acutely aware of what kind of leadership is wanted here and now and this means that leaders are expendable. *Balfour must go. Home must go.*

Yet, as Amery said of the British constitution, the leadership of the Conservative Party 'is not so much flexible as elastic, tending to revert to form as the influences which have deflected it in one direction or another have weakened or been superseded'.[1] The norm is character; style is anomalous. It is of course possible for the party to subordinate itself to the 'brilliant' outsider and even to take him into the tradition. Disraeli was assimilated; Lloyd George was not. Churchill was swallowed and perhaps has not yet been digested. It would be wrong to assume that the party is agape before these wonder-workers; they must all be capable of working within the spirit of the party.

Tories recognize known 'merit'. This does not imply either intellect as such or force. Wits like Birkenhead never had much chance and would-be Bismarcks like Milner no chance at all. Nor does it mean that the leader cannot rise from *relative* obscurity. A fund of 'merit' is available in a trained political class. Judging within this class has in the past been through private conversation and correspondence among those who hold the gates of the party. It is particularly true of the Conservative Party that 'a politician's advancement depends far more upon the opinion of his senior colleagues than upon the esteem in which he is held in the outside world'.[2] The 'ratings' made by outsiders have never, until recently, been seriously considered. Stirrings and flickerings of opinion in the constituencies towards the right men were interpreted and taken into account but no more. Opinion in the party in Parliament was not crucial.

The choice was, in effect, made by accepted leading men within the party but not, in spite of recent allegations, from a defined

[1] L. S. Amery, *Thoughts on the constitution* (1947), London, 1953, p. 2.
[2] David Butler, 'Political reporting in Britain', *The Listener*, 15 August 1963.

'magic circle'. It is not really very illuminating to explain the selection of a Tory leader solely in terms of social and cultural considerations. In recent times it cannot be said that any more than due consideration has been given to patrician background. It is surely difficult to place Bonar Law, Baldwin or Chamberlain within a charmed circle. And surely both Eden and Macmillan were raised up by more than just friendship and connections.

In choosing their leaders the Conservatives have always distrusted the *curriculum vitae*. Like Burke, Coleridge[1] insisted that the party must seek virtue and that virtue cannot 'depend on talent':

If superior talents, and the mere possession of knowledges such as can be learned at Mechanics' Institutions, were regularly accompanied with a will in harmony with the reason, and a consequent subordination of the appetites and passions to the ultimate ends of our being; if intellectual gifts and attainments were infallible signs of wisdom and goodness in the same proportion, and the knowing, clever and *talented* (vile word!) were always *rational*; if the mere facts of science conferred or superseded the soft'ning humanizing influence of the moral world... then, indeed, political power might not unwisely be conferred as the honorarium or privilege of having passed through all the forms of a National School, without the security of political ties...[2]

For Coleridge, the holder of political power should have *reason*, defined by him as 'the organ of the supersensuous', the power to discern spiritual realities; rather than mere *understanding* which measures, analyses and classifies. The leader is not a professional; he remains 'in the soft'ning humanizing influence of the moral world'. It does not seem to me that in recent times Conservatives have always been of one mind on this (some have been disturbed by outside critics who mock their method of choosing leaders and allege talents wasted and worth oppressed) but it seems clear that traditionally, it has not been usual for Conservatives, when making their selection, to think primarily in terms of a leader who can capture power. Conservation of power, party unity, have come first. It has not been political wizardry or masterful government or deeds that have been expected of the leader so much as certain personal qualities, what Timothy Raison has called 'the masculine qualities of vigour, courage, independence, self-reliance, and clearsightedness'.[3]

[1] *The church and state*, quoted in R. J. White, *op. cit.* pp. 66–7.
[2] Quoted in R. J. White, *ibid.*   [3] Raison, *Why conservative?*, p. 27.

Political scientists, political journalists and, perhaps, party managers seem now to consider these qualities obsolete: 'the function of leadership and the task of governmental office require other qualities than those customarily displayed by the traditional Tory politicians.'[1] Professional knowledge has now acquired a priority never given to it by Conservatives. Britain now 'needs more professional government, not just in possessing professional politicians but in bringing to politics an expertise equal to that which has already developed in the go-ahead parts of British life'.[2]

Political expertise means not only skill in 'the back alleys of power' and the arts of management and manipulation; it also means the capacity to *calculate*. The object of politics is to discover what people want or can be persuaded to want. The inner imperatives of politicians are obstructive and dangerous and there are many more qualifications for government than 'virtue and wisdom, actual and presumptive'.

Tories have appreciated managerial talents but no party seemed less likely until recently to choose a manager or technocrat to lead them. Experts have been there to be used. This is not to say that the Conservative Party with their concentration upon appraising the concrete historical situation, and governing within limitations, is unattractive to able outsiders, in law, business and the civil service, who appreciate efficiency but are not really political animals—Lindemann, Anderson, Mills, Monckton and possibly even Woolton are all good examples of men whose cast of mind was not deeply political but who liked the *business* of government. But to lead them, the Tories in the past have wanted a man trafficking in words, engaged in *political* debate, with inner imperatives.

Conservatives too seem to be losing faith in their ability to recognize their leaders. They are alarmed lest their men of character or style appear boobies on the television screen. Conservatives now analyse themselves more searchingly to discover that they themselves contain interest groups which need more managerial control, more skilled and knowledgeable conciliation than their dilettante leaders can provide. The tasks of government more and more seem to demand a kind of Presidential leadership with Bonapartist or Gaullist authority, a political leader who can

[1] Guttsmann, *The British political élite*, p. 312.
[2] Editorial in *The Economist*, 30 October 1965.

publicize himself and whose simple reputation can be widely appreciated. But Conservatives have not, until very recently, considered that an essential qualification of the leader should be in public relations. Their old criteria for procedures of selection are therefore all in doubt.

How modest have been the Tory expectations from their leaders; how surprisingly unobtrusive those leaders have often been; how wild are those criticisms which see the authoritarian personalities of Tories reflected in the authoritarian personality of their leaders (there seems to have been some confusion of 'authoritarian' with 'authoritative'); how much the usual emphasis has been upon the leader sealing the unity of the party, rather than commanding or inspiring followers, can be seen if the essentially political records of four of their leading politicians since 1911 are examined.

When Bonar Law succeeded Balfour as leader in 1911 and ended the Cecil dominance in the Conservative Party, Lloyd George, characteristically contemptuous of Tory judgment, said that 'the fools had stumbled upon the best man by accident'. Canadian-born, a Presbyterian by religion and a Glasgow iron-merchant by calling, with only eleven years in Parliament and no Cabinet experience, he was a most unlikely choice. Even as a 'sociological' choice to celebrate the rising influence of the manufacturing middle class in the party—the next three leaders were Austen Chamberlain, Baldwin and Neville Chamberlain—the selection is startling. For to compensate for his lack of political breeding and connections, Bonar Law had neither magnetism nor rough power.

What the Tories were looking for in 1911, after Balfour, was integrity, not style. The two contenders for the succession, Austen Chamberlain and Walter Long, both had political virtues. Austen Chamberlain, it has been said, 'perspired rectitude', never at any time played for himself, gave others the benefit of the doubt even when there was no doubt. Walter Long (like Chamberlain) had no parade of intelligence, was honest and spontaneous, had country character. Yet Bonar Law, the third candidate, won because the other two, locked in personal antagonism, might have *divided* the party.

Such a man was, as might be expected, politically ambitious: he had trained himself hard in the Glasgow Parliamentary Debating

Association for politics. He had more than just the clarity and realism of the good man of business and effectiveness in making and destroying arguments; he was also peculiarly suited in temperament and language to the strange, melodramatic politics between 1911 and 1914. He was not witty and he had no vanity. He did not want to know much but what he did know he knew well; he was 'honest to the verge of simplicity'.[1] What he found was hard words to defend acquired positions: and to expose the long-unexamined faith of his Liberal opponents in fine declarations of parliamentary solutions. The issues of this period, Ulster and Free Trade, engaged Law more deeply than any that came after. In Parliament, as we have seen, he was the author of what Asquith called the 'New Style'—a way of speaking which was stringent, direct and unaccommodating. Outside, he spoke the harshest truths, contemplated the possibility of mutiny in the army, and threatened violence. At a Conservative demonstration at Blenheim Palace in July 1912, he declared:

In our opposition to them [the Government] we shall not be guided by the considerations or bound by the restraints which would guide us in an ordinary Constitutional struggle. We shall take the means, whatever means seem to us most effective, to deprive them of the despotic power which they have usurped and compel them to appeal to the people whom they have deceived. They may, perhaps they will, carry their Home Rule Bill but what then? I said the other day in the House of Commons and I repeat here that there are things stronger than Parliamentary majorities.

The clever worldly men who led the Liberal Party underestimated and despised Bonar Law (Asquith called him 'the gilded tradesman' and said he had 'the mind of a Glasgow Bailie'[2]) but in the long run—with the aid of Lloyd George, Carson and Milner—he humiliated them. He bided his time more effectively than Asquith. Surprisingly, it was in the war years that Law became recognizably a Tory leader—primarily in his desire, to the point of self-effacement, for the preservation of party unity at all costs. As leader of the Conservative Party he was content with the Colonial Secretaryship in the Asquith Coalition of 1915—an office

---

[1] The six words which, said Baldwin, had won the election of 1922. 'One morning they [the voters] opened their papers and read that Lloyd George had said of Bonar Law that he was "honest to the verge of simplicity". And they said, "By God that is what we have been looking for."' G. M. Young, *Stanley Baldwin*, p. 43.

[2] Robert Blake, *The unknown Prime Minister*, London, 1955, p. 98.

so far below his deserts and abilities as to be considered a slight by others. In 1916 he refused the premiership and subordinated himself to Lloyd George in what Baldwin was to call 'the most perfect political parnership in history'. In 1922, it was only because the unity of the Conservative Party was in danger that he moved to destroy the Lloyd George Coalition.

Some light is thrown on Bonar Law's political character by his rejection of Churchill, who, he thought, had an 'entirely unbalanced' mind. Law's joining the Coalition in 1915 was conditional upon Churchill's leaving the Admiralty. Law is more notable for his rejections than his affirmations; his ability to control, check and pull down. Conservative politicians may sometimes have a melancholy stoicism but there is in Bonar Law an unusual dour and sad quality. The despondent realism of what he wrote to a friend in the dark month of March 1916 is characteristic:

'The whole political situation is as bad as it can be; so bad indeed that it seems to me to be very doubtful if the present condition of things can continue; but on the other hand I do not see the possibility of any change which would be an improvement.'[1]

There is one Tory attribute which is not there. Bonar Law was resistant, a rock upon which the old Liberalism foundered. It was this quality which made him such an admirable leader during a period when Toryism might have discredited itself in excess. But what he seems to have lacked was the strong conviction that he and his party must rule.

Another 'hard' Tory is Neville Chamberlain. As a public man Chamberlain was practical, egotistical, and hardly 'capable of being in uncertainties, Mysteries, doubts, without any irritable reaching after fact and reason'. Chamberlain, said Herriot, '*c'est du cristal*'. Here is a politician who does not ruminate like Baldwin but presses on to get things done, one who by his own admission could not contemplate any problem without seeking a solution to it. Baldwin's guiding principle, said L. S. Amery, was 'his ideal of what a Prime Minister should be'; he went to the House of Commons 'both to sense atmosphere and create it'.[2] Chamberlain created no atmosphere; he was combative and harshly contemptuous of a Labour Opposition which could not follow an argument. On one occasion Baldwin had to remind him

[1] *Ibid.* p. 281.
[2] *My political life*, III, London, 1935, p. 226.

that he was addressing 'an assembly of gentlemen'. But Chamberlain continued to regard the House primarily 'as the place where government is carried on'.[1]

Chamberlain 'admitted another power in Baldwin'. He might have the drive and design but Baldwin won the elections. What Chamberlain did was to labour indefatigably at the work in hand and to project even more. From 1931 to 1937 he was 'the packhorse' of the MacDonald and Baldwin governments. Not only was he—at the Ministry of Health and at the Treasury—one of the great departmental ministers of the century; he could also see around him, move forward and suggest policies to colleagues. There was a kind of administrative exuberance about him in those years. 'All his days filled by exacting pressures in foreign policy and finance, he rose and broadened under the full stretch.'[2]

The two great outsiders were critical of Chamberlain. Lloyd George said that his main quality was 'rigid competency', Churchill, that he would have made a good Lord Mayor of Birmingham in a lean year.[3] But one has only to contrast Chamberlain with another superb Conservative administrator, a Chamberlain man, and one who might even have become Prime Minister, to become aware that there were in Chamberlain certain gifts of initiative and even of imagination that Lloyd George and Churchill refused to see. For Sir John Anderson, mountainous in his wisdom and integrity, cared not at all about the substance of what he was administering. 'His inclination was to administer efficiently and smoothly within the limits of existing policy.'[4] When it came to the serious business of politics he had 'little room for fads and fancies or for those political nostrums that merely make a transient and meretricious appeal'.[5] Politically Anderson was a nullity, Chamberlain was not.

Chamberlain may not have had the popular appeal of Baldwin but he was intensely alive politically and made concentrated political impact at the highest levels. It is said that he did not bring to international affairs the same perception and realism that he had brought to domestic politics. Yet on the crumbling surface of the international order, Chamberlain seems to have been one of

[1] Amery, *op. cit.*
[2] K. Feiling, *Neville Chamberlain*, London, 1946, p. 233.
[3] Also attributed to Birkenhead, another outsider.
[4] J. W. Wheeler-Bennett, *John Anderson, Viscount Waverley*, London, 1962, p. 85.
[5] *Ibid.* p. 185.

the few who retained his footing. It is not true that he did not know what was politically relevant, that he was an innocent among forces that he did not comprehend. 'Mr Chamberlain perceived more clearly than any other political leader the growing danger of a policy of words not matched either by willingness or by capacity to act. He understood the paramount importance of re-establishing British credit by promising nothing which Britain could not perform...'[1]

The appeasement of Europe was, as Iain Macleod has written, 'neither a foolish nor an ignoble hope'.[2] Indeed, in the light of what force Britain could command and the weakness, unreliability or self-absorption of potential allies in face of a world conflict that might involve Britain in both Europe and the Far East at the same time, Chamberlain's policy, up to the fatal guarantee given to Poland in March 1939, to rearm and negotiate now seems, if not noble, neither unwise nor unenlightened. To separate, if possible, Italy and Germany (by securing a détente with either of them); to resist the temptation to make moral distinctions among the nations of Europe; to refuse to indulge in *verbal* knight-errantry on behalf of 'far-away countries': these made good sense.

In a skilful book,[3] Francis Williams insists that, like Baldwin, MacDonald, Montagu Norman and Halifax, Chamberlain was the wrong man for office. He was one of those, imprisoned in their own personal myths, who 'lacked the quality of living in their own time'. He had not the capacity for knowing the truth and telling it to his generation; he was unable effectively 'to link the past and the present, to facilitate the transition from one age to another...'.[4]

This thesis, with its implication that trustworthy leaders with keener insight into the needs of their times were conspicuously available, is not very convincing. With his wing collar, Victorian rectitude, corvine arrogance, emphasis upon 'strict administration', inner-directed decisiveness, Chamberlain often seemed archaically angular in public. (His private virtues and sensibility are well attested.) Yet how is it possible to consider the author of 'the great policy' of the 1930s so much out of touch with his

[1] E. H. Carr, *Britain: a study of foreign policy from the Versailles treaty to the outbreak of war*, London, 1939, pp. 166–7.
[2] *Neville Chamberlain*, London, 1961, p. 209.
[3] *A pattern of rulers*, London, 1965.   [4] *Ibid.* p. 252.

time? Who was really obsolete: Chamberlain, who sought within limits to redress what he (and many others) thought were legitimate German grievances; or Churchill with his instinct for a European balance of power which Britain by itself could not sustain? Chamberlain knew that the Russians could not be trusted, that French morale was low, that the League of Nations was useless and that little but words could be expected from America, and yet that a lasting European settlement had to be reached. Such a settlement he pursued with over-confidence in his own ability to the point of humiliation. Yet Munich was only a humiliation; it was not a disaster.

In what is Chamberlain Tory? Perhaps most notably in his reluctant entry to politics to prove himself, his clear aspiration to govern, to take charge, despite the irresistible 'nausea and revulsion' which 'the drudgery, humiliation and pettiness' of the public life produced in him. And there is also the 'exact correspondence between intimate thought and public deed',[1] the reluctance to develop style.

Bonar Law and Neville Chamberlain are the cutting edge of Conservatism in this century. They were necessary men to meet the challenge of Liberalism and Socialism. They were efficient, honest Tories, if not very prepossessing. Tory leaders may well possess virtues rarer than theirs.

'I do not hesitate to say,' runs the famous passage in Burke's *Reflections*, 'that the road to eminence and power, from obscure condition, ought not to be made too easy, nor a thing too much of course. If rare merit be the rarest of all rare things, it ought to pass through some sort of probation. The temple of honour ought to be seated on an eminence.' 'Rare merit' in recent British politics, seated on an eminence from the beginning and therefore needing only minimal probation, is perhaps best represented by Lord Halifax, Viceroy of India, Foreign Secretary and Ambassador to the United States. So universally was his merit recognized that there was no serious obstruction to his rise until that famous long silence—it seemed two minutes—followed Chamberlain's suggestion that Halifax should succeed him as Prime Minister on 9 May 1940.

Much taller than most men, much richer, he was also credited with loftier objectives. It was difficult to withstand such eminence,

[1] Feiling, *Neville Chamberlain*, p. 457.

graduating so smoothly, a version of pastoral, from five great country houses, Eton, Christ Church, All Souls, The Round Table and the Anglo-Catholic Congress. Even when unfledged, he had unmistakable promise for the gatekeepers of the Tory Party. Moderately effective despatch of business at the Board of Education and the Ministry of Agriculture—hunting two days a week—and he was ripe for viceregal office in India. Successful in conciliating liberal Indian opinion, and easing the way to self-government, he returned to England in all honour, an accepted reservoir of political wisdom. He was above faction, for as Viceroy he had carried out the policy of both Baldwin and MacDonald. He had not been involved in either of the two crucial splits in the inter-war years, in 1922 and 1931. He was above and beyond contention.

'He gave tangible form to a self-deception to which the English are prone, the belief that if they look long enough among those socially above them they will find an abstract public virtue untainted by political or hereditary interest.'[1] But is such hope entirely in vain? May not expectations encourage men to fulfil them? It is not impossible for a people to inculcate virtue in those that rule them. Rank can acquire obligations. It certainly seems to be true that denigration of politicians and the class from which they come does not improve their calibre.

What were the expectations? When he succeeded Eden as Foreign Secretary in 1938, Halifax was expected to bring to the foreign policy of Britain discernment and courage. Yet to the hard, knotted bitterness of Europe he brought not moral strength but moral detachment, indeed what seemed to be an unwillingness to make specific moral judgments about the foreign and domestic policies of others. He shared Chamberlain's realism and was prepared to work cautiously in uncharted territory:

'Unless you are prepared on the one hand to say: "I will fight in any case on behalf of peace which is one and indivisible," or on the other hand to say: "I will only fight when I am myself the victim of attack," there is an inevitable no-man's-land of uncertainty lying between which is quite incapable of antecedent definition.'[2]

Right to the end he was a convinced appeaser. Britain could,

[1] Francis Williams, *A pattern of rulers*, p. 228.
[2] Earl of Birkenhead, *Halifax*, London, 1965, p. 359.

he thought, do little to prevent growing German authority in
Central Europe and 'it would therefore seem short-sighted to
forgo the chance of a German settlement by holding out for
something that we are almost certainly going to find ourselves
powerless to secure'.[1]

He was not obscured by Chamberlain; he agreed with his
policy. He was remote but not necessarily, within his lights, ineffectual. He lacked concrete perception, *physiognomic tact*. He
mistook Hitler for a footman and could not see that behind the
junketing and the schoolboy zest of Goering there was a depraved
and desperate man. He was a good man trafficking in politics. He
knew too little—sometimes, it seemed, less than the least among
journalists.

Yet these things do not make him less of a Tory statesman.
Leaders are not elected for perception or wizardry but for public
virtue and perhaps for a capacity to remain 'above the battle'. It
was because he was a trust-creating and trustworthy man (in a
sense in which Churchill was not) that he proved, as has been said,
indestructible. Right up to the end of Chamberlain's premiership,
both Labour and Conservative leading politicians would have
accepted Halifax as Prime Minister.

Few worse things could befall British Conservatives than loss
of faith in their capacity to judge men. In the past they have not
hesitated to reject the 'brilliant' and raise the unobtrusively able.
Their criteria of man and occasion have not easily been shaken.
Balfour, Lloyd George, Curzon and Churchill were all judged
with few misgivings—no factions appeared.

Their recent failure to stand by the widely criticized choice of
Lord Home as leader of the party in 1963, the abandonment of the
'evolved' leader, may therefore considerably diminish Tory self-
confidence. It may be true that how a party chooses its own leader
is its own business. But if the method is one which cannot be
lucidly explained in public, it is surely better not to expose it
unduly. It was unfortunate that the choice of Home had to be at
the time of the Tory Party Conference in a period of high publicity, much of it unfavourable for the party. In this unnatural
limelight, Home seemed almost a parody of Conservative values.

Yet the choice was not irrational. Home may not have been the
best man but even the Americans, who appear to believe that the

[1] Earl of Birkenhead, *Halifax*, p. 374.

public can point an infallible finger at the right man, 'don't take', as James Reston has remarked, 'the best man available but the best-looking man among the very rich men from the very biggest states'. What critics ignored was that Home had given good service both as Foreign Secretary and as Secretary for Commonwealth Relations. He was experienced, honest and alert and there are good reasons for thinking he had reserves of energy. Some Conservative backbenchers thought he might make the best leader since Baldwin. Moreover, if it was plain for reasons that outsiders might find difficult to understand that the Tory gatekeepers would not have Butler as leader, there was no clear alternative. The soundings into the party at all levels, set in motion by Macmillan and more comprehensive than usual, did after all reveal a consensus for Home.

That the weathercock commentators of the weekly and daily press were unable to make much of Home, that the political public should have been bewildered, is understandable; what is more difficult to understand is why Home was forced to resign after only twenty-one months as leader, during which he almost won a General Election against the odds, even if it was true that he was unable to utter words like 'modernization' with much conviction and obviously had little zest for television politics—he thought the Nixon–Kennedy confrontation 'a deplorable piece of exhibitionism'.

Long ago Cyril Connolly had recollected him in *Enemies of promise* as the favoured one, Keeper of the Field and Captain of the Eleven at Eton.

He was a votary of the esoteric Eton religion, the kind of graceful, tolerant, sleepy boy who is showered with favours and crowned with all the laurels, who is liked by the masters and admired by the boys, without any apparent exertion on his part, without experiencing the ill-effects of success himself or arousing the pangs of envy in others. In the eighteenth century he would have become Prime Minister before he was thirty; as it was he appeared honourably ineligible for the struggle of life.[1]

This early insight might seem to confirm the opinion, widespread from 1963 onwards, that Home was something out of 'the palaeontology of the party', a man without the vulgar energy to carry out the tasks of a modern Prime Minister. Yet beneath the

---

[1] *Enemies of promise* (1938), London, 1961, p. 245.

irony there is the admission that Home, with his unobtrusive authority, was distinctive enough to be seen as the kind of man to become a head of government. His *ineligibility* for the struggle of life was not 'unfitness'.

The Tories were feeling for an identifiable leadership. (What had they had from Macmillan, that unabashed, *innovating* Conservative? What were they likely to get from the ambiguous Butler?) They wanted Tory character and they had to go right of centre for it. There was, moreover, something aesthetically appropriate about the choice of Home as leader and Prime Minister. Yet the party had doubts: they did not firmly endorse Captain Ernest Pretyman's famous dictum of 1921: 'The leader is there and we all know it when he is there.' And the journalists and political scientists would not bend the knee. They were indeed highly sceptical about this statesman who came out of the closet with every political limb fully formed. This was power growing 'like mushrooms in the dark'.[1]

Labour supporters commented freely and sometimes impertinently. Home, said Bernard Williams, had been selected by blackball and blackball 'is an institution for electing congenial members to clubs, not a device for deciding between the opinions of intelligent and passionate men on any substantive issue'.[2] Conservatives, however, believe that passionate men dividing on substantive issues will not long remain intelligent, and have never thought that their choice of leader should decide matters on which they are deeply divided. The model is, in fact, not that of a debating society but of a club. A leader selected by blackball will at least preserve amity. He will represent maximum agreement on personal merit.

Home may therefore be regarded as the paradigm Conservative who came in to hold the party together. He was a symbol of self-preservation, an archetype of 'character' in a dangerous period, and interesting in himself. His very 'amateurism', the awkwardness which he showed in resuming popular politics, underlined his integrity. Yet it seems that the middle-class professional people, 'sociologizing' in the best modern way, wanted more than an attentive statesman, a man visibly governing without ostentation. Like Labour, they were now anxious to have a man

[1] Bernard Williams, 'Mr Macmillan's successor', in *The Listener*, 24 October 1963.
[2] *Ibid.*

who could command 'a sociological majority' who could easily adapt himself to the mildly radical mood said to be permeating British politics, proclaim kinship with the 'salariat' and 'meritocracy'.[1] Home had to go because he could not command a lucidity foreign to his nature. He departed with dignity. 'All that being so, I come to two promises which I have always made to you. I have always considered them binding. The first is that I would never allow disunity in the party, least of all over myself; the second, that I would consider when the time was right to hand over the leadership to another.'

The Conservative Party has drawn its strength from the history of England, not from ideology but from reflection on insular experience and habits. Its leaders have been placed upon 'an eminence' so that they might rule with 'the sense of the country'. Conservatives have been trusted not because they were able or clever, but because they knew 'the old good humour of England'; they have ruled with assurance because the classes have never disliked each other for very long. Some Tory leaders have been clever, and most have known how to use the ability of others, but it has always been assumed that ability or cleverness must be mediated through what Burke called 'the presumptive virtue' of gentlemen.[2] Until recently Tory leaders have not been recruited from professional politicians—men wholly devoted to and living day in and day out in the business of politics. What the Tory leader had to bring to politics was an honesty and disinterestedness cultivated in the private realm. (This is not, of course, a quality confined to Conservatives. Early Labour leaders like Fred Jowett and George Lansbury and some later ones, like Hugh Gaitskell, had the same nurtured honesty.)

We have been told that Conservative leaders may be deposed and that three or four in this century have been virtually superseded. But they have not been denied or indicted; they have left

[1] Probably an unnecessary anxiety. See *The Times*, 14 January 1966, report on the views in the Liberal monthly, *New Outlook*, of William Douglas-Home, the playwright, on the fall of his brother. 'Mr Home says that voters abhor sharp practice, revere tradition (if enlightened), applaud an honest man, lack inverted snobbery, see beneath the surface, and deplore vote catching. The only thing the British public really liked, apart from racehorses, was character; the only thing the voters really liked was fair play.'

[2] The roots of this conception are very ably expounded in Mansfield, *Statesmanship and party government*, chapters 7, 8 and 9.

no legacy of faction. Only Balfour, because he seemed to trifle with the business of politics, because perhaps he was too clever, raised much rancour. Loyalties are quickly resumed and made fast again. Indeed Conservatism may well tend to 'drag the chain of lost loyalties, superannuated leaders and indefensible chivalries'.[1] Yet it seems doubtful whether in the *current market* of British politics this model and these attitudes can survive. Conservatives have developed too much appetite for power: they have had more office in recent years than has been good for them—and to retain it they have (unlike the old Liberal Party) too often sacrificed principles for office. Today they often seem over-anxious to prove that they are not 'the stupid party'. The young men of *Crossbow* appear almost too anxious to catch every Radical straw in the wind. Have Conservatives lost some of their old confidence in their ability to mediate and criticize fashionable modes of thought and opinion?

It may well be true that the present political climate in Britain is Radical. This does not mean that the Conservative Party should try to do the work of other parties. In seeking to show that it is not obtuse, the Tory Party may well lose all sense of what it is. A depersonalized party may well find itself short of leaders of character and style—men who know what they have to do.

[1] Keith Feiling, *TLS*, 26 September 1929, quoted in F. J. C. Hearnshaw, *Conservatism in England*, London, 1933, p. 33.

WORDS AND ACTION:
CHURCHILL AND EDEN

'Only one man in a hundred', wrote Milner, 'dares give effect or utterance to the statesmanship that is in him.' But the opportunity to devise and execute grand policy is given to very few. In recent times, only two British politicians have had it: one was, as we have seen, Neville Chamberlain; the other was Churchill. There is little that one can say about Churchill that is not supererogatory. He is an illustrated book that has been turned leaf by leaf too often. We are all grateful to the almost extinguished politician who became 'the great deliverer' but are now almost too well acquainted with the face that could hide nothing, the long watchful crouch for action, the words 'wheeled up for battle', as Aneurin Bevan observed, 'like an enormous gun'.

What can be seen in Churchill is not so much prescience, sustaining mission or attentive statesmanship, as heroic political energy. Those famous words 'In War: Resolution; in Defeat: Defiance; in Victory: Magnanimity; in Peace: Good-Will' do not tell us what he stood for; only that he stood fast. He gives a lesson in human conduct, in adversity and success. He proved that the values of politics could be those of life. He was the least Machiavellian, the most transparent, 'the most truthful of politicians'.[1] And although moralistic, indicting both sloth and inattention, he opens up an unexpectedly rich vein of politics—so rich that the unpolitical can appreciate Churchill as they can no other politician.

There is much in Churchill that seems to be the spontaneous politics of character, the visible acting out of political impulse. To an unusual degree he was self-moving, an individualist who read his own auguries. Yet almost everything he did in public was deliberated; there was very little off the cuff. The speeches were written out, learned and delivered verbatim. If it is true, as Asquith remarked, that, like Lloyd George, he thought with his mouth, it was in council, in Cabinet, in conversation that he

---

[1] Lord Moran, *Churchill: the struggle for survival, 1940–65*, London, 1966, p. 773.

conducted his transitory verbal exploration of ideas and schemes. In the public realm, even his vituperation was prepared. There is Balfour's rebuke of long ago:

> It is not, on the whole, desirable to come down to this House with invective which is both prepared and violent. The House will tolerate, and very rightly tolerate, almost anything within the rule of order which evidently springs from a genuine indignation aroused by the collision of debate; but to come down with these prepared phrases is not usually successful...If there is preparation there should be more finish, and if there is so much violence there should certainly be more obvious veracity of feeling.[1]

A similar judgment might be passed on his wit. He made himself into a wit, harbouring aphorisms, repartee and rejoinders in kind as some might harbour grudges. Churchill, said Birkenhead, spent years of his life preparing impromptu speeches. He waited to deliver his witticisms. They were carefully composed and concentrated, and therefore often worth waiting for. Nothing, for example, could be more obviously composed and polished for delivery than his famous remark on Attlee's surprisingly effective performance as Prime Minister: 'Feed a grub on royal jelly.'

It is doubtful whether, although he had great activity of mind, such activity that Sir Edward Grey said that he would very soon become incapable of being anything in a Cabinet but Prime Minister, Churchill was in any sense a constructive thinker.

> In nearly every case an *idea* enters his head from outside. It then rolls round the hollows of his brain, collecting strength like a snowball. *Then*, after whirlwinds of *rhetoric*, he becomes convinced that it is *right*; and denounces everyone who criticizes it...He sets ideas to Rhetoric as musicians set theirs to music. And he can convince himself of almost any truth if it is once allowed thus to start its wild career through his rhetorical machinery.[2]

'He can only think in phrases, and close argument is really lost on him,' wrote Amery, 'the only way to get home with him would be in equally striking counter-phrases.'[3] In his early days in the Commons he could not think on his feet. And although he could play the demagogue and was aware of the People in an almost

---

[1] Lady Asquith, *Winston Churchill as I knew him* (1965), London, 1967, p. 127.
[2] C. F. G. Masterman, quoted by Lucy Masterman, 'Winston Churchill: the Liberal phase, part two', *History Today*, December 1964.
[3] Amery, *My political life*, London, 1935, II, 510.

eighteenth-century sense, he was seldom in peacetime closely in touch with popular feelings. He could be inspiring, dominating, intimidating, but he was not a persuasive man.[1]

Some extravagant claims have been made for Churchill's speeches and prose. John Connell in a British Council pamphlet went so far as to write that 'of English prose he is one of the greatest known masters, ranking with Addison or Swift for clarity and masculine vigour of exposition, with Gibbon for lapidary pungency, with Macaulay for romantic colour, and with (on the loftiest, most difficult plane of all) the compilers of the Authorized Version of the Bible for a supreme combination of majesty and homely simplicity'.[2] This is hardly true. Much of Churchill's rhetoric is tiresomely windy, difficult to read for very long, and impressive only for the force which sustains it. Late in his political life he did make great utterances but these are at least as remarkable for the effect that they had on himself as on others. They instilled *him* with purpose and courage.

This cannot be said of his early speeches. There is, for example, his attack on the 'Birmingham policy' of the Edwardian Tory Party: 'Corruption at home, aggression abroad, sentiment by the bucketful, patriotism by the Imperial pint, the open hand at the public Exchequer and the open door at the public house, dear food for the million, cheap labour for the millionaire.' This is succinct; the phrases to hand have been carefully 'gummed together'. But, in an ex-Tory, one doubts the 'veracity of feeling'.

The ring of words made him. Words carefully turned led to action. Often he seemed to be pressing on regardless of consequences. But he was not, as has been pointed out, a true adventurer. Birth, connections and friends cushioned him. He had not risen from nothing and would therefore never pay the full penalty for incaution. Yet although he was a man from the top he was a 'would be', wished to excel, and had all the energy of the self-making man—his closest political friends tended to be men of this kind.

There is now some agreement that he was a passionate, imaginative man who did not reason things out; that he was a poor judge

[1] Anyone reading steadily through Lord Moran's court memoir, *Churchill: the struggle for survival, 1940–65*, will surely find it progressively more difficult to agree with Brendan Bracken and Macmillan that the mind and sensibility of Churchill really deserve a Boswell.

[2] *Winston Churchill*, London, 1956, p. 8.

of men (How could he find out about people, asked Lord Norman-
brook, when he did all the talking?[1]); that he had a curious
liking for quacks and hard-backed men, for those 'with tearing
spirits'; that he was not particularly effective (although unduly
depreciated) either as an administrator or a strategist unless someone like Anderson or Alanbrooke was guiding him; that, most
surprisingly, he did not like making decisions.

Many others—John Morley, Margot Asquith, A. G. Gardiner
—have gone further, to say that Churchill was not even redeemed
by high purpose. Yet what impresses most about Churchill in the
1930s is his constancy, his set position, his willingness to lie
becalmed until the wind filled his sails again. Perhaps only a
politician as impervious to atmosphere as he (as a diver in his bell,
says Lady Asquith), could have exhibited such valour. His lack of
sensibility and his obsessive sense of situation were his strength.
His long sojourn out of office, his persistent political and historical research deepened his solipsism, belatedly gave him
'character'. He remained unaware of 'the needs, the interests, the
legitimate preoccupations of others'[2] but he became predictable:
a known focus of discontent for politicians, military men and
diplomatists out of favour. His views on Russia, India and the
General Strike might be archaic. His political life might have
come to an end with an inept performance as Chancellor of the
Exchequer, but here was a man to stand fast at the centre of things,
who, 'when all but courage failed...made courage conscious
of itself, plumed it with defiance, and rendered it invincible'.[3]

The ring of words continued after him, passed into the rhetoric
of lesser politicians; and most of the hollower statements—the
wood upon the metal—about Britain's place in the world today
and so on have Churchillian origins. Through sheer *panache*
Churchill still attracts the politically innocent. For he is still the
central figure in that incredibly simple but probably indestructible
historiography of the inter-war years which divides British
politicians into those who stood firm round Churchill, or in broad
sympathy with his conception of a grand alliance against Hitler,
and those who sought by negotiation the appeasement of Europe.
He appealed and still appeals to those who think that there are

[1] Moran, *Churchill*, p. 701.
[2] Goronwy Rees, 'Churchill reconsidered', *Encounter*, November, 1965.
[3] Leading article, 'The great deliverer', in *The Times*, 25 January 1965.

certain clear political truths to be spoken at the right time by the right person.

When the ultimatum to Germany expired on 4 August 1914, Margot Asquith saw 'Winston Churchill with a happy face striding towards the double doors of the Cabinet room'.[1] He was probably the only happy man in Asquith's Cabinet. Whether it was the River War, the Boer War, the Great War or Hitler's War he took fiercer and more prolonged delight in action than any other politician. Goronwy Rees thinks that his one profound interest was war and that there was nothing archaic about this. 'It was Churchill's merit as a politician which also gave him his claim to greatness as a statesman, precisely that from youth upwards, he instinctively understood that war was the determining factor in the history of the twentieth century and had the courage to face and accept the consequences.'[2] We all owe more than we think to those war games on the nursery floor in the house in St James's in the 1880s.

Yet love of action did not mean desire for change. Churchill did not really challenge the system. He approved of the social order, of the way in which things had gone and were going.

Why is it that life and property are more secure in Britain [he once asked] than in any other country in the world?...The security arises from the continuation of that very class-struggle which they lament and of which they complain, which goes on ceaselessly in our country ...a struggle between class and class which never sinks into lethargy, and never breaks into violence, but which from year to year makes possible a steady and constant advance...We are always reaching a higher level after each change, but yet with the harmony of our life unbroken and unimpaired.[3]

Within this social order Churchill took up such postures as events or his own words made appropriate. He could appear as Liberal, Radical or Tory.

His Liberalism was (as Mrs Lucy Masterman says) merely a phase; his Radicalism, where his words occasionally took him. There is much more to his Toryism, errant and idiosyncratic though it seems. ('The fact is, David,' he once said to Lloyd George, 'I am a Tory.') At heart 'he desired in Britain a state of things in

---

[1] *Autobiography* II, London, 1922, p. 196.   [2] *Encounter*, November 1965.

[3] Lady Asquith, *op. cit.* p. 164.

which a benign upper class dispensed benefits to an industrious, *bien-pensant* and grateful working class'.[1] It is true that he was more of a Tory than a Conservative. 'The symbols of Toryism—Crown, Country, Empire—which might seem abstractions to some were to him realities.'[2] Yet he was without Tory insularity: no man was more conscious of Europe and the British stake there.

Powerful English politicians frequently outgrow their parties over a period of time. From very early on Churchill treated parties as vehicles for his ambition. The labels he bore, Conservative, Liberal, Independent, Constitutionalist, never meant much to him. What gives his protean political life coherence is the energy with which he reflects on it, his persistence in adversity. Tories do not habitually 'walk with destiny'; they are not much given to grand designs; being is as important as doing. But Churchill was re-absorbed in the Party and became its leader. What is more he associated the leadership with deeds, reinforced its resistance to the course of history.

'The Chest—Magnanimity—Sentiment—these are the indispensable liaison officers between cerebral and visceral man. It may be even said that it is by this middle element man is man: for by his intellect he is mere spirit and by his appetite he is mere animal.'[3] Churchill is the middle element.

After Churchill, one leading British politician of the post-war period seemed capable of deeds. At the end of the Second World War, Anthony Eden had already been at the centre of politics for fourteen years and was still young. He was recognized as a skilful and potentially creative diplomatist (potentially, because during the war years he had been in the shadow of Churchill) who had never lost his honesty, who, despite his professionalism, had never seemed to be 'in business for himself'.

Views differ on Eden's complexity but it is clear that the hero of the three-volume memoirs, *Facing the dictators*, *The reckoning* and *Full circle*, sees himself as a simple man. His principles never drooped like flags on a windless day. What lessons he learned he never forgot; he engraves them again and again:

'Whenever the nations fail to insist on respect for international engagements, they lay up trouble for themselves later on. This

[1] Lucy Masterman, *loc. cit.*   [2] *The Times*, 25 January 1965.
[3] C. S. Lewis, *The abolition of man*, London, 1946, p. 21.

bilking is the modern equivalent of Ethelred the Unready's attempt to buy off the invaders of his land. It can have no more success.'[1]

He might acquiesce in the decision not to resist Hitler when he re-occupied the Rhineland in 1936 but was nevertheless taught an *academic* lesson that he 'was determined to apply...twenty years later':

'A military dictator's capacity for aggrandisement is only limited by the physical checks imposed upon him. Hitler was not challenged until his power had been swollen by a succession of triumphs, and the price to be paid changed the history of our planet.'[2]

In the fluid perplexing situation[3] of the 1930s, Eden was rigorously formal, sticking to the Covenant of the League of Nations and voicing popular sentiments on collective security. He used the safest of current words, was studiously professional and always moderate, yet could still seem to many Tories, because of his deportment and the kind of approval he won, both too ostentatiously professional and too showy. He had come too easily by his style. He had both a greater concern for Europe, greater feeling for Britain's responsibility there and correspondingly less fear for the unity of the Commonwealth and Empire under the stress of action than those who had most power and influence in Britain. Unlike All Souls, Cliveden and other dominant centres of persuasion, Eden did not regard the search for accommodation *per se* with the European dictators as a policy.[4] Before one came to terms with Mussolini, offered *de jure* recognition of his Abyssinian conquests, one must test his good faith, probe his intentions. From an agreement there must result an increased and not decreased sense of security. For 'to enter upon publicized discussion in order to cover broken engagements, without any evidence that a better fate will befall the new engagements than the old, is to run the most reckless of hazards'.[5]

[1] *The Eden memoirs: Facing the dictators*, London, 1962, p. 244.
[2] *Ibid.* p. 351.
[3] This perplexity is nowhere better expressed than in *The Times* of 28 June 1933, 'Europe in fact is placed in the dilemma of having to refuse to face what reason suggests should at least in part be conceded, or else of yielding to extremism what earlier was refused to moderation'—quoted in John Connell, *The 'Office'*, London, 1958, p. 141.
[4] See John Connell, *The 'Office'*, pp. 136 ff.
[5] *Facing the dictators*, p. 597.

Eden too wanted appeasement but a lasting appeasement, carefully and professionally achieved. It was just this professionalism that Chamberlain offended with his dislike of and impatience with the formalities of diplomacy. Chamberlain wished to move, Eden to stand firm: 'The more critical the negotiating position of a democracy, the more important it is to hold to the tested forms of diplomacy, to proceed step by step, to make sure of agreement on the preliminaries before embarking on the detailed negotiation.'[1]

And yet in welcoming the Roosevelt initiative for a peace conference in January 1938, he could lower his professional criteria. His elders were all against it. 'Rightly or wrongly,' writes Hoare, 'we were deeply suspicious, not indeed of American good intentions, but of American readiness to follow up inspiring words with any practical action.'[2] Hoare makes a good case against both Eden and Churchill. Roosevelt could not bring the United States out of isolation, and 'ecumenical conferences and general statements of moral principles' would certainly not stop the dictators.[3]

As Foreign Secretary in Baldwin's Cabinet, Eden was faced at the table by three former holders of the office and by colleagues who thought that he was often merely a professional voice for Vansittart,[4] the somewhat unprofessional Permanent Under-Secretary at the Foreign Office. Yet, for one so young, Eden brooked little interference. Baldwin observed him bridle at a Cabinet meeting and wrote him a note: 'Don't be too indignant. I once saw Curzon burst into tears when the Cabinet was amending his despatches.' When Horace Wilson, Chamberlain's confidant and emissary, appealed to Eden for a more flexible attitude to the European dictators, he was told that he had no understanding of foreign affairs. When Chamberlain pursued his own policy and circumvented the Foreign Office, Eden resigned with honour.

For he knew that in the country he was a force transcending party. In 1935 he had told Baldwin that he 'held a certain point of view on foreign affairs, the country knew it, foreigners knew it'.[5] His appearance and convictions had given him not only popularity but also a personal following.

What were his affinities? Some have seen him as a voice of

---

[1] Eden, *op. cit.*   [2] *Nine troubled years*, p. 263.   [3] *Ibid.* p. 269.
[4] 'The truth is that Vansittart was seldom an official giving cool and disinterested advice based on study and experience. He was himself a sincere, almost fanatical crusader, and much more a Secretary of State in mentality than a permanent official.' *Facing the dictators*, p. 242.   [5] *Ibid.*, p. 217.

resolution and independence, a sober, modern rendering of Canning. He has also been commonly linked with Winston Churchill and was for long, during the war and after, his heir-apparent. Before the war, Churchill distinguished him as 'one strong young figure standing up against long, dismal, drawling tides of drift and surrender'.[1] Churchill would later say that on questions of foreign policy, nine times out of ten, Eden and he would agree.[2] Randolph Churchill, whose historiography was as simple as but less magnanimous than that of his father, insisted that Eden was never dissociated from the pusillanimous foreign policy of the MacDonald–Baldwin régime, that he was a docile man who 'embodied all the hopes which the silliest people in the country entertained about how Geneva and not their own strength would bring them peace',[3] one with no dauntless Churchillian courage in him. He resigned on a matter of principle but there was also a sense in which he was throwing off an authority that would not allow him to make policy. He refused to be subordinated but, Randolph Churchill implied, if there was valour in the government it was represented by Duff Cooper rather than Eden.[4]

That Winston Churchill was more valorous than Eden cannot be doubted but Churchill was, after all, a platform man, publicist and parliamentary *frondeur*, a considerable distance from power and responsibility; his *irresponsible* valour was fortuitous.

The ambiguity in the early Eden was resolved by his resignation. When he passed over to and was assimilated by the right-wing patriots—he joined 'the Group' chaired by L. S. Amery and including in its membership Macmillan, Sandys, Cranborne and, later, Duff Cooper—he remained muted, responsible, professional. But the long period in the shadow of Churchill during and after the war left its mark. Together the names of Churchill and Eden (and oddly enough of the Labour patriot, Ernest Bevin, whose policy Oliver Stanley subtitled 'The importance of being Anthony') lent a reassuring solidity to post-war British foreign policy. It was appropriate that Eden, as heir to the assertive politics of Churchill, should have attempted the last act of will within that policy. The irony is that, in spite of all the lessons committed to memory, in spite of the fund of rectitude stored up

[1] *The Second World War*, I, 201.　　[2] *The Eden memoirs: Full circle*, London 1960, p. 247.
[3] Randolph Churchill, *The rise and fall of Sir Anthony Eden*, London, 1959, p. 106.
[4] *Ibid.* p. 63.

and invested during and after the war, Eden failed. Not all the didacticism, the strenuous argumentation of the three-volume memoirs can change that.

The theme of the memoirs is that Eden was impelled to his last fatal action by his whole experience. Even Korea reinforced the lesson of the 1930s:

The fighting in Korea achieved a balance of power, recognized and respected as such. Had the United States not acted to halt the northern irruption, the decision would have gone to the communists by default. Further attempts must have followed, on a larger scale and bearing more imminent danger of world conflict. That was the lesson of Europe in the 'thirties. It was also the lesson of the Middle East in the 'fifties.[1]

There is much else to confirm Eden's interpretation of his record; there is, for example, his firm stand over Trieste and over Musaddiq's threat to Anglo-Iranian oil; his resourcefulness, on the failure of the European Defence Community, in committing British troops to Europe to maintain the grand alliance of nations (even if a worse alternative to the supra-national army favoured by Dulles).

Yet in seeking and obtaining a diplomatic solution by partition in Indo-China in 1954, Eden was surely not so simply instructed by what happened in the 1930s. It was Dulles, not Eden, who saw 'that the situation in Indo-China was analogous to the Japanese invasion of Manchuria in 1931 and to Hitler's reoccupation of the Rhineland'.[2] It was Dulles who was reluctant to reach agreement with the Communists, who would not acknowledge Chou En-lai's existence at the Geneva Conference. It was Eden who was actively diplomatic, made all the proposals, while Dulles sulked.

In the Middle East, Eden sought accommodation with Arab nationalism and peace between Israel and Egypt through the Tripartite agreement of 1948. At the same time he hoped that the American-sponsored alliance among the 'northern tier powers', the Baghdad Pact, would both seal off the whole area from Soviet penetration and protect tangible British interests in oil and communications. It is true that he was not prepared to concede too much to Egypt, potentially the strongest power in the Middle East. On the eve of Sudanese independence, when the Egyptians were angling for an Egyptian-Sudanese Union, he told the

[1] *Full circle*, p. 28.   [1] *Ibid.* p. 97.

Americans that Britain 'could not keep the Egyptian Government alive by feeding the Sudanese to them'.[1] Particularly delicate were the relations with Iraq and Jordan, each with a ruler inclined to accommodation with Britain, but each at the mercy of unpredictable popular impulses from below. Yet it was the maintenance of just such relationships that lay within the range of Eden's esoteric craft.

Why then, on becoming Prime Minister, did he, in this chosen area, pass over from diplomacy to force? The Middle East was part of the world that he knew a great deal about. He had signed both the Anglo-Egyptian agreements of 1936 and 1954. He *knew* the Arabs and was contemptuous of Dulles, who would talk about 'public opinion' in Saudi Arabia, and of Dulles's advisers, who naïvely thought that the whole of the Arabian peninsula should belong to Saudi Arabia. Yet he could not see, either that Arab nationalism might well not be willing to accept a settlement on British terms, with due deference to British interests, or that the methods of national assertion would necessarily be rough, disruptive and destructive of international order and morality and yet have validity in the eyes of much of the world if used against colonialist or 'neo-colonialist' régimes.

What alarmed Eden was Nasser's wild demagogic appeal, uncultivated politics, constant intrigue (*intense* activity reminiscent of Hitler's) against those Arab rulers who might reach an accommodation with Britain. In 1956, there were many Englishmen who could not accept the inevitability of such rough power, such stridency, in the Middle East. The unruliness of Nasser seemed to Eden to threaten all order. This was why Eden abandoned law for force. As in the 1930s, he saw the danger of drift and inactivity. When Nasser nationalized the Suez Canal in July 1956 and struck directly at those interests which Eden had thought he could preserve by diplomacy, the diplomat of Geneva saw that diplomacy was useless:

'The question was, how long we could pursue diplomatic methods and economic sanctions, which very likely would not succeed, before the possibility of military action slipped from our grasp.'[2] This was no time for mediation, but for will. The situation had to be seized and changed.

Like Chamberlain, he was aware that time was slipping away.

[1] *Ibid.* p. 235.   [2] *Ibid.* p. 456.

Chamberlain had been advantaged: in his day Britain was still a power in the front rank, capable of independent policy. But in the 1950s it had become obvious that the only major initiatives which Britain could take were those sanctioned by the United States. Even at Geneva during the Vietnam settlement, Eden had felt the advantage of having the American bomb behind him at the conference table. It was surely clear that in this conflict between a metropolitan and a 'colonial' country, both Eisenhower and Dulles would not give Britain the consideration which as an ally in difficulties she might expect. Rather they would disengage themselves from a hazardous colonial enterprise.

It was Eden's second illusion that a British statesman could still act against the grain of public opinion. It is true that British foreign policy has generally been more insulated from public pressures than that of the United States. Yet when actions or situations have raised moral issues, Disraeli's support for the Turks, Gordon's predicament at Khartoum, Chanak or the Hoare–Laval plan, the country has been divided, the political élites have been divided; and much of the country has dissociated itself from what the government has done or allowed to come about.

Eden knew the importance of going with the current. Had he not become a name in the 1930s by uttering popular catchwords? He had always had a good 'public'. It was this public's response to patriotic action that he counted on more than he counted on support in Parliament. In Parliament there were problems of persuasion and he solved them much less successfully than Chamberlain. To his own backbenchers, suspicious of his placatory Middle East policy, he appeared indecisive. From the beginning of 1956 the Tory Press was critical. 'Most Conservatives,' said the *Daily Telegraph*, 'are waiting to feel the smack of firm Government.' The criticism extended to domestic affairs, where he did not seem to be sufficiently Tory. This line of criticism ran on until August 1956 when *The Times* let itself go in a leading article entitled 'Escapers Club' which came out strongly against the advocates of 'playing the [Suez] crisis slowly'. Suez was not Abadan. The note was of exasperation:

Public opinion, despite what the dissidents angrily say, is remarkably firm. Of course, it wants to avoid the use of force. So does everyone and we hope no one does so more than the British Government. But this is a far cry from saying that because there seems little that we can do about it, the best thing is to find excuses for, and forget, the whole business. Nations live by vigorous defence of their interests. Even Mr Nehru, who so conscientiously sermonizes the rest of the world, does not let a trick go in Kashmir. As G. M. Trevelyan reminded us many years ago, the sun of Venice set because of the double event of the Turkish blocking of the caravan routes and the discovery of the Cape route and America. A pleasure-loving people more interested in their revels than in their responsibilities did the rest.

'During the eighteenth century the material decline of Venice was complete, accompanied by a degeneracy in public spirit that made her a by-word even in the Europe of the *ancien régime*. Atrophy was not, however, followed by dissolution. The corpse lived on.'[1]

Eden needed success and he could only gain success in foreign policy. Success in foreign policy required mastery of the House of Commons. And Eden was never really sure of himself there. If his own supporters suspected his will (for which they had no real cause), the Labour Opposition regarded him as a romantic, not as aware as he should be of the realities of emergent nationalism.

Resolute words on the floor of the House, backed by firm preparations for action, would probably have given him mastery of the House and a public prepared for Suez. But the situation in the Middle East was too uncertain for firm metropolitan words to be used. In a world in which it was said King Hussein of Jordan had dismissed Glubb Pasha because of an article in the weekly *Illustrated* which implied that Glubb was the real ruler of Jordan, Eden had to pick his phrases. He himself admits that he made a bad speech and cut a poor figure in the House on one crucial occasion in March 1956 simply because he could not tell all.

His disabilities were those hampering all parliamentary statesmen. 'There was a time', he writes, 'when the fixing of a foreign affairs debate was related to concern for British interests abroad. Speeches were even sometimes couched in moderate terms so as not to increase the difficulties of Her Majesty's Ministers.'[2] Yet Eden knew that foreign policy, like domestic policy, had become 'a free for-all' and 'never mind the consequences'. Was not Eden therefore counting far too much on his luck in plunging into the deed in 1956?

[1] *The Times*, 27 August 1956.   [2] *Full circle*, p. 352.

For not only did he need approval on the floor; he also needed the acquiescence of his senior partner, the American Secretary of State, John Foster Dulles, perhaps a less inventive man, but nevertheless with a great wallet of diplomatic knowledge on his back, conscious of wider consequences, with a strong sense of what was proper. From Dulles, opaque and devious, yet obviously bent on cultivating just such men as Nasser and hostile to remaining British pretensions to power, Eden counted on a consideration he could not hope to get. Dulles had declared that Nasser must 'disgorge' but had never abandoned diplomacy—in this case a series of odd, stalling expedients which merely gave Nasser time to establish his position. At no time did he countenance a force solution, although he knew that the British government might well resort to it.

In these circumstances Eden turned from the 'uncertain ally' to France, unashamedly intent upon destroying the power of Nasser in the Arab world, particularly in North Africa, and already arming Israel against her neighbours. An Anglo-French expedition to coincide with an Israeli attack on Egypt through the Sinai desert was plotted. American neutrality was hoped for.

The Eden of 1956 was a righteous man. What then of the alleged 'collusion' between Israel, France and Britain from somewhere in the middle of October? Was an Anglo-French mission to take over the Suez Canal physically after an Israeli initiative first broached by two French emissaries at a secret meeting at Chequers on 14 October? What was decided 'in common prudence' at dinner at the Hôtel Matignon on 16 October by Eden, Selwyn Lloyd, Mollet and Pineau? Or between Pineau, Ben Gurion and Lloyd at Sèvres on 22 or 23 October? It seems certain that there was dissimulation in order to strike hard and effectively. Yet whatever things were hid from America and undivulged to the Commonwealth, whatever deceptions were practised, it cannot yet be said that they are conclusive in forming a judgment on Eden and Suez. For, surely, if Nasser were to be brought down because of his illegal action, he had to be brought down expeditiously. Politics were being continued in war. Planning for military action may well mean fixing circumstances and times, may well involve *collusion*. In making preparations the British government was prudent. The imprudence lay in dispensing with politics.

Suez shows Eden as a Conservative with too much passion for order in the world. The Conservative sees the world as it is as conveniently ordered even if not according to strict canons of justice. Within this given order, within a civilization, men can talk with each other and adjust their interests. This makes sense. What is dangerous is the attempts of unlettered men to turn the world upside down in the name of some new moral order, aspiring nationalism and so on. In face of these, Eden appears as the Anti-Jacobin, opposed to all the dishonouring of covenants and treaties, the disruption, the terrorism, the blind destructive energy of national revolutions. As Martin Wight has pointed out, Eden was tolerant of nationalism abroad only so long as it behaved itself.[1]

Yet the United Nations Organization itself does not insist on new nations behaving themselves; rather, in Eden's words, it prefers to 'obtain a temporary easement' by condoning breaches of international agreements.[2] The nationalists are, it seems, regarded as bold, unbiddable children entitled to use force to break the mould of colonialism. Eden's tragedy was that there was so little concurrence with his insistence that their breaches of the international order were portentous. So 'in trying to preserve the political conditions of international life he became doctrinaire; in trying to enforce the moral conditions of international life he allowed himself to become unscrupulous...'.[3] But the scruples returned: Eden did not complete his enterprise. American power made him look a forcible-feeble man.

Eden insists that it is not immoral to recognize and mark down an enemy. He cites a Turkish proverb: 'Though your enemy be an ant, imagine that he is an elephant.' The dictator should be struck down when growing. In this, Eden was passionate but he could not carry the country. For a brief while, after Nasser's nationalization of the Canal, it seemed that he had the backing of responsible Labour leaders. But they fell away from him because of their characteristic reluctance to use force to settle disputes, because of unwillingness to endorse Eden's world order, because of certain sympathies and affinities with Nasser as a ruler, and because political advantage might be derived from dissociation from government policy.

---

[1] 'Brutus in Foreign Policy', *International Affairs*, July 1960.
[2] *Full circle*, p. 579.   [3] Wight, *loc. cit.*

Eden seems to have set himself for action. Capacity for decision had been something markedly lacking in both British and French rulers since the war. Yet it was still difficult in 1956 to accept the fact that real decision-making power lay with Dulles, that Britain was capable of no more initiatives, that she was in perpetual tutelage to the United States. Had Eden been able to muster a broad undivided support at home, it is possible that American objections and obstruction might have been overridden. Eden was taking a risk: but, as he himself says, diplomacy is not all prudence. Risks have to be taken: situations to be seized.

What is to be remarked about Eden's conduct in October 1956 is that he seems to have acted alone or with only minimal counsel. Much was hidden not only from his own party, from Parliament and from the people but also from officials. He dispensed with much of the apparatus for decisions. He seems to have meditated alone before action, drawing upon principles hardened in his own experience, congealing to an inflexibility not associated with his recent diplomacy, and relying upon his own touch, his own professional knowledge.

Bismarck once made a grand declaration of his humility before events: 'A statesman cannot create anything himself; he must wait and listen until he hears the steps of God sounding through events; then leap up and grasp the hem of his garment.' Eden knew events very well and if anyone was capable of sensing just how much could be made out of them it was surely he. He did not seem the kind of man to fly in the face of Providence.

English leading politicians, wrote Ernest Barker, have normally been Ministers of the Interior: their preoccupations and experience, domestic rather than foreign. On coming to office as Prime Minister, they have therefore had to adjust themselves to world affairs. Not so Eden. Eden was a specialist in foreign policy, so capable of taking pains, so deeply versed and immersed in his craft that he might well consider himself peculiarly fitted to divine and take right action.

Before Suez Eden seemed a prudent man. But prudence did not mean that there were no occasions on which Britain would not stand firm. Eden was tired, as was *The Times*, of withdrawal before threats, tired of off-loading responsibilities abroad. His vanity was affronted. Although a diplomatist he was not a busybody, not committed to perpetual mediation and trimming. Eden gave utterance and effect to the statesmanship that was within him but found that prestige, experience in foreign affairs were no substitutes for power. He presumed too much.

Martin Wight[1] has noted the effect that Churchillian cadences have had on Tory writing for a generation and implies, I think, that the results have been unfortunate. There can be little doubt that the Churchillian model for Eden was not a good one. It forced him into postures which did not suit him, gave him words that all too faithfully echoed the grand master:

'We have many times led Europe in the fight for freedom. It would be an ignoble end to our long history if we accepted to perish by degrees' (to President Eisenhower, 6 September 1956).[2]

'In external affairs a democratic state has to be on its guard against certain dangers. The most insidious of these is to take the easy way, and to put off decision. Drift is the demon of democracy' (to his constituents at Leamington, 1958).[3]

Because of Churchill, Eden cultivated an untimely *will* in foreign affairs—untimely because Britain no longer had the economic strength to stand alone. It was this, allied to his irascibility and to his sense of professional superiority, which made Eden less of a Tory man than he might otherwise have been. Action could not go along with intentions. In this, at least, Chamberlain could teach him something.

What Churchill gave Eden was a kind of recalcitrance to the way the world was going. (It is out of just such recalcitrance that De Gaulle has made high politics, but De Gaulle, through long adversity and long silences, was much better schooled for it.) Under party and newspaper provocation (at one point *Punch* likened him as an appeaser to Neville Chamberlain), Eden was tempted to an act of imperial will, almost of temper, when there was practically no imperial will left.

---

[1] Wight, *loc. cit.*   [2] *Full circle*, p. 467.   [3] *Ibid.* p. 509.

II

THE QUILTED ANVIL

Nations, wrote Adam Ferguson, 'stumble upon establishments which are indeed the result of human action but not the execution of human design'.[1] English politics has not only fortuitously inherited a tradition of agreement and timely concession but also, it has been said, two prerequisites of stable relations between leaders and people: 'independence qualified by deference, an independence springing from the sense of personal responsibility, a deference rendered to moral as well as intellectual authority...'.[2] 'Deference,' which Bryce presumably took from Bagehot, is perhaps an unfortunate word—it has certainly been used uncritically by political scientists ever since, usually to imply *social* deference to the exclusion of other kinds. A reading of history hardly establishes deference as the prime or perennial element in English political life. England has not always been known for bending the knee to those who are established. Up to the end of the seventeenth century insurrection seemed the English mode— her medieval liberties were secured by persistent rebellion—and customary or casual riot was almost one of the liberties of Englishmen until well into the Victorian age.

It might be more perceptive to say that during the last two centuries or so Englishmen have put their trust in their rulers, because, while operating under more persistent criticism than elsewhere, they have met expectations. Englishmen have expected to find in their politicians a feeling for the whole country, private virtue, serious application when necessary, and spirit. The cleverness of a politician has been less important than his ability to give the sense of the nation. Indeed, if we remember Shelburne, Brougham, Haldane and Webb as exemplars it would seem that intellect hardly flourishes in English politics. In his recent essay on Bagehot there is this surprising testimony from R. H. S. Crossman on the primacy of the sense of touch of those who rule:

[1] *An essay on the history of civil society*, Edinburgh, 1767, p. 187.
[2] Bryce, *Modern democracies*, II, 616.

'When he was not describing the Cabinet as an ingenious contrivance, Bagehot saw more clearly than anyone that the British
ruling class would never tolerate a Machiavelli for long, and that
its real strength was not cleverness or clarity of thought, but a
sense of tradition which it shared with the common people, and
its native ability to know the time for firmness and the time for
concession.'[1] English stylists, it is true, have sometimes been men
of intellect, but they have been stylists in a political society which
checked the adjectives and tempered the metaphors. Character has
been fundamental and even the stylists have, with one or two hard
cases, passed for honest men.[2]

Now it would not be difficult to work out a sociology of this
kind of politics, to trace connections between this persistence and
its social base, to explain the higher in terms of the lower, to make
classifications.[3] 'But no classification can be exclusive; and just as
British classes have merged readily into one another, so British
statesmen have sometimes combined in their persons the gifts and
attributes of different classes.'[4] Nor should we forget that such
competence is unusual over a long period of time and remains
meritorious, however it is kept up. Where there is a settled tradition, governments renew themselves by continual co-optation and
accretion. Much turns on who set the pattern, on who was there
first. The subsequent story may be one of amplification and
criticism:

British democracy is not an abstract idea. It is a way of living and a
manner of politics which first began to emerge in the Middle Ages. In
those distant times almost the whole outline of this way of life and
manner of politics was adumbrated, an outline which has since been
enlarged by experience and invention and defended against attack from
without and treason from within.[5]

Moreover, Englishmen in their insular security have usually
had time to reflect on a continuous stream of political experience,

[1] Introduction to Walter Bagehot, *The English constitution*, London, 1963, p. 32.
[2] Character will even excuse failure. Cf. Lord Moran to John Winant in *Churchill: the struggle for survival, 1940–65*, p. 128: 'Whereas we English rather like a man who hasn't come off, anyway if he is staunch and uncomplaining in adversity. You see it's a man's character that counts with us, not his achievement.'
[3] Leo Strauss, 'An epilogue', *Essays on the scientific study of politics*, ed. Herbert J. Storing, p. 311.
[4] Ernest Barker, 'British statesmen', *Essays on government*, Oxford, 1945, p. 22.
[5] Michael Oakeshott, 'Contemporary British politics', *The Cambridge Journal*, May 1948, pp. 489–90.

to make distinctions among the kinds of régime in the world (ever since Sir John Fortescue's *Governance of England*), and to see that some are better than others, to evaluate their politicians on a scale determined within their own tradition. The breathing spaces have not always been there—even the Whigs were on the burning lake in the seventeenth century—but without them the temperate politics of the eighteenth century would not have been possible; without them the ground would not have caked so solidly under the feet of the master politicians in the nineteenth century.

Americans, particularly American political scientists, occasionally play a game (odd in a country which puts laws before men) in which their 'positive' Presidents are placed in a kind of League table of greatness. These attempts to relate and compare personal bent, public persuasion and public deeds, the *gesta Dei per Americanos*, are simplifications. Yet history must be simplified if it is to be used. And no people at present seem more determined to use their history than the Americans. It is probably a less conclusive exercise than weighing novelists in the scales of a Great Tradition but it is a way of arriving at canons for the Presidential office. In Britain the game is hardly played at all despite a longer roll of worthies, probably as much natural ability, and certainly more schooled talent in politics. There is a more impressive array of good 'lives' covering the whole modern era, but the biographers have rightly been concerned with the man and his world as it was and not with his lengthened shadow, his projection, his relationship to those who came before and after. No one has yet written a book upon the Image of Chatham or of Gladstone in English history. To Americans, Washington, Jefferson and Lincoln all seem proper subjects for such treatment.

Historians are not supposed to 'use' history—although most, in fact, do. Political scientists may do so under strict conditions. Literary critics should and do use it without repining. Ordinary men (Aristotle's citizens) will always use what history they have to judge leading politicians. Involuntarily or voluntarily, both scholars and ordinary men will make distinctions. 'A man who refuses to distinguish between great statesmen, mediocrities, and insane impostors may be a good bibliographer; he cannot say anything relevant about politics and political history.'[1]

The reputation of politicians is a matter of critical response to

---

[1] Leo Strauss, *What is political philosophy?*, Illinois, 1959, p. 21.

them, to what they precipitate in the memory. The scholar has a longer memory and a wider range of references than the ordinary man but both are in effect limited to their own political tradition; for both the centre of reference is 'the given political situation in the individual's own country'.[1] And the men remembered are not what Maurice Cowling calls the 'diminutive practitioners' who determine the 'judgment of political possibility',[2] but the politicians of virtue and imagination who made the political weather.

Only those who cut a great figure and at the same time brought to public life virtue or imagination are assessed in this essay and even so the gallery is incomplete. I have said little about those who brought to politics only sound judgment and capacity for business. These men, the masters of the arrangements, the indispensable 'second rate which can co-operate readily with its like',[3] make English politics more effective and cumulatively give it weight but are not remembered. Yet if politics is duly professionalized in this country it is likely that this kind of politician will predominate. Certainly, it would seem that if ever Britain is assimilated to a federal or 'interdependent' structure, European or North Atlantic, these men of business will be more fitted to operate within it than politicians of character or style.

It is said that Britain is too deeply steeped in her past but it is doubtful if this is still true. Both the quality and effectiveness of civic education have perhaps always been low in Britain compared with France or the United States. The criticism of and within British politics today seldom invokes the past; the slogan, even of the Conservatives, is 'modernization'. 'We have not for some years', writes Raymond Williams, 'seen the Conservatism of the empire, the gentleman and the Christian and classical pieties.'[4] And he goes on to point out that 'the whole modernization programme is the bourgeois attack on all institutions and habits of mind that limit or hinder the aggressive and expanding operations of the market, which is seen as the only important social process'.[5] What we are witnessing is 'an indiscriminate rejection' of traditional bearings by both Conservative and Labour parties. The

[1] *Ibid.* p. 16.
[2] Maurice Cowling, *Mill and liberalism*, Cambridge, 1963, p. 109.
[3] Barker, *Essays on government*, p. 44.
[4] 'Towards a socialist society', in *Towards socialism*, Perry Anderson and Robin Blackburn (ed.) London, 1965, p. 380.
[5] *Ibid.*

emphasis is upon the current 'consumer', the man in the *contemporary* market, not the member of community reaching into past and future. The past is obstructive; for the future no responsibility is accepted.

The weakness of the until recently prolific 'state of England' literature is not so much that it is so often uninformed and intemperate in its indictment of 'stagnant societies', inert establishments and so on, as that—in the name of efficiency, restoration of 'British influence in the world'—it so often urges the country to be something so very different from what it has been and is, to transform itself by, say, adopting new institutions, recruiting more effective *personnel*, applying the radical 'sociology of equality' to the education and training of the nation.

Professor Brian Chapman, for example, seeks a resurgence of will through institutional reform. What he invokes in *British government observed* is the power in the French state, its administrative energy and doctrinal assurance, its *governing* authority rooted in both the 'despotic paternalism' of the *ancien régime* and the 'revolutionary egalitarianism' of the Jacobins. The failure of Britain has been the failure to take correct decisions, not only because of a lack of the best information and the best machinery for making decisions, but also, apparently, because of the absence of *étatiste* self-confidence and Cartesian rationalism in her civil service, in which, Chapman surprisingly adds, 'there is no sentiment that public office should involve public responsibility, or that public power should involve the exercise of dispassionate and disinterested judgment'.[1] British civil servants, it appears, do not carry with them the sense of beneficent state power borne by their equivalents on the continent.

Chapman is concerned with reforming 'policy-making institutions', with improving British government by releasing policy-making talents within the bureaucracy, rather than with strengthening the impact of truly political forces upon it. He does not really distinguish among instigators. Politics and policy are the legitimate business of civil servants and valuable initiatives are at least as likely to come from them as from the politicians—who indeed will be able to do very little unless they organize, professionalize and syndicalize themselves within Parliament.

These criticisms are brisk but in the end restricted and un-

[1] *British government observed*, London, 1963, p. 61.

helpful. Chapman seems unable to make distinctions between régimes and is, for example, capable of seeing a parallel between what he calls a 'social and economic' tyranny in Britain and the 'open political tyrannies' of Hitler and Mussolini. In the same way he can discern in the anonymous obedience of the British civil service a portent of something like the *Gehorsamkeit*, the supine instrumentism of the Nazi bureaucracy.

It is true that in recent years the British government has some-times failed to *govern*. But its current *malaise* is hardly likely to be cured by infusing French *étatisme* into that ancient, central initiating force, the British Crown, by equipping the queen's servants, 'wise, politic' if rather backward, with that 'intellectual arrogance' (combining 'superb self-confidence with a distrust of other people's motives') which Chapman so much admires in his Frenchmen. They may do things better abroad, but England can hardly be other than she is, proceeding within her own tradition to her own undetermined ends.

The more profound our understanding of political activity, the less we shall be at the mercy of plausible but mistaken analogy, the less we shall be tempted by a false or irrelevant model. And the more throughly we understand our own political tradition, the more readily its whole resources are available to us, the less likely we shall be to embrace the illusions which wait for the ignorant and unwary...[1]

A state of England by Anthony Hartley is closer to the grain of British politics. Hartley does not think that we can improve our-selves 'by placing a barrier between us and our history'.[2] The tone of voice (though less certain) is that of Matthew Arnold, sober and perturbed. What perturbs him is not only the general sense of power on the wane but also 'the dissociation of that emotion which we call patriotism from the ordinary business of govern-ment and administration', the lack of authority in the state. 'We are Englishmen despite the British state...'[3] There is a marked reluctance to give politicians the confidence they need to rule effectively, a general suspicion of dominative attitudes, a con-fusion in the mind of the political nation between *authority* and authoritarianism. The implication is virtually the same as Lord Radcliffe's,[4] that a society in which no statesman can appeal with

[1] Michael Oakeshott, 'Political education', in *Rationalism and politics*, p. 133.
[2] *A state of England*, London, 1963, pp. 23–4.
[3] *Ibid.* p. 230.   [4] 'The dissolving society', *The Spectator*, 13 May 1966.

confidence to a public interest over and above sectional interests is likely to be 'a dissolving society'.

Hartley writes as if the sense of the state were something England had once had and then lost. But it is precisely this consciousness of public authority that Arnold maintained was so lamentably missing in English society as long as a century ago. Moreover, until quite recently, the English were actually being admired for their unawareness of 'a communal life above the individual life'. '...it is good for the world,' wrote Wilhelm Dibelius in 1930, 'and good for nations with other ideals, that the world contains a state such as has made the State well-nigh superfluous...'[1] Here in English society was a model of 'self-reliant and self-controlling citizens'. In truth, it seems that the most distinctive characteristic of British society has always been the absence of any clear conception of paramount state power.

In peacetime, the British people have always been likely to exercise a *liberum veto*, a Calhounian *negative* on all grand projects; they themselves have *will* (Dibelius, Madariaga and others have testified to this) but they are reluctant to be the objects of *will*. As for masterful rulers—'England can live without great men comparatively longer than any other country'.[2]

There are Neo-Marxist critics like Perry Anderson and Tom Nairn who *use* history to disinter what they call the 'full, effective past'. Out of it they hope to provide the Socialist theory necessary to transform the social order. So, in some startlingly vehement essays,[3] they try to compress the dense, complex history of England into Marxist categories. Within this myth all the English virtues of moderation, empiricism, scepticism about political ideas become vices. The distinctiveness of England becomes mere provincialism, the continuity of England is merely 'centuries of stale constipation and sedimentary ancestor-worship'.[4]

Everything has gone wrong. When the English working class was most militant—in the early nineteenth century—there was no Socialist doctrine (i.e. Marxist theory) upon which it could draw. When Marxism eventually came to England in the 1870s and 1880s it came too late: the working classes had by then settled down as an estate of the realm under aristocracy and middle class. In the twentieth century other (fortunate) countries were fissured

---

[1] W. Dibelius, *England*, London, 1930, p. 503. [2] *Ibid.* p. 504. [3] *Towards socialism.*
[4] Tom Nairn, 'The nature of the Labour Party', in *Towards socialism*, p. 212.

by war and economic calamities. There were not enough disasters in Britain to break up the hegemony.

The politics of adjustment and compromise, in particular the 'lead-heavy "moderation"' of Labour, is therefore scorned for a transforming politics demanding a common will never seen on land or sea. It seems that what makes people really mature is barricades and Jacobin revolutions. It is not only that Anderson and Nairn are, like Chapman, applying standards outside the tradition. The history itself, strictly subordinated to theory, is history without regard for men and the context within which they worked. As E. P. Thompson has pointed out in a very thorough critique, the approach is too schematic; the serious historian must always be prepared to see his model break up under the impact of facts.[1] The rigidity of this Neo-Marxist 'trajectory' of history is in the end dismissive of history.

Much trouble is being taken at present to detach Britain from her history either because as received it inhibits her or because it is erroneous. But, in truth, the danger is that Britain will, without exhortation, emancipate herself from her past, not just from her 'greatness', her economic and imperial achievements which were to some extent accidental, but much more significantly from 'the public philosophy', the sense of responsible *imperium*, from the quality of politics which made her distinctive. It is this dissociation from the past—Ortega y Gasset thought it the generic fact of our time—which makes men feel that they 'have suddenly been left alone on the earth, that the dead did not die in appearance only but effectively; that they can no longer help us'.[2] It is the transmission of codes, standards, human exemplars from the past which is threatened. Already there are too many messages reaching us laterally from all over the world to let us reflect on what has come through from the past.

Modern communications, the media of technology, tend to erase all but current impressions. Journalism and television celebrate so many ephemeral events and heroes, D. J. Boorstin has told us, that the past is crowded out. 'In our always more overpopulated consciousness, the hero every year becomes less significant.'[3] He is replaced by the celebrity. 'The hero is made by

---

[1] 'The peculiarities of the English', in *The socialist register*, 1965.
[2] *The revolt of the masses*, pp. 39–40.
[3] *The image*, London, 1963, p. 63.

folk-lore, sacred texts, and history books, but the celebrity is the creature of gossip, of public opinion, of magazines, newspapers, and the ephemeral images of movie and television screens.'[1]

And although there is more scholarship than ever before it has little countervailing authority. Much is produced but little is absorbed—except by colleagues. Moreover, historians have long since ceased to make any kind of convincing narrative out of history and under their scrutiny the old men of mark have lost much of their heroism. American biographical works 'are often merely professional exercises; scholars ply their tools, and the chips fall where they may. We have thus learned a great deal more about our national heroes than earlier generations cared to know.'[2]

In the nineteenth century the leading politician was visible only at great public meetings; his speeches in small type were read only by the initiates. Today he is seen by the whole nation as he unbends in fireside chat, as he enters or leaves the aircraft. On these occasions there is a danger of being misunderstood by the inattentive and being deliberately misconstrued by the attentive. No one knows better than the modern politician that 'the word you have not spoken is your slave: the word that you have spoken is your master'. Edgeless words, possibly a studied colloquialism, are therefore safest.

For the journalist, the politician is copy, a profile, a characteristic stance, and one stance is as good as another as long as it generates news. In the course of his business, the journalist fabricates both 'news' and men, seeks to activate and shape politics and politicians. Political eminence which was once laboriously achieved is now built up over a short period. 'Was there ever a time when power belonged less to the inwardly strong than it does now; when a man's influence on his fellow men depended so much on the image of him created by propaganda?'[3] One of the most desolating words in the language is 'image', the picture in the mind which can be 'dinted', 'shaped', 'blurred', by journalists, public relations men, or party headquarters. What they project is the irrelevant private life, rehearsed responses, studied presence, unexceptionable intentions and, on set occasions, the rhetoric or wit of speechwriters.

It is true that the users of other men's wit are sometimes intelli-

[1] Boorstin, *The image* p. 72.   [2] *Ibid.* p. 61.
[3] J. Plamenatz, *On alien rule and self-government*, London, 1960, p. 97.

gent and appreciative patrons. There will be some who will make the speechwriter's reach-me-down their own. It is understandable too that the professional politician of the future may be too busy as manager, decision-maker, symbol or presence to fuse his own imagery. Yet there is something inexcusable about putting wit, low or high, into a man for public purposes. There is the tale of Lord Lauderdale, who on hearing one of Sheridan's stories insisted on telling it to a friend. Whereupon Sheridan said to him earnestly: 'For God's sake don't: a joke in your mouth is no laughing matter.' To goldless gold and silkless silk we can now add witless wit.

The public delivery of public words remains peculiarly the politician's task. It is by words at the right time that a politician teaches his generation.[1] He will not be able to get them to listen unless he can charge his words with meaning. 'Your legislator can't legislate for the public good, your commander can't command, your populace (if you be a democratic country) can't instruct its "representatives", save by language.'[2] Yet the politician has many rivals and is often without an audience, or is not sure which one he is addressing.

There are so many other words: the newspaper word, the radio word, the television word. Here is an endless succession of speeches without answers, of unconnected essays, discontinued contributions, editorials written against time, to soothe, to warn, to excite. What is produced is a fusillade of watchwords, catchwords, standpoints, meeting-points. 'Event' succeeds 'event' in bewildering profusion. Attention swings from Berlin to Zanzibar, from Delhi to Saigon, from banking to housing or immigration. The information varies in 'thickness', much is specially generated for the media, but with a hundred or more sovereign states in the world, the cables carry a lot of politics. Here are the materials of history but no historians to filter them. There are perplexing changes of tone or matter. Desperate issues suddenly disappear from sight. Arguments which seemed valid are suddenly heard no more.

In circumstances such as these it might be wise for the politician to maintain long silences and then speak with deliberation. Only De Gaulle among contemporary politicians does this. American

---

[1] Richard E. Neustadt, *Presidential power*, New York, 1960, pp. 100, 103 f.
[2] Ezra Pound, *ABC of reading*, London, 1934, p. 17.

Presidents[1] and British Prime Ministers talk too much and too casually.

There is another sense in which the current language of politics is at the end of its tether. Unobtrusive revolutions in the higher criticism make little difference to the public. But the politician at one time was accustomed to use words like 'democracy', 'human rights' and 'freedom' and 'rule of law' as if they had meaning. He is not at all certain today. Like many academics he has some difficulty in making distinctions. He is, of course, a practical man and does not either habitually seek metaphysical justifications for his actions or use 'words as divining rods for truth'. He knows very well that when he speaks of 'freedom' he may only be using the word to establish a preference. So when philosophers clear up our political vocabulary, as Weldon and others have done, and say that no answer can be given as to the worth of a system until it has been examined in a great deal of detail, they would seem to be doing a good job. 'A demagogue with an impediment in his speech' will be less dangerous than one with a silver tongue.

Yet the full implications of this rigour are disquieting. In political discourse, writes Professor Aiken, only two forms of expression now seem to be legitimate: 'realistic, verifiable statements of fact' and 'bald, undisguised expressions of first-person (singular or plural) interest'. He continues:

> Thus to put an end to eloquence would be to put an end, not only to 'moralism' (which is usually nothing more than the morality of those with whom we disagree) and to 'ideology', but also to any form of politics in which the great issues are stated or argued in terms of human rights and responsibilities and in which it is essential to gain the approval of the people, or their representatives, before any fundamental change in governmental policy is made.[2]

So many tell us that it is dangerous to let eloquence loose in politics that we are apt to forget how rare it is. Everyone is ready

---

[1] Cf. Douglass Cater, *Power in Washington*, London, 1965, p. 112. 'There are an old-fashioned few, of whom I count myself one, who are troubled by the declining sense of solemnity when a President talks to his publics. The preparation may require more drudgery, and the immediate response may not always seem worth the effort, but if the President offers good rhetoric, with disciplined ideas for content, it can have a percolative effect that lasts longer than the moment of delivery and goes further than the listening and viewing audiences. It extends the persuasive power of a President beyond his term of office, perhaps even beyond his lifetime.'

[2] H. D. Aiken, 'The revolt against ideology', in *Commentary*, April 1964, p. 36.

to put snaffle and curb upon what may be becoming, in fact, in those in authority, as hard to come by as the unicorn—the moral imagination. In the modern politics of developed countries, the words tend to creep along with phased programmes and the slow accretion of experience. Political style, i.e. words promising imaginative action, is rarely possible. Past action provides only dead metaphors and dead analogies. The language of battle and beleaguerment is incongruous to projects for raising national production by one per cent. The honest politician must learn to use the words of the plan, the technical vocabulary, prefabricated, neutral and innocuous.

Certainly it should be the duty of the English politician to keep his eye on the object and speak the language of politics circumspectly. For while the language was, at least to the end of the eighteenth century, tempered in the English experience, today it is a compost of slogans from other traditions and breaches with tradition, from France, Germany, Russia and America. It is a welter from which it is hard to extract coherence.

George Orwell thought that political language was bad because politicians could not say what they thought.[1] But it is not just evasion and the strain of defending the indefensible which rob political speech of raciness and vigour. The politician is not always in a corner: he may well be expressing convictions and clear preferences. Yet, at one and the same time, he may feel that he must relate the 'practical activity' of politics—quite legitimately but often without sufficient meditation—to larger intentions and purposes and, simply because circumstances may alter everything, that he must also put in those saving clauses which will enable him to move to another position.

Worn, chipped or gilded, this current language is the only one we have. 'Few ideas are correct ones,' wrote Disraeli in *Contarini Fleming*, 'and what are correct no one can ascertain, but with words we govern men.' At no level can political discourse be demonstrative, but we must continue to use it. Words remain guides for action and the quality of words can still sometimes influence the nature of action. And, reciprocally, events, real events, may burn away the excrescences, as in 1940, when Churchill's 'republican' style was miraculously refined into plain and moving speech, and the British people who had been moralizing the

[1] 'Politics and the English language', in *Shooting an elephant*, London, 1950.

situation in some confusion were able at last clearly to identify the enemy.

The British have always wanted to know who governed them, have always resented anonymous authority. Who were the evil counsellors, who had the ear of the king, were questions for which in the past they always stayed for an answer. Today they often seem to be governed by no one in particular. And yet the whole of English constitutional history may in one light be regarded as a process for determining who governed and under what conditions.

Because within that history it was accepted that the power that was in king or Court was something not to be destroyed but to be contended for by appeal to the political nation—this was the eighteenth-century solution—there was brought into operation a ritualistic two-party competition in which the object was not to establish a new régime but merely to capture the machinery of government and give fresh impetus to it.

Thus there matured, only the day before yesterday, a model for the books which secured a concentration of authority together with sensitivity to public opinion, to the primary social forces. There was a place for instigation, a place for endorsement or correction, and a place for action. There was a Prime Minister, *primus inter pares*, dominant or chairmanlike, an inner ring at his shoulder; a full deliberative Cabinet; in the Commons, a forum where sparks might be struck, inquests held and political leadership appraised. There was an obedient, neutral bureaucracy, responsive to the lightest political touch.

The system was one which differentiated between politician and bureaucrat. It was assumed that in a truly political régime, the civil servant, even though he absorbed the dominant political values so well that he could anticipate the reactions of his political masters and even prompt their priorities, still remained part of the machinery of execution, with his world largely rationalized for him. He cherished his discretion but it was only a fragment delegated from the top. Under the dispensation he must not only intuitively grasp the political premises of others; he must also honour the stock responses evolved by his department over the years. The lower one went in the hierarchy, the more axiomatic seemed the rules, the more adamantine the departmental attitudes, the more remote and arbitrary the political impulse.

In contrast, the politician was thought of as one inhabiting the region of the unresolved, the area where no clear preference has been stated. What has been resolved falls to the administration.

We are in the realm of politics [writes Mannheim] when envoys of foreign countries conclude treaties which were never made before; when parliamentary representatives carry through new methods of taxation; when an election campaign is waged; when certain opposition groups prepare a revolt or organize strikes—or when these are suppressed.[1]

The line of demarcation was never, of course, as clear as this. When you had policies that were given, when the politician presided *de haut* over a machine which received its impulse long ago, the men in power were administrators rather than politicians. And if there were bureaucratic politicians, there were also political bureaucrats working within the prerogative of the monarch, outgrowing the mere Court politician, developing an appetite for major choice, perhaps even for grand design.

We have been made aware of a 'policy-administrative continuum' in which it would be difficult to say who instigates and who does not. What we learn from war-histories, the indiscretions of ministers, the inferences of scholars about the Cabinet shows that it is not the centre of command we might expect such a supreme governing organ to be. What is to be done is often decided elsewhere, perhaps at a recognized political level by the Prime Minister and a few colleagues, or in Cabinet committees, but also in official steering committees, in the departments or outside. For the departments no longer make policy out of their own tissues. Lobby, advisory committees, research organizations all make their contributions; administrator, lawyer, technician, professional body and interest group all say their piece. The Cabinet is in fact not just 18–24 men deliberating but the visible head of a complex administrative structure within which the key points cannot be precisely traced. There may always have been some truth in this picture; today, we are fully aware that the politician bobs like a cork on the surface of a pond whose depth cannot be accurately plumbed.

Both managerial politicians and political administrators are concerned with continuity of government. It is a mistake to think that because one knows much more than the other he will want or

---

[1] Karl Mannheim, *Ideology and utopia*, London, 1936, pp. 100–1.

be able to use the other as a tool. Knowledge can be a burden and it is a mistake to believe that those who have long lived professionally with problems know best how to deal with them and need no help. Many successful enterprises have been based on felicitous relationships between outsiders and insiders, between amateur and professional, 'gentlemen' and 'tarpaulins', squire and gamekeeper, patron and artist. There can be mutual respect between him who decides and him who provides the material for the decision. And it is probably a mistake, too, to assume a positive civil service that always knows where it is going. Although the civil servant, like the politician, makes a policy, he is *attentiste* in attitude, is predisposed to take cue and tone from others. The will and promptings of outsiders may well be welcomed. For most of the time the civil servant 'steers what may appear to be a craven course among the various pressures of public and still more of semi-public opinion...'.[1] He is distinguished by his freedom from ideas: 'he deals with them as rising forces'[2] from outside. He remains obedient within a closed and collegiate world which none dares politicize.

What actually goes on between minister and civil servant remains a matter of surmise until the historical particulars have been revealed long afterwards: circumstances and persons are all-important. The sheer growth of apparatus and staff does not therefore mean that politicians have necessarily lost the initiative. Political régimes, well endowed with heroic energy, live ideology, or even just aristocratic presence, can control and move vast bureaucracies fairly easily. Individual ministers with clear and limited objectives can normally get their way. It is a misconception to think bureaucracies are characteristically resistant. Yet without inspiration, dogma or 'authority' the minister is not likely to make much of a mark on 'the wall of experienced opinion'. For within the experience and enduring responsibilities of the department nearly everything has been done before.

Where the political impact upon the department has been fully absorbed or has been barely felt anyway, the opportunities for the civil servant to invade the ministerial mind, to devise, to set things in motion, are very great. And today more than ever he may feel that innovation is expected of him. He knows very well that there are some activities which he should skirt or observe dispassionately

---

[1] Sisson, *The spirit of British administration*, p. 23.   [2] *Ibid.* p. 131.

and that if he too officiously mobilizes his values, departs from 'stoical realism', he may find himself through too much zeal identified as an overt politician, like Robert Morant, Vansittart and Warren Fisher, or the civil servants of Crichel Down. But his very immunity from detailed parliamentary scrutiny into the *origins* of policy gives him an unadvertised yet well-understood authority.

Within this complexity, roles seem interchangeable. If it is the activity and not the office that has political content, the higher civil servant may be the politician and the politician the administrator. When cards of identity are switched like this, little wonder that there is doubt about who rules. Dispersion of the decision-making power not only makes for unintelligibility at large; it also diminishes the representative and responsible politician who so often seems to be little more than the outworks of the bureaucracy, contenting himself with expounding its meanings to all and sundry and giving the department 'a small or greater impulsion'.[1] It is sometimes even doubtful if he knows better than the 'permanent politicians' of the bureaucracy 'what the public won't stand'. He often seems to be doing very little. 'There is a long concatenation, and the people in it are so numerous, their activities so multifarious, the organizations they form are so permanent, as compared with the relative impermanence of what are thought of as elected governments...that it is more usual to speak of what a Minister is *responsible for* than of what he does.'[2]

One measure of the politician is in his public deportment, in his individual responsibility to Parliament. Here in the Commons he is in the place of estimation and the place of censure where 'every vat must stand on its own bottom'. But both the peril and the self-reliance are illusory. Only rarely does he fall. Partly, this is due to the hypersensitivity of the department to public and parliamentary warning signals: to the acquired premonitory sense of the higher- and middle-range civil servants.[3] The minister takes upon himself the criticism directed against his department; in return civil servants anticipate squalls, build breakwaters for him. But what has reprieved the minister more effectively than anything else has been the extension of collective responsibility. His sins, they are so often forgiven him, assumed by the whole government, ultimately by the Prime Minister.

[1] Sisson, *op. cit.* p. 13.   [2] *Ibid.*
[3] F. Dunnill, *The civil service, some human aspects,* London, 1956, pp. 125 f.

For there is one politician whose authority within the realm has not diminished. Whoever he is, the Prime Minister surely has power. With a faithful party in Parliament, in direct communication with the nation, commissioned to appoint and dismiss his colleagues in the administration, he wields, in fact, the prerogative of the Crown, has become, it is said, a kind of 'elected monarch'.[1] No one can doubt that there is, as Churchill insisted, a great deal of difference between No. 1, No. 2 and No. 3. Increasingly he symbolizes both the party and the régime. Today the national expectations for new bearings in politics focus mainly on this 'wild man at the top'. Indeed his rising authority may make his associates into Court politicians.

Party too has its organization. The energy of its leader and the enthusiasm of his supporters are not enough. Hence the staff, the headquarters, to give persistent attention to the business of gaining or sharing power. At the end of the nineteenth century each of the great historical parties developed central machines and national organizations in the country to secure votes. But in each case the extra-parliamentary organization deliberately brought into being was, after twisting for a while in the hands of its creators, subordinated to the parliamentary leadership. The Labour party grew up on the presumption of an extra-parliamentary sovereignty, that the movement should control the politician, but it has, in accepting the legitimacy of parliamentary politics, followed the older parties. The parliamentary leadership has independent authority and expects, at least when in power, some 'deference' from the rank and file.

The British politician in power or with power within reach (Labour leaders notably grow in stature as the prospects of office ripen) is neither a puppet of the machine nor a delegate of the extra-parliamentary party. The battles which Gladstone fought against Chamberlain and Salisbury against Randolph Churchill were battles for parliamentary government and independent power in politicians. The politician is enlisted by the party, projected by the party, but he is, while remaining responsive, never exclusively responsible to it. Indeed, ultimately—in office—he must be capable of detaching himself from rank-and-file pressures. Then we have the politician as the filter for sectional interests.

[1] R. W. K. Hinton, 'The Prime Minister as an elected monarch', in *Parliamentary affairs*, XIII, 1959–60, pp. 297–303.

There is nothing new about this. Analysis is merely unearthing what was always presumed in the political world, that Whitehall and Westminster are places where interests come to terms with power. Persistent pressure focuses mainly on the kinds of decision made by the civil servants rather than those made by politicians. But here, nevertheless, is the democratic politician as broker, bringing things into balance; the politician as editor, deciding what the public wants or will stand. This is the politician as Bosola in *The Duchess of Malfi* described him, 'the devil's quilted anvil. He fashions all sins on him and the blows are never heard.' But although much occupied with conciliating interests, the politician still has command of the situation as long as there is a strong party behind him and his own view of the public good—and those of his colleagues—remains clear. Pressure groups do not diminish the politician; they are the element in which he has his being; they are the touchstone of his character and the material of his craft.

The milieu, political and bureaucratic, is denser, more complex than it was. It is not necessarily more resistant but the politician probably has to do more to claim attention, to make the simplifications expected of him, to discover which tasks he can do well. He probably needs a less exercised but more authoritative voice. He must be able to gauge the forces at work in society with greater exactness than ever before.

Yet it is possible that too much is being asked of the politician. Our perspective is still short and we still tend to see the idealized parliamentary politician of the nineteenth century as the archetype. Over a longer historical span he seems ephemeral. There is a sense in which popular institutions and representative politicians are ancillary to the business of government.[1] They may give it intelligence, awareness and impetus but are not persistent. What persists is the service of the Crown; the use of prerogative power by the queen's servants.[2] It is just this awareness of the continuance of an ancient governmental authority, within which political office-holders have long operated with only a fleeting consciousness of popular will, that nineteenth-century liberal modes and archetypes still tend to weaken and obscure today.

The Victorian period produced a culture, 'an area of intercommunication, living and alert in all directions at once'[3] which was

---

[1] Sisson, *op. cit.* p. 158.   [2] *Ibid.*   [3] G. M. Young, *Victorian essays*, p. 213.

conducive to general politics. Idealism, religious or secular, was close to the surface, forcing its way through associations within society, flooding down the affluents of the parties through their famous men. Familial connections, local industrial authority or territorial prestige, pressure groups were important, but they were not the only wind in the sails of the nineteenth-century politician. He had to moralize on events and society and acquired the confidence to endow the most modest step forward—the end of Church rates, the disestablishment of the Irish Church—with ecumenical significance. Political watchwords might last a generation, not a year, or a month.

The Victorians tended to be optimistic about history, and 'the light on the hill' made the political journey itself more exhilarating. When Felix Holt, the Radical, is sceptical about the suffrage: 'A Radical—yes; but I want to go to some roots a good deal lower down than the franchise', the Reverend Lyon, while admitting that 'there is work within that cannot be dispensed with', insists that, as a preliminary, men must be freed 'from the stifled life of political nullity' and brought 'into what Milton calls "the liberal air" wherein alone can be wrought the final triumphs of the Spirit'.

Politicians in Victorian times were closer, as John Holloway[1] has said, to those who reflect on 'history, society, human value and indeed the whole order of nature' than they are today. Behind the conduct of public affairs in the 1870s there were such reflections as *Unto this last*, *Culture and anarchy*, *On liberty*, Disraeli's great speeches at the Crystal Palace, and Gladstone on Butler—in all 'a major achievement of imagination and thought'. Today the divorce between politics and general literature is almost complete. 'It is impossible,' says Holloway, 'to imagine any of our leading political figures, in any party, giving a serious public address on any literary, speculative, or indeed just cultural subject...' No contemporary leading politician today, hardly any man of letters writing on politics, seems able to set the imagination in motion. One might add that nothing better illustrates the insulation of the modern practice of politics from general ideas than the unmistakable Philistinism of some of the most 'successful', 'adept', 'adroit', etc., of recent leading politicians.

Moreover, the Victorian leading politician spoke to men who

[1] 'Walter Bagehot and the divided present', *The Listener*, 28 April 1966.

were hungry for politics, who wanted to be taught. So for a brief period iniquity was attacked, enemies identified, principles and programmes stated. It was a process of re-grouping the isolates within the community and it was edifying and stimulating to both speaker and audience.

The hunger for politics could not last. Political action was to prove fatiguing, its results disappointing. Expectations have changed. To unsympathetic observers today, Victorian politics seem like a confidence trick—a bombinating in the void which took everyone in. Sir Ivor Jennings asked what it was all about: 'Was Church and land reform in Ireland so very stupid?'[1] The introduction of passion into politics had been unfortunate: it had produced an oratorical posturing, worlds away from the slow grinding friction of effective political settlements. Today we have, it is said, a much better knowledge of the grain of politics, of what can be achieved through politics. Time and again we have been told that it is a mistake to see politics as a technique for achieving or demonstrating ideals, that it is in fact a practical activity which may perhaps bring settlements but never solutions. Politics is the better for being disencumbered from passion, from principles which deteriorate into slogans, from exhortations which either merely warm the air or become injunctions.

The general politics of ideals and ends is therefore either useless or dangerous. Effective politics is achieved below the level of debate, within the caucus, group or union, by those who prepare the agenda. And the general politician remains useful only as oracle or symbol. For John Bright or Joseph Chamberlain the world became what they thought it was. Density of information had not yet choked the power to generalize. They retained subjectivity and creative power. So too, in this century, did Churchill by refusing to admit that the world had changed.

Ordinary men as well as scholars seem to have turned away from deeds and men. Most of the leading politicians have been judged and found wanting. All are seen as finding conditions difficult and only one recognized as having mastery. Asquith was 'decent', had manners, voice, and judgment, but lacked a really vitalizing political awareness: he never came to life. Balfour was distinguished in grasp and sensibility but always *seemed* disengaged from his tasks. Lloyd George had all the political gifts but was

[1] *Party politics*, 1, *Appeal to the people*, Cambridge, 1960, p. 130.

never trusted. Baldwin, the trustworthy man, was charged with deception, *ex ore suo*; MacDonald, 'head and shoulders' above his Labour colleagues, became in their eyes a renegade. All these were 'guilty men' not merely because, in another age, they might have been indicted as 'evil counsellors' but also because they failed to live up to past standards.

Churchill alone redeemed himself and then only by a stroke of good fortune. Before the war his writing and oratory were judged perversely fustian. Was he not classed (with Laski) by one literary critic as 'a master of second-class prose'? Such opinions might be fastidious but it cannot be said that Churchill was a popular hero either. His audience admired 'the galloper' in him, recognized will and force, but his powers of persuasion were limited. Oddly enough he lacked 'weight'. The aspersions of 'careerism' stuck. What at last gave him authority was unremitting hostility to hegemony on the continent of Europe.

There were others who might have won general approval. Beatrice Webb was impressed by Oswald Mosley's oratory and 'lithe' beauty.[1] But his leaving the Labour Party showed more than lack of political judgment; it also revealed inordinate vanity and an unawareness of where he was in the course of English history. The left has always had some difficulty in producing a *national* leader (because of an acquired suspicion of talented leadership itself) but Ernest Bevin had shrewdness, a stabilizing obtuseness and immunity from the intellectual excitations of the left, real demotic force, and above all 'a sense of the country'. Even so it is difficult to see the kind of England to which he could have given prolonged leadership.

It is of course just possible that up to 1926 Britain might have been the land of the demagogue. He might have been Tom Mann (only just possibly), Lloyd George or George Lansbury. He might even have been Horatio Bottomley, 'the greatest lay lawyer in England' with his 'fine natural vulgarity' and 'mind wonderfully quick, light and limber'.[2] Bottomley was a rogue—'behind the public personality there was, in any serious sense, no character at all',[3] and it is highly unlikely that those who held the gates would ever have let him in. Yet he was heard: men swore by *John*

[1] For a while. In time she realized that he had 'bad health, a slight intelligence and an unstable character...' —*Diaries 1924–1932*, p. 267.
[2] Julian Symons, *Horatio Bottomley*, London, 1955, p. 17.   [3] *Ibid*. p. 274.

Bull. Today people are not listening. Politics has become opaque, perplexing; the politician, probably well-meaning but necessarily disingenuous, not heartless but agile and in the end not to be trusted.

One insight into the dispersion of political certitude is to be found in Joyce Cary's novel, *Prisoner of grace*. The central character is Chester Nimmo, a Radical politician of the first quarter of the century. The model is obviously Lloyd George. Nimmo achieves and keeps power through his lay-preacher oratory, his ability to manage men and master situations. 'When you are dealing with men like Chester,' says his wife Nina, 'facts simply turn round the other way; and as for situations, it is their business to change them.' Yet she respects the shaping power: 'I really think that politicians (I mean good honest ones who have good principles) can be more admirable than saints, because they do far more difficult work and are not allowed just "to save their souls".' Without a persistent interest in politics she retains some belief that human hopes can be translated into political terms. Yet at the same time the medium of politics has become bewildering and daunting. For after Nimmo had acquired valuable political notoriety at a rowdy public meeting she admits:

It was at this time I began to feel among 'political' people the strange and horrible feeling which afterwards became so familiar to me (but not less horrible), of living in a world without any solid objects at all, of floating day and night through clouds of words and schemes and hopes and ambitions and calculations where you could not say this idea was obviously selfish and dangerous and that one quite false and wicked because all of them were relative to something else.

When politics becomes impenetrable the goodness must go out of it.

For this puzzlement and consequent inattention it would be impossible to allocate precise blame. Perhaps it began with the failure of the Liberals, as the People's Party from 1906, or with the ill-tempered, ungenerous politics of 1911 to 1914. Or one might concur with D. H. Lawrence's judgment that the virtue went out of English politics in 1917 when the old political society capitulated to things it did '*not vitally believe in*', gave way 'to mere current baseness'.[1] 1917–18 was the winter of the rejection of the Lans-

[1] In April 1917 he was writing to Lady Cynthia Asquith: 'I feel angry with you,

downe proposals to end the self-destructive war and thus preserve
some of the civilities of the pre-war European world; the year
when 'the patriotic press' reached its nadir of mendacity; of the
'super-patriotism' of Bottomley and Pemberton Billing. And of
course it was the year of Lloyd George himself, 'brilliant', innovating, yet bewildering and destructive of the old *imperium*.

The agile, political trafficking of 'the first-class brains' in the
immediate post-war world must also have contributed to public
disillusionment, followed as it was by the necessary 'corruption'
(through assimilation into the political system) of Labour's
leaders in the 1920s. And there is truth in the view that British
politics, so unabashedly and securely insular (so provincial, said
its critics), lost some of its confidence under the pressure of alien
ideologies in the 1930s. Both MacDonald and Baldwin played
difficult bridging roles, the one without a supporting party, the
other without the full weight of party conviction. Neville
Chamberlain, the third National government leader, had genuine
strength and indeed temporarily 'the sense of the country' but,
despite real success domestically, lost his public by staking his
reputation in a sphere in which different experience, differently
matured convictions, were required.

There are plenty of reasons why the British public should have
have become progressively more reluctant to invest a great deal of
faith in their politicians. Yet many of the vulgar judgments
passed on recent politicians are unduly harsh simply because they
do not take into account the peculiar tasks of this century. One
obvious reason why the politician so rarely illumines the political
scene is that his decisions are less momentous than formerly. The
strength of British politics, said Augustine Birrell sixty years ago,
derived primarily from its representation of 'a people who were
always destined to play a great part in the world'. The tasks,
necessary and prudent, upon which Britain has been recently
engaged are not likely to lengthen the shadow of a statesman. The
decisions of a mid-twentieth century Prime Minister are different
in range and kind from those of Lord Salisbury or even of Lloyd
George. In the constricted circumstances of today the politician

the way you have betrayed everything that is real, by admitting the superiority of
that which is merely temporal and foul and external upon us. If all the aristocrats
have sold the vital principle of life to the mere current of foul affairs, what good
are the aristocrats?' *The letters of D. H. Lawrence*, ed. Aldous Huxley, London,
1934, p. 406.

can say little that is remarkable. For what makes words memorable is reality of choice and the power to act and govern in the light of that choice.

What England has known is the free politics of the independent state. But in an *interdependent* world, possessed of only modest power and declining influence, she will almost certainly become municipal, i.e. confined to home affairs. Beyond Britain there may well be a long-maturing will and decision, 'an immense and tutelary power'.[1] But with the loan sanctions, the ambit for projects, the inducements to co-operation coming from outside, the interstices left for politics will surely become very narrow. The national politician will accept as given the outlines of the general plan and concern himself primarily with what is going on in his own municipality. And for these modest, careful tasks neither character nor style will be necessary—only attention to business and the professional skills necessary 'to methodize success'.[2]

This would seem to entail certain moral loss. For in the Greek *polis* where political modes began, the first of merits was courage, possibly desperate courage, in the public eye. To leave the idiocy of the private realm was to experience another and higher kind of being, 'to know equality and freedom for the first time'. Here was felicity and also danger. This perilous politics has long been etiolated by processes which Hannah Arendt describes in *The human condition*, but courage in the public eye has remained a virtue in modern liberal politics: the courage to make a stand and not only by those out of power, those who are oppressed, but also by those in power; not only by those contending within the realm, like Peter Wentworth walking in his garden and rehearsing what he was to say in the Elizabethan House of Commons, or Baldwin meditating his speech at the Carlton Club in 1922; but also those speaking for the realm like Churchill in 1940.

This kind of political courage (still cultivated, I suppose, by De Gaulle) is likely to be at a discount in the future. Yet it remains, as Churchill proved, the most widely appreciated of political

---

[1] 'Above this race of men stands an immense and tutelary power, which takes upon itself alone to secure their gratifications, and to watch over their fate. That power is absolute, minute, regular, provident, and mild.' Alexis de Tocqueville, *Democracy in America*, tr. Henry Reeve, London, 1875, II, 290.

[2] A slight modification of a phrase used by H. J. Blackham, *Political discipline in a free society*, London, 1961, p. 135.

qualities. William James once wrote an essay on 'The Moral Equivalent of War'. 'Militarism,' he said, 'is the great preserver of our ideals of hardihood, and human life with no use for hardihood would be contemptible. Without risks or prizes for the darer, history would be insipid indeed; and there is a type of military character which every one thinks the race should never cease to breed, for every one is sensitive to its superiority.'[1] Yet in a world in which militarism has become suicidal, it seems that military virtues cultivated in 'the supreme theatre of human strenuousness'[2] must go. Is it possible that the virtues cultivated in liberal politics will disappear too—not toleration and compromise, of course, but the kind of political courage which either generated or expressed moral power in society?

D. H. Lawrence saw men's 'collective activities' everywhere becoming 'cook-housemaid to their sheer individual activities'.[3] 'You, you Cabinet Minister—what are you? You are the archgrocer, the super-hotel-manager, the foreman over ships and railways. What else are you?' The issue is a universal one. Is the *uomo singolare* who formerly took men out of themselves, absorbed them in his vision and gave them vicarious pride, a dangerous anachronism? Is even the memory of great deeds, which made communities what they are, 'dangerous'? And what of political passion? 'In order to do great things,' said Saint-Simon, 'one must be impassioned.' In 'Politics as a Vocation' Max Weber concurred. Passionate devotion to a cause, passion governed by responsibility, should be the hallmark of the great politician, the man who is to put his hand on the wheel of history. But today we feel that he had better not put his hand on the wheel: we are fearful lest he give it a shove. Neither the tensions of the Athenian assembly where orators in passionate debate settled once and for all the fate of the *polis*, nor the plastic power of the great nineteenth-century tribunes, are appropriate to a time when nearly everything, and much that cannot be contemplated, is historically possible. So it is safer to detach the imaginative vision from the process of politics and agree with Lawrence 'that man no longer expresses himself in his form of government, and his President is strictly only his superlative butler'.[4]

---

[1] William James, *Essays on faith and morals* (1897), London, 1943, pp. 316–17.
[2] *Ibid.* p. 320.
[3] D. H. Lawrence, *Selected essays*, London, 1950 (Penguin ed.), p. 79.   [4] *Ibid.* p. 77.

William James saw the leader as one who 'gave form to the unstructured moment' and it is still difficult to visualize politics without creative activity of this kind. Yet the idea of leaders imposing themselves upon associations, actively challenging others for leadership, is fading; the contemporary concept is rather of the group intimating what it stands for and what it wants and concurrently 'outlining roles to be filled'.[1] The men with requisite qualities emerge to assume them. Today, we are told, the political leader is functional and needs specific managerial talents; he should be skilled in the use of mass media, know how to administer large organizations and how to advance in the party.[2] He need be neither robust nor passionate but he should be selected from as wide a field as possible, have a career structure; be, like the rest of us, well trained and professional. The nineteenth-century politician often made decisions with an imperfect knowledge of what was going on. This must not happen again.

The art of the new politician will be 'a deliberate, bold, resourceful, and sustained social art'—to secure the 'conditions of secular salvation'.[3] His rule will be sober and knowledgeable, 'provident and mild', in an age in which there is 'a fundamental convergence in our thoughts and aims'.[4] In a politics thus dissociated from the imaginative vision, there will be little room for those who 'give form to the unstructured moment'. The safe politician will be the one for whom the knives are all blunted, the corners padded.

The moral loss may be less in England than elsewhere. England has always expected integrity in her politicians and occasionally has called men of style to her service. But she has given them only very brief authority and has never sought a master. The politician has never been allowed to think of the realm as material for his art; statecraft must be practised within strict limits. Leadership in England, as Trotter insisted many years ago,[5] tends to be an expression of the common impulse rather than a substitute for it.

[1] See D. W. Harding, *Social psychology and individual values*, London, 1963, p. 101.
[2] D. V. Verney, *The analysis of political systems*, London, 1959, p. 159.
[3] Blackham, *Political discipline in a free society*, pp. 119–20.
[4] Gunnar Myrdal, *Beyond the welfare state*, quoted in C. A. R. Crosland, *The conservative enemy*, London, 1962, p. 237.
[5] W. Trotter, *Instincts of the herd in peace and war*, 2nd edition, 1919. There is an excellent discussion of Trotter's insights into English political attitudes in D. W. Harding, 'Political scepticism in Britain', *The Political Quarterly*, January–March 1959, pp. 18–28.

Leaders are not the creators of a unity which comes out of an ancient people whose ways have been little disturbed; cohesion is attained without external shaping power.

England can develop her own will and seek her objectives with a persistence which makes her formidable but she is resistant to the will of men who would make something out of her—like Joseph Chamberlain, Milner and Cripps. Moreover, it is England that is resistant, not her political institutions. She remains a free spirit, drifting, seemingly aimless. 'She poor thing was born upon the road, and lives in such a dust of travel that she never knows where she is.'[1] She pays little attention to rhetoric about unity and purpose and has been unimpressed by grand invocations of her political destiny. The ideologies of her enemies have usually been more highly organized, more intellectually impressive, their knowledge of what was going on in the world much superior. Yet, with what has often been only the most elementary grasp of her predicament,[2] England has usually had *time* in crises and conflict to generate greater moral power than her enemies, to gain friends in the world through diffusion of her ethical certitude (which others call cant[3]). Her leaders do no more than express her; they are expected to grow and catch her spirit; they are exhaustible and dispensable—even the greatest.

England is therefore not unfitted as a nation for the 'sober and disinterested choices' of municipal life in a post-political age—once she has rid herself of those myths which Enoch Powell[4] has said still haunt her corporate imagination: first, that she was once a secure and long-established imperial power and has now fallen from greatness through 'weakness, benevolence or some other cause or causes'; second, that she was once the natural workshop of the world and has now supinely lost her pre-eminence. Both these concepts are misleading in that they solidify very brief moments in the English past.

At heart England has always been content with herself, has been, even if she has undertaken missions, a country without ambition (compare her with France or Germany). 'She has had no theory of herself, no consciousness of her destiny, no will to

---

[1] Joyce Cary, *To be a pilgrim*.
[2] England can, says Trotter, 'scarcely accomplish an intellectual process more complex than the recognition of an enemy', *op. cit.* p. 228.
[3] See Dibelius, *England*, pp. 181 and 499.
[4] *A nation not afraid*, London, 1965, pp. 137 ff.

power. She has had almost no national heroes, and has always been constitutionally frigid to her great men, grudging them the material for their experimentations on her people...'[1] She should have little difficulty in recovering her pre-imperial past.

English leaders and the English people 'connect'—without undue familiarity. But England does not expect to be saved by her leaders. She will save herself—if she must be saved. And this she will only do under pressure. For in peacetime national consciousness has been barely discernible. The prevailing attitude of Englishmen is one of detachment from politics, detachment while being fully conscious of the reserve power to intervene if necessary.[2] Her politicians are not harassed: they are given free use of accepted prerogative power. They are left to determine their own recruitment, their own hierarchy, their own criteria of leadership. And in spite of the protests of journalists, there is no great popular demand to break down their relative immunity from searching and irreverent publicity.

No great English politician has ever embodied England although many have tried to express her. De Gaulle has said of his wartime authority: 'I was France. I was the independence and sovereignty of France, and it was for this reason that everyone obeyed me.' No Englishman has ever presumed to have such a sense of moral power—not Churchill, not even Cromwell. Even today when the parties have lost much of their conviction and drive, it is not easy to see an English politician invoking the state (*pays légal* or *pays réel*) against them. Some observers, like Lord Gladwyn, have tentatively forecast the coming of a kind of Bonapartist or Gaullist régime in England, authorized by quinquennial plebiscites.[3] It is true that exasperated young men frequently demand power in government, clear-cut effective administration with the sense of the state behind it, a régime explicitly recognizing, even in quiet times, the existence of a perennial public interest over and above the interests of individuals and groups. But there are few signs that the people have lost their temper yet, that they want other than the kind of leaders they have now and have had, honest, responsible, accessible and disposed to co-operate with history rather than to set their stamp on it.

[1] Trotter, *op. cit.* p. 202.
[2] See Harding, *art. cit.* pp. 25–6.
[3] As reported in *The Times*, 2 August 1965.

INDEX